The Book of
Herne Hill

*Four Miles South
of the Standard Cornhill*

Patricia M. Jenkyns

HALSGROVE

First published in Great Britain in 2003

British Library Cataloguing-in-Publication Data
A CIP record for this title is available from the British Library

ISBN 1 84114 235 2

HALSGROVE

Halsgrove House
Lower Moor Way
Tiverton, Devon EX16 6SS
Tel: 01884 243242
Fax: 01884 243325
email: sales@halsgrove.com
website: www.halsgrove.com

Frontispiece photograph: *Brockwell Park gates, Herne Hill, 1940. The park was the venue for family outings at weekends and holiday times. In this photograph the gates and railings remain but high lampposts have replaced the more decorative gas lamps and the blue police box and red telephone box are present. The two lodges have disappeared and there is not a rook's nest to be seen.*

Printed and bound in Great Britain by Bookcraft Ltd, Midsomer Norton.

CONTENTS

Children gathering with jugs to collect milk from the milkman's cart in Water Lane. Delivery was often twice daily for there was little refrigeration.

The main entrance to Brockwell Park at the junction of Norwood and Dulwich Roads. The park was one of the most photographed areas in Herne Hill. Very few alterations were needed when the Brockwell estate became a park. The gates and railings remained and the lodges were used to house the park staff and their families. The island opposite the entrance was one of the few 'official' bus-stops. Elsewhere passengers were able to stop horse buses and, later, trams anywhere along the routes.

Chapter 1
ϾᏜᎶᎴ
HERNE HILL IN PRE-MODERN TIMES

Anyone who enjoys history knows that it is a story of past happenings, as exciting and interesting as any tale of fiction. Local history is rarely concerned with earth-shattering events, but is usually about ordinary men and women endeavouring to earn a living and provide for their families.

Local history also concerns the buying and selling of land and the development of an area – often in response to events taking place at some distance from a community. The building of Westminster Bridge over the River Thames, and the subsequent construction of roads south of the river, had a profound effect on Herne Hill.

The River Thames was London's main thoroughfare, with many landing stages along its banks. For centuries the only bridge over the Thames in the region of the City was the extremely congested London Bridge.

South of London Bridge was Southwark (the South Works) and the Kent Road leading to Dover. On the south bank of the Thames were the areas of Lambeth, Greenwich and Bermondsey, in the counties of Kent and Surrey, which had grown up around two palaces and a monastery. Further afield were villages such as Camberwell, Dulwich and Brixton, which originally developed around natural crossroads and water-supplies.

Before the Reformation, much of the land that now makes up the area known as Herne Hill was owned by the Church. Land in the vicinity of St Saviour's, Herne Hill Road, was part of the Archbishop of Canterbury's hunting ground – it was well wooded and suitable for chasing deer. Brockwell Common was held by the religious body of the Hospital of St Thomas, Southwark, the proceeds from the land being used for the good of the sick poor of Southwark, and much of what is now Dulwich was the property of the Monastery of Bermondsey.

In the late 1530s the Church was forced to surrender its property and income to Henry VIII – the properties then being sold to the highest bidders. Just over a century later the Interregnum took place.

Again properties changed hands and for Herne Hill and its environs there was a considerable loss of woodland as trees were felled for Cromwell's naval shipbuilding programme. The Great North Wood (Norwood) lost many oaks, as did the old hunting grounds. Thereafter the land became more arable and in time it was chiefly used for market gardens and smallholdings.

Herne Hill's name did not come into use until the 1760s. It cannot be said for certain how or why the old roadway was so named but several suggestions have been put forward (see chapter 7).

Herne Hill's modern history began with the building of Westminster Bridge over the River Thames. At first there was opposition to its construction but, with generous compensation to the ferrymen and to the Archbishop, who owned the 'Horseferry' plying between Westminster and Lambeth, building began.

This was quickly followed by the construction of Blackfriars, Southwark and Vauxhall Bridges. Then came the development of an extended system of roads. These were not winding country lanes following natural contours, but straight, wide roads leading to such areas as Kennington, the Elephant and Castle, Brixton and Camberwell. These routes encouraged the movement of people across the river to more pleasant and cleaner areas in the counties of Kent and Surrey.

There had always been vestiges of roads to London. Legend has it that in Roman times a road led through Brixton to the Thames Embankment and that pilgrims walked along roadways (now Acre Lane, Dulwich Road and Croxted Road) to join the Pilgrims' Way to Canterbury. William of Normandy's troops are thought to have foraged in the Camberwell area before crossing the Thames to converge upon London and demand its surrender in 1066.

Early maps show roads linking villages. In Herne Hill, with the exception of Herne Hill Road, the main thoroughfares were once the old country lanes which later became coach roads and are now bus routes.

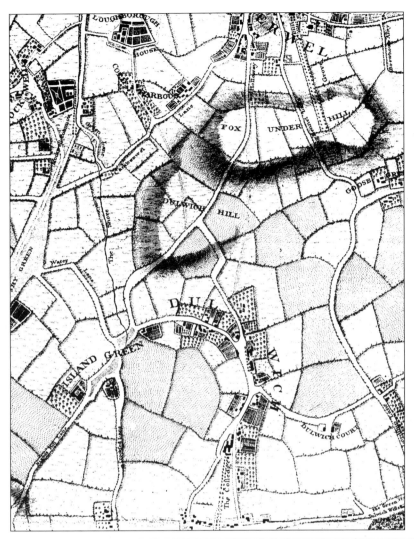

Left: *Rocques' Map, 1760s. One of the first known maps to show the area that was later called Herne Hill. The River Effra's tributaries can be seen meeting at Island Green and flowing onwards to the Thames at Vauxhall. In 2003, the river flows underground and the country lanes have become roads.*

Below: *A view of Herne Hill in 1823. This drawing by W. Robb shows the first generation of houses on Herne Hill and the lodge of the Blades estate (not easily seen). The road to Brixton and the bridge crossing the River Effra are visible. The horse and cart is probably carrying ale to the Half Moon Inn, just around the corner.*

Chapter 2

ᴄᴥᴥᴥᴥ

THE BEGINNING OF MODERN HERNE HILL

In the 1770s, Samuel Sanders, a timber merchant with premises on the south bank of the Thames, bought land on Denmark Hill and, later, on Herne Hill. It is not known how he heard that the land was for sale, but he could possibly have been told by a farmer, Robert Bulkeley, who had property 'north east of Red Post Hill' and who, in 1775, was fined £150 at the Guildford assizes (Surrey's county town) for cutting down 2,000 trees. Such a large number of trees must have been felled to fill an order and who but a timber merchant would have purchased such a quantity of new wood?

These events coincided with the building of Westminster Bridge, the architect of which was Charles Labelye. The River Thames, which was the source of domestic water for the Lambeth and Westminster areas, was becoming increasingly polluted. Samuel Sanders may have wanted to move his family away from the river to an area of clean air and safe water. The land on Denmark Hill answered this need and Samuel built a substantial house there. Not long afterwards he began to grant long leases of land on Denmark and Herne Hills to well-to-do city merchants and bankers, who then constructed large houses in spacious grounds. The dwellings were so fine that the area soon became known as the 'Belgravia of South London'.

The Sanders estate covered the area that became Ruskin Park and stretched back to the now Fawnbrake Avenue and Brantwood Road, up Denmark Hill and down Herne Hill. The long leases

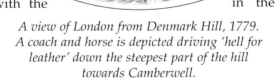

A view of London from Denmark Hill, 1779. A coach and horse is depicted driving 'hell for leather' down the steepest part of the hill towards Camberwell.

that Sanders granted, and the family management of the land, ensured that over the years the area's growth was gradual and controlled.

At about the same time that Samuel Sanders bought his property on Denmark Hill, Hugh Minet (a descendant of a refugee Huguenot family) bought land in the vicinity of what is now Coldharbour Lane. This land later bordered upon the estate of Samuel Sanders where Finsen Road and Ruskin Park are found. Some of it was low-lying and proved more suitable for market gardening than property development. It remained so until the arrival of the railway in the Denmark Hill/Camberwell area, and the building of the embankments to Loughborough Junction.

The land purchased by Samuel Sanders bordered the parish of St Mary at Lambeth and the parish of St Giles', Camberwell. The borders of the two parishes on Denmark and Herne Hills were by no means regular and it was not until the formation of Borough Councils that agreements were made to straighten the boundaries down the middle of both hills.

In the early 1600s Edward Alleyn bought a very modest estate in Dulwich which had increased to 1,300 acres within five years. His foundation of a school for boys (later Dulwich College) and the management of the estates ensured that Dulwich and Herne Hill remained far more pleasant than many of South London's suburbs and did not later have to be cleared of slums.

It was very fortunate that much of the land in Herne Hill and Dulwich was purchased by people

Above: *No. 154 Denmark Hill was built in the 1780s and the architect was William Blackburn. It can be seen in the background of a number of photographs of Ruskin Park's conservatory. The house later stood in the grounds of King's College Hospital, until it was demolished in the 1960s to make room for the hospital's new ward block. It was one of the fine houses noted by Mr Edwards on his journey to Brighton. The house was owned by Mr Richard Lawrence, a near neighbour of Samuel Sanders.*

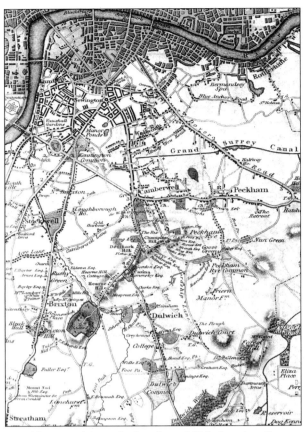

Above: *A map dating from 1823 showing the beginning of modern Herne Hill. The owners of the estates and the footpaths that later became roadways are marked. The River Thames runs along the top of the map and the area south of the river is surprisingly clear of housing and roads.*

Westminster Bridge opened in 1750 when the development of Westminster made another bridge over the Thames necessary. The new bridge led to the growth of the north area of Lambeth.

who intended living upon it. Thus it was saved from the ugliness of speculative over-development, which, in 1900, had caused Walter Besant to write that it was difficult to imagine 'how wonderfully beautiful South London was, before the builders seized upon it' and covered it with 'villas, shops and streets'.

In 1789 a young man called Edwards made a journey from London to the South Coast. He later published a 'Companion' describing his experiences and the route of his journey. He recorded what he saw as he climbed Denmark Hill. On the left was 'The Fox Under the Hill' and a little further up, where Ruskin Park is now, was a group of houses, one of which was the house of Samuel Sanders, 'the owner of the land on which the houses stand'. The hill ascended 'more sharp' where a road branched off on the left (now Champion Hill) leading to 'Grove Hill, the seat of Dr Lettsom'. Several houses were under construction on Denmark Hill (including one for Mr Sanders), and further up the hill was a tearoom run by 'Mr Lightfoot'. Just beyond the 'IV mile stone from the Standard Cornhill' he turned left by 'The Red Post'. Edwards did not mention any buildings on Herne Hill, noting only the fact that 'on the right, about 60 yards distant, is a small genteel white house, just built by Mr Smith' and that 'a gradual descent began'. Edwards descended Red Post Hill to Dulwich and passed 'The White Hart', 'The Crown', 'The Greyhound', the Long Pond, and 'Miss Tolk's boarding school for young ladies'. He eventually reached the 'V mile stone from the Standard Cornhill' and Dulwich College.

Edwards thought Dulwich was 'a very pleasant place' and mentioned the stagecoach that left for London and returned twice daily. He took the road to Island Green from Dulwich, passing 'a genteel house where Mr Kitchen, the surgeon, had a shop', a 'remarkable large elm tree', and the 'Half Moon Public House' kept by Mr Humphry. At the junction of Herne Hill and Half Moon Lane was Island Green. There Edwards crossed 'the stream' (the Effra) and entered Brockwell Common. On the right was Water Lane, leading to Brixton Causeway. And so to Knight's Hill, the seat of Lord Thurlow, and Norwood Common.

The development of Denmark and Herne Hills on both sides of the roadways must have been rapid, for when the Wilsons, the Beneckes, the Bicknells and the Ruskins moved into their houses between the late 1790s and the 1820s the properties were already well established.

Some of the houses were set in extensive grounds. Those on the Dulwich side were fewer and their grounds larger, in some cases stretching down to Half Moon Lane. Most grounds included kitchen gardens, producing fruit and vegetables for the families. Some households also had smallholdings elsewhere with livestock. Elhanan Bicknell had a small 'home farm' at the top of Poplar Walk, with a resident farmer who kept pigs and other livestock.

The passing of the Lambeth Manor Enclosure Act of 1810 enabled John Blades, a glass manufacturer of Ludgate Hill, to buy and enclose Brockwell Common. He demolished the house by Norwood Lane, which the young Mr Edwards had thought 'pleasant' (perhaps due to dampness caused by the occasional overflowing of the River Effra at Island Green) and built a house on one of the hills.

The grounds of the estate had several springs to supply the establishment. No house in that position would have been built without a water-supply and it is thought that Mr J.B. Papworth, who had laid out the gardens and roads and designed the fencing of the estate, had built in the supply of water. The architect of the house at Brockwell was Mr D.R. Roper.

Later Mr Papworth designed a house in the park called Clarence Lodge which was leased. In John Blades' will he bequeathed a life interest in the lodge to his daughter Caroline, who had married the Revd Edwin Prodgers, the first vicar of St Matthew's, East Brixton. The will also bequeathed a life interest in two houses called Brockwell Terrace, also designed by Papworth. The intention had been to build a full terrace of houses but John Blades died before the plan could be completed. He had previously purchased land in what is now Water Lane and built houses there which were thought to provide accommodation for the estate staff.

The development of Brixton Water Lane had been advancing slowly in response to improvements in the transport services. Land suitable for housing adjacent to Water Lane was unexpectedly released by the early death of a local landowner called Robert Stone in 1820. The estate had to be sold in order for him to be able to support his wife and young children and to pay his debts. Part of the land was purchased by the Westminster Freehold Land Society who, in time, laid out the roadways of the 'Poets' Corner' (Chaucer, Spenser, Shakespeare and Milton Roads). House construction began and the many styles of housing extant here indicate Poets' Corner's gradual development and the various builders involved in its growth. This area has a distinctive character, although some new development took place as a result of war damage and many of the houses have been subdivided. The construction of Regent Road and the neighbouring areas followed, later hastened by the coming of the railways.

St Paul's Church, Herne Hill. This photograph was taken before the road was tarmacked. At the time of writing there has been little change to the layout of the roadway and the houses, church and gardens. Remarkably, the two great trees are still standing, as is the church wall. Below the church, many of the trees and bushes have gone and a new block of flats and houses have been built in their place.

A view of St Jude's Church, Dulwich Road, from Brockwell Park.

Chapter 3

ᴄᴑᎶᏇᴼ

DIOCESAN BOUNDARIES

The parish of St Mary at Lambeth stretched from the Thames to what is now Denmark and Herne Hills and had been within the diocese of Winchester for centuries, despite Lambeth Palace and St Mary's Church being neighbours. St Mary's Church was the church of the Archbishops of Canterbury and a number are buried within its precincts. The parish of St Giles', Camberwell, was also administered by the diocese of Winchester.

In 1877, a rearrangement of diocesan boundaries became necessary because the diocese of Winchester had grown too populous and was difficult to administer. A new diocese of St Albans was created and among other changes the old areas of Lambeth and Camberwell passed to the care of the diocese of Rochester.

In 1905, as the suburbs spread and population increased, further boundary changes became imperative. A new administrative area was founded, that of the diocese of Southwark with the Cathedral Church of St Saviour's and St Mary Overie. Since that time these boundaries have remained essentially unaltered, despite the continued intensive urbanisation of South London and its environs.

The Fosberys of Dulwich Road and Water Lane in the 1880s.

CHURCH ATTENDANCE

Surveys of church attendance were carried out during the Victorian era. The most famous was that of 1851. However, this was not a survey carried out by Church authorities, but by a government department. The results were surprising for they showed that only 35 per cent of the country's population attended church or chapel on Sunday 30 March 1851 and, of these, 47 per cent were Church of England and 49 per cent were Nonconformist. The area of Camberwell had greater Church of England attendance but there were more Church of England establishments in the area than of other denominations.

It would be difficult to be dogmatic about church attendance in Herne Hill at that time. St Paul's, Herne Hill, was only seven years old and there were few other churches in the immediate area. It is known that many people kept their allegiance to other places of worship even though some had in fact contributed money towards the founding of St Paul's.

The Bicknell family were Unitarians and attended the Essex Street or Effra Road Chapels. However, two of the sons were practising Church of England members. The eldest, Elhanan, who lived in South Place off Herne Hill, was a friend of the vicar of St Paul's (who was later to conduct Elhanan's funeral service) and the youngest, Clarence, was a graduate of Cambridge University who became a curate of St Paul's, Walworth Road.

The Ruskin family attended the Camden Chapel, Peckham Road, or the Beresford Chapel, Walworth Road, and occasionally St Matthew's, Denmark Hill. The Blades-Blackburn family attended either St Bride's, Fleet Street, or St Matthew's, Brixton, for Caroline Blades had married its first vicar. In the past the family had worshipped in a private chapel in the grounds of Brockwell estate. The Gurney family on Denmark Hill were staunch Baptists. A number of residents of Herne Hill and Denmark Hill were of German descent and attended establishments sympathetic to their Lutheran and Catholic backgrounds. The Fosberys ran 'cottage meetings' in their home on Water Lane and attendance at these was growing. The meetings attracted people from all Nonconformist denominations for there was a dearth of places in which such people could worship.

In October 1886 another census was recorded, by which time the population had increased considerably and more places of worship had been built in Herne Hill and the surrounding area. Again, overall numbers showed more Nonconformists than Church of England worshippers (figures included those attending services held in hospitals and workhouses – there were none in Herne Hill). One service each, morning and afternoon, was recorded. In some instances numbers were inflated for particular celebrations, such as the harvest festival when children attended with their parents. In other cases they were lessened because early-morning services had taken place before the main service.

In Herne Hill it is impossible to give accurate figures because most local Nonconformist establishments were built later, around the turn of the century, and those of such beliefs would have attended worship outside their residential area.

The Parish Church of St Mary at Lambeth.

Church of England Attendance (Herne Hill) 1902/03

	Morning	Evening
St Jude's, East Brixton (Dulwich Road)	759	1,197
St Saviour's, Herne Hill Road	534	584
St Paul's, Herne Hill	499	328
St Matthew's, Denmark Hill	515	560
Holy Trinity, Tulse Hill	708	734
Alleyn College Chapel, Dulwich Village	479	359

Nonconformist Attendance 1902/03

Unitarian, Effra Road	128	55
Methodist Church, Railton Road	293	244
Congregational, Camberwell Green	490	376
German Evangelical, Windsor Road, Camberwell	97 (morning only)	

Just over 25 years later another census was taken, this time over the year 1902–03. This showed that since the 1886 census the number of Nonconformists nationwide had continued to increase. Churches and chapels of different denominations had been built in Herne Hill and the neighbouring area and the population had increased as the area developed, reaching a peak in the first years of the twentieth century. New parishes were formed and there were several Church schools in the locality. Improvements had been made to transport services making it easier for worshippers to attend churches elsewhere.

THE PARISHES

The Parish Church of St Mary at Lambeth (the foundation of which dates back to Saxon times) predates its neighbour, Lambeth Palace, which is the official residence of the Archbishop of Canterbury.

In the late-eighteenth century, the boundaries of the parish of St Mary at Lambeth stretched from the south bank of the Thames to Camberwell, Streatham, Dulwich and Croydon. The size of the parish reflected the sparseness of its population, particularly in the south, but the building of the first bridge between Westminster and Lambeth and then Blackfriars Bridge rapidly changed its structure.

St Mary's parish bordered upon the parish of St Giles' with two bulges roughly from Sunray Avenue to Green Lane and Champion Hill and from Ruskin Walk to Red Post Hill. Over the years the bulges were eliminated as Vestries became boroughs and boundaries were straightened. St Mary's also had a border with Streatham Detached (Brockwell Common, Norwood and Croxted Lanes).

In the 1820s, the four 'Waterloo' churches were built: St Matthew's, Brixton; St Mark's, Kennington; St Luke's, West Norwood; and St John's, Waterloo. In 1840 the parish of St Mary at Lambeth was divided into four district parishes.

Throughout the history of the area it is noticeable that after a new parish was formed its boundaries, and those of the surrounding districts, changed every 20 years or so. First, there was the founding of the church and parish followed by the founding of a sister church which led in time to a new parish or, less often, the creation of a new church and new parish.

By the 1820s Brockwell Common had been enclosed (itself part of Streatham Detached) and many substantial houses had been built on the hills leading from Camberwell to Half Moon Lane, and along the roads from Brixton and Water Lane.

Few of the early residents on Denmark and Herne Hills would have attended their Parish Church of St Mary at Lambeth because it was too far to travel, even by carriage. It was more convenient to attend the Church of St Giles in Camberwell. When, inevitably, the church became overcrowded, a small chapel of ease was built which was replaced 20 years later (in 1848) by St Matthew's Church, Denmark Hill, and a new parish was instituted.

The coming of the railway to Denmark Hill and Camberwell triggered another population explosion, which in turn led to the building of St Saviour's Church south of Coldharbour Lane, the construction of the railway embankment (in Herne Hill Road) and the formation of a new parish. Part of St Matthew's parish was transferred to St Saviour's parish.

In the 1840s the residents on Herne Hill felt that they were sufficient in number to warrant a church of their own. In 1844 St Paul's Church, Herne Hill, was consecrated and another parish instituted. Parts of the parishes of St Giles', Camberwell, and St Matthew's, Brixton, were transferred to the parish of St Paul's, Herne Hill.

By the 1860s the area south of St Matthew's had developed to such an extent that a new church became a necessity and so St Jude's was constructed in Dulwich Road and a new parish, St Jude's, East Brixton, formed. In time, the boundaries between the parishes of St Paul's, Herne Hill, and St Jude's were adjusted, and parts of the parish of St Matthew's were transferred to St Jude's, which bordered upon Streatham Detached. In 1856 the Holy Trinity Church, Tulse Hill, had been built on the other side of Brockwell estate and a new parish had been formed. The Brockwell Park estate was within its area and had boundaries with Norwood and Croxted Lanes. It covered the area that became Rosendale Road to Park Road and Lower Tulse Hill.

In 1894, 50 years after the formation of St Paul's, St Barnabas' Church was built in Dulwich Village and a new parish was constituted. In 1902 parts of the parish of St Paul's were transferred to St Barnabas', including those bordering the railway in Village Way and at the bottom of Red Post Hill.

Before the construction of the Casino estate after the First World War, a church hall was built at the lower end of Red Post Hill, which was known as the district of Herne Hill, St Faith's. After the construction of the Blanchedowne estate in the late 1940s a new church was built and in 1951 a parish was formed called St Faith's, North Dulwich. The part of the parish of St Paul's covering the roads to Ruskin Park and the new Blanchedowne estate was transferred to St Faith's.

In response to the changing population and the formation of a bordering parish, both St Matthew's, Denmark Hill, and St Saviour's had transferred some northerly parts of their parishes to the new parish of St James', Knatchbull Road.

In 1956, following the destruction by fire of St Matthew's in September 1940 and its refounding in Lilford Road, the two churches and parishes of St Matthew's and St Saviour's were united with one vicar. With the demolition of the bomb-damaged St Saviour's Church, the change in population and the retirement of the vicar of the united parish, the boundaries of the parishes were altered. In 1985 the area north of the railways, previously in the parish of St Matthew's and St Saviour's, was transferred to St Giles', Camberwell, which made the parish of Camberwell St Giles' with St Matthew's. The parishes of St Saviour's, Ruskin Park, and St Paul's, Herne Hill, were united to form the parish of Herne Hill. In 2003 both parishes remain within the diocese of Southwark, the northern parish being within the deanery of Camberwell and the southern parish of Herne Hill in the deanery of Dulwich.

Left: St Saviour's Church, Herne Hill Road. The architect was Alexander Gough and the church was built 1867 in response to an increase in population in the Herne Hill Road area. An infants' and girls' school was founded shortly afterwards and the church thrived. It was demolished in the 1980s following irreparable wartime damage and the land was released to provide a larger play area for the school. The 'church' moved to the parish hall.

St Giles' Church, Camberwell. Before St Matthew's was built on Denmark Hill, the nearest church for people living in the vicinity was St Giles'. In time it became overcrowded and the construction of a new church close to the members of the congregation was necessary.

Above: *The parish hall, St Saviour's Church, was opened in 1914 just in time for its use by the convalescent service patients of King's College Hospital and Ruskin Park.*

Above: *St Matthew's Church on Denmark Hill. This church was destroyed during the Blitz and a new St Matthew's was eventually built in Lilford Road off Coldharbour Lane.*

Left: *A. Beresford Pite, professor of architecture at Brixton Technical College.*

Chapter 4

❧☙

PARISH CHURCHES

ST MATTHEW'S CHURCH, DENMARK HILL

When seating in the Parish Church of St Giles', Camberwell, proved insufficient for the new parishioners in the Denmark and Herne Hills area, a chapel of ease was built at the lower end of Denmark Hill. The De Crespigny family (descendants of Huguenot refugees) gave the site just outside the parish boundary of St Giles' and the official care of the parish vicar.

This caused difficulties over the years and led, strangely, to the auctioning of chapel shares. They were purchased by a member of the free church and presented to the evangelical party of the Church of England. Matters were made more difficult in February 1841 when St Giles' Church was destroyed by fire. It was rebuilt and reconsecrated in November 1844 by the Bishop of Winchester.

When in the same year the Revd Stephen Bridge was appointed to the chapel of ease he made a condition that a consecrated church be built in its place. Eventually, in July 1848, St Matthew's Church was consecrated by the Bishop of Winchester.

The Revd Stephen Bridge was vicar of St Matthew's for a further 25 years, during which time an infants' school was added to the new girls' school in Camberwell New Road. The original girls' school had been built in 1832 by the congregation in thanksgiving for their deliverance from an epidemic of cholera.

The church was fortunate in its clergy and its reputation grew over the years. It was so well attended that to be certain of a seat for any service, one would have to arrive at least 30 minutes early and after the service the hill was lined with carriages waiting to take the churchgoers home.

One of St Matthew's most ardent worshippers was the artist Samuel Prout who lived in De Crespigny Terrace where the Salvation Army College stands in 2003. When he died in February 1852, the Revd Stephen Bridge conducted the service of burial before his interment in Norwood Cemetery. John James Ruskin wrote to his son John, in Venice, to tell him of his friend's death, saying that it had been announced during that day's service.

During the 1860s the railway arrived in Denmark Hill and great changes took place. The De Crespigny family had sold their estate in 1840 and many of the larger houses were turned into hotels or were demolished and smaller houses built in their place. Generally it was thought 'the Hill lost much of its exclusiveness'.

However, St Matthew's maintained its reputation and high attendance. It invested in a fine organ and gradually built up a good name for its standard of music and choir singing. Its schools prospered and the boys' school, which was built in the 1860s, helped raise money for the construction of King's College Hospital on a site next to the church. There is a plaque in the chapel of the hospital noting the efforts of the headmaster, Mr Knapp, and the boys.

As with all other churches in the area, St Matthew's was closely involved with the hospital throughout the First World War.

At the outbreak of the Second World War, most of the children were evacuated to safe areas and the congregation numbers fell. The church had no time to recover and on the night of 26 September 1940, at the height of the Blitz, a stick of incendiary bombs fell on St Matthew's and the building was devoured by flames. The congregation took refuge in the girls' school in Camberwell New Road but that was also destroyed by enemy action – except for its great iron bell. The congregation then met in the house next to the old church until the modern St Matthew's was built in Lilford Road.

St Matthew's Church had been declared redundant but the Ecclesiastical Commission eventually realised that huge numbers of people were moving into the area in order to inhabit the blocks of flats that were being built. When the new church was dedicated in 1960 the vicar of St Saviour's also became the vicar of St Matthew's and the two parishes were conjoined. The great iron bell, saved from the school, was incorporated into the new church building.

St Saviour's Church

For years, as transport services improved, houses and villas had been built along the ancient Coldharbour Lane. Fields that had lain behind Denmark and Herne Hills disappeared under roads and terraces. The development of roads east and west of the present Herne Hill Road stopped at the land boundaries of the Sanders estate. The population grew so rapidly that the Revd Stephen Bridge of St Matthew's Church felt a new church was needed. A site was initially suggested in Coldharbour Lane but when a new branch of the London, Chatham and Dover Railway reached Loughborough Junction the Ecclesiastical Commission changed its mind.

A solution was eventually provided by James Minet who gave an acre of land adjacent to the Sanders estate to the Revd Bridge. The architect, A.O. Gough (who had built St Matthew's) was engaged and building began. The foundation-stone was laid by the wife of W.H. Stone of Casina House and in June 1867 the new church was consecrated by the Bishop of Winchester. The first vicar was installed and a new parish was formed.

As the population of the area increased, concern was felt for the large number of children who had no means of education. In 1869, a year before the 1870 Education Act was passed, a girls' school with adjacent schoolhouse was opened. By the 1890s, 2,500 more people had moved into the area and pressure mounted for the Church school to be enlarged to include infants. This resulted in some rebuilding and a lessening of pressure for school places.

During this decade a Benevolent Society was founded for the care of poor parishioners and their families. Thus, some of the problems associated with the care of its members were eased.

In 1914 Sir Robert Sanders MP presented the church with half an acre of land for the building of a parish hall. The architect was Professor Beresford Pite of Brixton Technical College; he was the brother of the architect of King's College Hospital and the son of the architect of the Milkwood Road estate.

War was declared a year after the opening of King's College Hospital next to the newly-opened Ruskin Park. Part of the hospital (later also the park) was taken over by the War Department. Huts were built for convalescent soldiers and the parish hall was put to use as a workroom for the wives of absent servicemen and as an entertainment centre for the men in the park, in King's, and the lst London General Hospital (St Gabriel's College, Myatts' Fields). A memorial to the war dead was unveiled in 1920 and for years the church was crowded each Armistice Sunday. The congregation responded to the bishop's appeal for 25 churches to be built in the new outer-London housing estates (among them Downham and Mitcham) and a club for the unemployed was founded.

At the outbreak of the Second World War, the Sunday school emptied but as elsewhere the evacuated children eventually returned and the school grew. In August 1940 the bombing of London began. A number of incidents occurred in the area surrounding the church, causing damage to its structure. It never really recovered and later subsidence occurred. The church was eventually considered unsafe and was closed and demolished after a long period of disuse. The vicarage had been rebuilt and every Sunday the parish hall became the church.

Prior to these occurrences, the congregation had been involved in the rebuilding of St Matthew's Church in Lilford Road. In July 1960 the new St Matthew's was dedicated and the vicar of St Saviour's was appointed as joint vicar to the two churches. When he retired a new vicar was not appointed until the 1980s when a solution was found – the parishes of St Saviour's and St Paul's joined to form the parish of Herne Hill, and St Matthew's Church returned to the parish of St Giles'.

St Paul's Church, Herne Hill

In the 1840s the Anglicans in the area decided that they were sufficiently numerous to warrant a church of their own. Those living near Dulwich Village could attend the college chapel but for most of those on Herne Hill there were the two St Matthews' (Brixton and Denmark Hill) or the prospect of travelling even further afield.

Blanche in *Ye Olde Parish of Camberwell* noted that the lease of a site was given by Mrs Simpson and the freehold acquired from the Dulwich College estate. Money was contributed by those living on Herne Hill and in some cases by those who were not Orthodox Anglicans. George Alexander was engaged as architect and building commenced. The church was consecrated by the Bishop of Winchester in December 1844. The new vicar, the Revd Anderson, and his family lived in a house opposite St Paul's until a vicarage was built behind the church.

Some 14 years later the church was burned down but fortunately the vicar had had the foresight to insure it. He had considered fire inevitable, in view

St Paul's Church, Herne Hill, 1930s.

of the siting of the boiler flues. With the insurance money and further contributions from parishioners, it was possible to start rebuilding. The architect A.G. Street (later of Law Court fame) presented a plan which pleased John Ruskin. He had not admired the first St Paul's and after its destruction had distressed many people on Herne Hill by visiting them and congratulating them on their loss!

St Paul's was very fortunate in its vicars. It had only three in the first 50 years. The second was the Revd Powell whose son married the daughter of the resident of the Abbey, which had stood just above what is now the Mansions and the garage at the bottom of Herne Hill. The third vicar was the Revd Stephen Bridge, the son of the vicar of St Matthew's, Denmark Hill. It was during his ministry that the daughter church of St John's was built. There are memorial tablets to him in both churches.

At this time the parish was becoming very populous and by the 1880s many of the original properties on the hill had been replaced by smaller but well-to-do villas. It was still a prosperous place in which to live and on Booth's survey map of 1899 the area was painted yellow as a sign of wealth.

In the great freeze of 1895 and during the nationwide agricultural depression when so many of the country parsons were unable to let their glebe lands, the hill community was able to respond to appeals for help. It also joined other churches and schools in the area to celebrate the Golden and Diamond Jubilees of Queen Victoria. In 1901 a memorial to John Ruskin was unveiled by William Holman Hunt, the last of the pre-Raphaelites. (It had been Ruskin's support that helped turn the tide of public opinion in their favour.) In 1921 a memorial was also unveiled in memory of men lost during the First World War.

During the Second World War St Paul's was damaged on two occasions. In the first Blitz an incendiary bomb set light to the south aisle but, as with St Paul's Cathedral, swift action on the part of fire-watchers helped extinguish the flames before too much damage was done. In July 1944 a flying bomb fell in Carver Road and caused widespread local damage, a fatality and other injuries, and blew out the glass in the east windows.

As in many areas of South East London, the population demographic changed when a number of young people were evacuated or called up. After the war the population in the area around the church increased and the need for a parish hall became evident. This had been planned during the pre-war period and land had been purchased next to the church grounds. Fund-raising for the building began and when the first flush of rebuilding of damaged properties had been carried out, construction started on the church hall. It was opened in 1958 and since then has played an important part in the life of the community.

Unlike most parish churches built in the area during the Victorian era, St Paul's survived intact after its first destruction by fire. It seems that it will continue into the millennium.

ST JOHN'S CHURCH, LOWDEN ROAD

When the Milkwood Road housing estate was built, it added 3,000 more souls to the parish of St Paul's. At the time, access to St Paul's was not easy as none of the roads between Lowden Road and Herne Hill existed, except the long Milkwood Road and Poplar Walk, both of which were only partially made up.

A curate was engaged with special responsibility for those living in the vicinity and for raising funds to build a small church. In 1881 St John's was opened on an island at the junction of Lowden and Heron Roads, very near Jessop Road School. Neville's Bakery was built between the church and the school and provided employment for many of those living on the estate. The firm had provided houses around the bakery for some of its workers and beside the railway embankment there was a garden where employees could spend time. Many of the workers also attended the church.

The new church was greatly needed in the community and was soon so full that an extension became necessary.

A very large proportion of the children living on the estate attended both Jessop Road School and St John's Sunday School and it was logical that the vicar of St Paul's and the curate should become members of the school committee.

St John's became an integral part of the community. It had a reading room where a year's membership could be obtained for a small fee (1s. for youths, 1s.6d. for men). During the week many activities took place at the church hall and the Girls' Friendly Society, Boys' Brigade, and Women's Unions flourished until the outbreak of the Second World War.

St John's never recovered its vitality after the war. Jessop Road School had to be rebuilt and Neville's Bakery was sold to Westons, the biscuit manufacturers, who closed it after a period of neglect. Most destructive of all for the community was the end of so many of the 99-year leases of houses on the estate.

Property neglect led to many people moving away and a general degeneration of the area. The church was used increasingly as a community centre and the Heron Club, which met regularly, was very active.

In 1981, the centennial year, a new community association was formed which promised to give new life to the church and centre. A week-long celebration took place and among the events was a civic service, and entertainments and an exhibition based on the history of St John's and St Paul's. A grant was received from the Borough Council, which helped in the renovation of the church as a community centre. The organ was sold and the kitchen revamped. The Heron Club continued and luncheon clubs were started. After-school projects and holiday projects were tried but failed. The site of Neville's Bakery was joined to the church grounds to form an open space and a fenced playground was provided for young children and used mainly by the adjoining school. However, few people were interested in taking advantage of the area for its intended purpose and, despite their prohibition, dog walkers are the main users.

ST JUDE'S CHURCH, DULWICH ROAD

By the 1860s the area of Herne Hill bordering upon the parish of St Matthew's, Brixton, had become sufficiently populous to necessitate the building of a new church. This became even more urgent when the railway embankment divided the area, and St Paul's Church, Herne Hill, seemed even further afield to those living beside the railway and the Brockwell estate. St Matthew's Church, Brixton, felt the pressure of overcrowding; two men named Joseph Moore and Herbert Dalton were particularly aware of this problem. In 1867 they purchased land from Joshua Blackburn (heir to John Blades) for £736 and freely conveyed it to the Ecclesiastical Commission. The architect E.C. Robins won the contest for designing the new church and fund-raising began. In 1867 the foundation-stone was laid by Joshua Blackburn, who had returned the purchase money as a contribution to the building fund. In October 1868 the new Church of St Jude's was consecrated, a new parish formed, and the Revd Ransford, the curate of St Matthew's, Brixton, was appointed as the first vicar. Within four years the church building debt had been discharged and money had been raised for the purchase of an organ.

Adjustments were made to both St Matthew's and St Paul's parish boundaries and St Jude's accepted responsibility for the area on the Brockwell estate side of the railway, including the school, the name of which was changed from St Paul's to St Jude's.

Soon a parish hall became necessary to cater for the needs of the 5,000 people then living in the area. There was sufficient land on which to build a hall next to the school in West Place. It was opened in 1887 and, as a result of a bazaar held in the Brockwell estate grounds, was free of debt within a year.

St Jude's Church, Dulwich Road, was built in the 1860s on land purchased from the Brockwell estate. It was so successful that its debts were soon discharged and a new parish was formed. A parish hall was built in Railton Road and a school was established.

The hall was used as part of the school and for church activities. The caretaker lived above and Sunday school was held there. During the 1920s the Sunday school provided for more than 600 children who were taught by at least 60 teachers and the boys overflowed into premises in the Effra Road Board School. The Mothers' Union, the Boys' Brigade (with a bugle band that won many competitions), the Girl Guides, the Girls' Friendly Society, the Young Empire Builders, the Band of Hope and needlework and singing classes all met in the hall.

Over the years St Jude's Church, the vicarage and the parish hall suffered the usual wear and tear of time and use and often needed repair and maintenance. The vicarage suffered from dry rot, but hardest to bear was the arson attack which destroyed the newly-renovated organ and the entire music library, so valuable to the choir and musical life of the church.

Parts of the community around St Jude's were considerably impoverished. Certainly during the period of the First World War the vicar of St Jude's visited the Docklands to collect carcasses of meat and other foodstuffs sent to Britain from the Empire to give to his needy parishioners. There was no form of rationing other than that imposed by personal finances.

The church lost many of its young men during the First World War and, in common with other churches and chapels, erected its own memorial on oak panels with names in gold.

The church appointed a parish nurse whose services were available on application to the vicar – contributions were welcome if the patients could afford to pay.

The church was badly damaged by fire in 1923 but was repaired and, despite hard times nationally, prospered in the 1920s and '30s. It was reputed that some of the congregation had transferred from St Paul's in Herne Hill because the services there were considered 'too high'.

At the beginning of the Second World War, St Jude's found itself with a small congregation and a practically empty Sunday school. However, within a few months many of the children had returned from evacuation and the population adjusted to wartime conditions. The quiet time did not last long and in the summer of 1940 bombing began and the church, vicarage, school and parish hall were all damaged. Some of the damage was repaired and the vicarage was rebuilt as soon as possible after the end of hostilities. The church never recovered. Services were held in the side chapel and Sunday school in the

St Jude's Church, 1920s. The church was built during Victorian times on the edge of what is now Brockwell Park. It has had a chequered life and was eventually passed to a commercial concern. The vicarage was rebuilt and every Sunday the church shares the premises of St Jude's School in Regent Road.

vestry and vicarage. Some people did not return to Herne Hill from evacuation and the bigger houses were nearly all subdivided.

By the 1960s the church was derelict, although the roof was intact. The local population had changed entirely by the 1970s and in 1974 it was decided to transfer the freehold of the church to a budget office-furniture firm. In October 1973 St Jude's School, Railton Road, had moved to new premises in Regent Road, and the old St Jude's School and hall passed to a Pentecostal church. In the design of the new school, provision had been made for religious observance and church activities. In 1974 the church was transferred to the new school and since then services have been held at the school every Sunday. St Jude's parish remains intact.

St Faith's Church, North Dulwich

During the first decade of the twentieth century it was thought probable that a new church would be necessary in the North Dulwich area of Herne Hill, which was fast being developed. Land at the junction of Red Post Hill and Sunray Avenue was acquired from the Dulwich College estate and a parish hall was built and consecrated by the Bishop of Southwark in 1909 for all church purposes, including services.

In 1924 this was made a Mission District and a temporary parsonage was taken on Denmark Hill. In 1941 it changed to a Conventional District, prior to its separation from St Paul's, Herne Hill, and its first minister was appointed. A new parsonage was built in the church grounds and plans were made for the building of a new church. The foundation-stone was laid in 1956 and the church was consecrated in October 1957.

Additions were made to the parish hall, which connected with the new Church of St Faith's. The cost was met largely by the War Damage Commission

from funds awarded for churches destroyed but not rebuilt and a bequest for stained-glass windows for one of these churches was transferred to St Faith's.

At the time of writing St Faith's is very much a church of the community and in May 1989 a centre was opened by Princess Margaret. The church hall was renovated to accommodate the thriving and varied programme. A major refurbishment began in 1996 using money raised by the congregation.

Holy Trinity Church, Trinity Rise, Tulse Hill

Holy Trinity is not strictly speaking in Herne Hill but it is known that residents of Herne Hill have always attended the church. There was opposition to the founding of a church in the Tulse Hill area, particularly from the vicar of St Luke's, West Norwood, who felt it would deprive his church of income. He did not foresee the increase in population that would follow the arrival of the railway. The Church Commission rejected his argument and in 1856 Holy Trinity was consecrated and later a new parish was formed.

The church is said to be in 'early geometric decorated style' in Kentish ragstone and has the unusual feature of an unsupported nave. A parsonage and parish hall were built next to it.

The surrounding area was damaged during the Second World War and the church structure was undermined. It was eventually declared unsafe and all functions were briefly conducted in the parish hall, until that also needed renovation. The congregation moved to St Matthew's Church, Brixton, which had been damaged by bombs and then partially converted into a community centre. There the congregation of Holy Trinity remained until 1996 when it thankfully moved back into its own, beautifully renovated church, next door to its parish hall.

The parishes of St Matthew's, Brixton, and Holy Trinity, Tulse Hill, have been united into the new parish of Holy Trinity.

Holy Trinity Church, Trinity Rise.

Holy Trinity Church, Trinity Rise, is not strictly in Herne Hill but numerous people living in the area have walked through the park to attend services there.

ST PHILIP AND ST JAMES' CHURCH, POPLAR WALK

Built in 1905, St Philip and St James' is the only Catholic church in Herne Hill. It is known as an Ellis church, after the donor who gave money for funding churches in the South London area. At the time there was a dearth of churches in which those of the Catholic faith could worship.

A priest's residence was built on the site, very much a house of Edwardian times, with two storeys and steps leading to the front door. There was a garden laid out between the church and the house.

In the late 1960s land next to Rutland Court was given for the founding of a replacement church. It was later felt that the site was too narrow to accommodate a church, a house and a parish hall, and that car parking would be very difficult on a main highway. It was instead decided that St Philip and St James' Church should be refurbished and a parish hall built next to it for parochial use. This coincided with the arrival of Father Clements.

The axis of the church was changed. The altar was moved from the east to the middle of the south wall and the fitted pews were replaced with chairs. Stained-glass windows made at Buckfast Abbey were fitted and a small pipe organ was installed. Partitions can be slotted into the structure between the hall and church and can be opened to allow for a more expansive use for church purposes, parochial matters or social events. The garden was lost in the process of reconstruction.

For a number of years, the parish hall was the venue for meetings of the Herne Hill Society.

CHURCH OF THE NEW TESTAMENT OF GOD, GUERNSEY ROAD

In 1896 a small wooden chapel was built as a temporary measure in Guernsey Road to serve the population of the newly developing Rosendale Road, Peabody estate and Guernsey Road. It was replaced a little later by a tin building and in 1911 by a small Church of England chapel, a branch of Holy Trinity Church.

It remained an outreach chapel of Holy Trinity but in the early 1970s began to share its facilities with the New Testament Church of God. In 1979 the chapel passed entirely into its care and has continued so ever since. It has been refurbished and, at the time of writing, has many other functions during the week. It is cared for by a pastor and committee.

Chapter 5

⋘⊙⋙

NONCONFORMIST CHURCHES

THE METHODIST CHAPEL, RAILTON ROAD

At the time of writing there are a number of Nonconformist chapels and churches in Herne Hill and the surrounding area. Few worshippers bother about boundaries – instead attendance depends upon allegiance, family tradition, congregational friends and community activity.

However, this was not always so. The Methodists were among the earliest Nonconformists in the area. In the 1830s cottage meetings were held in the Dulwich Road home of the Fosberys, a postman and his wife. Later the meetings moved to Water Lane where they continued for more than 30 years until the 'congregation' became too large for comfort.

In 1869, the foundation-stones of London's first iron chapel were laid in Milton Road. Shortly afterwards, the chapel was included in the Lambeth circuit and soon every 'sitting' was let; a system similar to that practised by the Church of England. The congregation continued to grow, along with the surrounding population. In the absence of chapels of their own, members of other denominations attended, including Baptists, Congregationalists, Presbyterians and Swedenborgs.

Five years later it became necessary to build a new chapel in Railton Road (on the site of a redundant sandpit) with seating for 600 people. A jar was laid under the foundations containing newspapers, posters and tickets to both the opening ceremonies of the Railton Road chapels. The jar came to light nearly 100 years later when the bomb-damaged Railton Road Chapel was demolished to make way for the present foundation.

When the Railton Road Chapel opened in 1875, the Fosberys were still members of the congregation. Alderman Hubbart, who had been a member of the cottage group, said that he had felt that they were saints, such as one read about but 'seldom met in life'.

By 1895 the chapel's building debt had been considerably reduced by energetic fund-raising but as the metropolis crept nearer, many well-to-do members moved further out into areas like Streatham and membership dropped to 250. This was despite the union of several branches of Methodism to create the United Methodist Free Church. (It was not until the late 1930s that all national branches joined together; the small Primitive Methodists had rejected the idea of an amalgamation because of differences of political approach.)

Congregation numbers fell drastically at the beginning of the Second World War. The chapel was badly damaged by bombs and, although emergency repairs were carried out in the postwar period, the passing of time and a changing population again made rebuilding a necessity.

In 1969 the foundation-stone of the new chapel was laid by the Revd Urwin who had been minister

The Railton Road Methodist Church, 1905. This photograph was taken before the installation of street lighting and a tarmac road surface.

during the First World War. A year later the chapel was opened – a light, modern building with good acoustics. A jar containing information about chapel members and the local area was again placed under the foundations.

By this time the Dulwich Road Mission had closed and the members had joined the Railton Road Methodists, bringing with them their Scout troop and women's group. Many alterations took place in the area around the chapel and community projects were established. At the time of writing the chapel is shared with other groups.

THE METHODIST CHURCH, HALF MOON LANE

During the late-Victorian and Edwardian periods a number of Nonconformist churches and chapels were built in the neighbourhood of Herne Hill.

The building and dedication of the Half Moon Lane Methodist Church coincided with the formation of the parish of St Barnabas', Dulwich Village, some 50 years after the parish of St Paul's was formed.

Land at the junction of Half Moon Lane and Beckwith Road was purchased and dedicated in time for the turn of the century. Dyos commented in *A Victorian Suburb* that the cost of over £8,000 was raised almost entirely by the efforts of the Ladies' Committee. Money was also raised for the building of halls and rooms on the site adjacent to the church in Half Moon Lane.

The church and halls were badly damaged in bombing raids during the Second World War and although the halls were rebuilt in 1953 the congregation was continually involved in the expense of repairs to the church. In 1960 the members

celebrated the sixtieth anniversary of its dedication.

Soon after that happy event, the members were involved in the debate on unification of the Anglican and Methodist Churches that was taking place nationally. The Methodist Conference agreed the measure but not the Anglican Synod.

In 1971 the Methodists and members of St Faith's Church agreed to share worship. The site of the Half Moon Methodist Church was cleared and a block of flats, Wesley House, was built, the halls being retained for their separate activities. The two churches worshipped together for 14 years but in 1985 the Methodists and the United Reform Church (originally the Red Post Hill Congregational Church) agreed to join together under the title of the Herne Hill United Reform Church. The halls of both churches were again retained separately. Both partners agreed to maintain commitment to their respective faiths but to be united in their community. At the time of writing they share their minister with another church in Barry Road, East Dulwich, which also has joint membership.

DENMARK PLACE BAPTIST CHURCH

Just over 100 years before the Baptist church in Half Moon Lane was built, a small Baptist chapel was opened in Denmark Place. By the 1820s it was very poorly attended but the appointment of a new pastor saw the congregation revived and soon much larger premises were needed. The new chapel opened in 1825 but within a few years it had to be enlarged by the addition of galleries. It continued to prosper and a school was built next door, which was eventually demolished. A prominent member of the original chapel was William Brodie Gurney who lived on

The Methodist church at the junction of Half Moon Lane with Beckwith Road and Village Way (above left). When carts and horse buses were the only traffic it was safe to pose here for photographs. The church was damaged during the war and demolished in the 1960s. The Methodist halls and Wesley House occupy the site in 2003 (above right).

Top: *A notice announcing the reopening of the Railton Road Methodist Chapel after extensive repairs in 1949.*

Denmark Hill. He was involved in the Sunday School Union, the British and Foreign Bible Society and in educational projects. He was an official shorthand writer for the Houses of Parliament.

Charles Booth's 1900 report on religious influences mentioned that about 100 women attended the mothers' meetings on Monday afternoons. They came with their babies and sewing to have books read to them as they worked. There were other women's meetings where parcels were packed for the parish poor, and there was a monthly sewing day when the women worked to provide articles for the 'maternal society' and the families of poor ministers.

At the time of writing the chapel is well attended despite the opening of several Baptist chapels in Brixton, Dulwich, Camberwell and Herne Hill.

THE METROPOLITAN TABERNACLE

In 1859 the Metropolitan Tabernacle, Elephant and Castle, was built to accommodate the congregation of the charismatic young pastor Charles Spurgeon. Space for 6,000 worshippers (3,500 standing) was provided but, when Spurgeon preached, this was not enough. Every seat was taken well ahead of time and all the standing space was filled as the crowds flowed out onto the portico of the huge building. There was a lecture hall for 900 and a schoolroom for 1,000 children. The young pastor had already founded the Stockwell Orphanage and the Training College for Pastors.

The tabernacle was rebuilt in 1899 following a fire and was destroyed by enemy action in 1941. It was again rebuilt and reopened in 1959, 100 years after the original opening, but the seating capacity was substantially less (only 1,750 persons could be accommodated). In 1923 a Residential Training College was opened in Norwood at Falkland Place, the original home of Viscount Falkland.

THE BAPTIST CHURCH, HALF MOON LANE, WINTERBROOK ROAD

In 1897 a group of people who met in premises under the arches of Loughborough Junction railway felt a Baptist church was needed in the southern part of Herne Hill, where new roads were being laid and many houses built.

A site was acquired from the Dulwich College estate governors and building commenced. Foundation-stones were laid in 1898. The 'Church' was officially founded and the first pastor appointed in January 1899, and in May of that year the church hall was opened.

In 1904 the building of the present church commenced. Concrete foundations and special arching were necessary because of the proximity of the River Effra. In June 12 foundation-stones were laid and in March 1906 the church was opened amid celebrations and thanksgiving – particularly for those who had worked so hard for its foundation and to pay off half of the debt.

The church flourished, increasing its membership, widening its horizons to overseas missions and working to pay off its remaining debt. During the devastation of the First World War membership increased and, in common with St Saviour's and St Matthew's, convalescent soldiers from the 4th London General Hospital (King's College Hospital) were entertained. In 1920 a memorial pulpit was erected for the men lost during the war.

In 1923 the building debt was entirely cleared. Over the years many improvements were undertaken and a number of societies formed, especially for the younger members of the congregation. At the outbreak of the Second World War children were evacuated and young people joined the Forces, but when a large number of children returned, Guides, Brownies, Cubs and Scout troops were formed. A canteen was opened for the men and women of the Royal Corps of Signals stationed nearby (at least one signaller married a church member) and an Air-Raid Wardens' Post occupied part of the church premises. Later, the rent paid for the Wardens' Post contributed towards the insulation of a gas-fired hot-water system to heat the radiators.

In 1974 a decision was made to convert the church into a two-storey building. The plans of the original structure allowed for this eventually but it did mean a large debt had to be accepted. The work was carried out and the subsequent debt paid off within eight years. Since then other projects have been undertaken, such as the re-slating of the roof (churches usually require re-roofing every 100 years or so) and the church has been thoroughly modernised, including the introduction of an electronic organ and the setting up of a music group.

Recently the church has moved out into the community to the Effra Parade School. The River Effra links them together, even if it does flow underground.

THE CONGREGATIONAL CHURCH, DENMARK HILL

Most of the churches built in the Herne Hill area around the turn of the century were founded as a direct result of the housing developments in their vicinity. By the 1890s housing developments were gradually spreading towards the two hills from all directions and many new houses on the Lambeth side of Herne Hill had replaced the first generation of larger, more opulent villas. A little later the houses on the Dulwich side of the road were being replaced by houses similar to those on the Lambeth side.

Left: *The Baptist church in Half Moon Lane was opened in 1906. It has two storeys and central heating.*

Right: *The interior of the Baptist chapel, Half Moon Lane. The chapel's congregation has always moved with the times and a band has often led the singing during services. The chapel was fortunate in that it suffered little damage during the Second World War.*

Left: *Alfred Conder's (the architect) illustration of the Gothic-style Congregational church in Denmark Hill. The church was built in response to the area's growing population and was designed to allow for expansion to 800 sittings. Ground space was reserved for future development. A 500-year lease had been granted by the Dulwich College estate governors. The spire of the church stood as a landmark for many years.*

Right: *Herne Hill Congretional church at the junction of Denmark and Red Post Hills, before 1914. The Casina estate was on the opposite corner. During the Second World War, nearby bombing caused subsidence, which subsequently led to the demolition of the church. It was rebuilt in an entirely modern style, but is still a landmark.*

Much of the land between the Casina estate and Simpson's Alley was redeveloped.

The Congregational churches in Camberwell and Barry Road, East Dulwich, continued to increase their own membership but were supportive of plans to found a new church in Herne Hill. Contributions came from many sources: the London Congretional Union gave £1,000; Miss Keen, of Streatham, paid for the tower and spire; and Alderman Evan Spicer of 'Belair', later chairman of the London County Council, helped secure the 500-year lease from the Dulwich College estate.

In 1902, whilst awaiting completion of the church hall (facing onto Red Post Hill), services were held in the billiard room of Casina House. The charge was 2s.6d. for a single service and 5s. for two services. When the hall was completed, work began on the church and in June 1904 the Gothic-looking building was ready for occupation and the Church body officially founded. There was seating for 450 people, the church was lit by electricity and it had a hot-water radiator system for heating. For a number of years it was necessary to fund-raise before the building debt was discharged.

As the population in the surrounding area grew, so the church prospered. A summer fête was held annually in the grounds of the church and spread to those of Aylesford House opposite.

The church stood as a landmark at the junction of Denmark and Red Post Hills and featured in many photographic postcards sold in Herne Hill.

In 1941 the Loughborough Park Congregational Church, situated near the junction of Herne Hill Road and Coldharbour Lane, closed. It had been considerably bomb-damaged during the London Blitz. Many of the congregation walked up Herne Hill Road to worship at the Red Post Hill church. To accommodate the expanding attendance a temporary hall was built in 1940 next to the original one.

Sadly, over the years that followed and partly due to the bombing, the foundations of the church began to slip downhill and in 1949 it had to be demolished. Unfortunately no compensation for war damage could be claimed as there had been no direct hit and the expense of rebuilding was borne by the congregation. Services and other activities were held in the church hall until the new building was completed.

A light and modern church replaced the old Gothic-style one. Like its predecessors, it continues to be a landmark.

In 1970 the Congregational Church body held talks with the Presbyterian Church of England and Wales. Unlike those talks between the Church of England and the Methodists they were successful and in 1972 they amalgamated to become the United Reformed Church of England and Wales, later joined by the Church of Christ. The Denmark Hill church had welcomed a number of new members from the Blanchedowne estate when the small Baptist outreach group ceased to meet. The group started in the village hall of the estate but closed several years later due to lack of support. Its congregation then moved to other local churches, according to their inclinations.

In 1985 the Herne Hill Methodist Church (formerly Half Moon Lane) negotiated with the United Reform Church on Denmark Hill. The two united to become the United Reform Church/Methodist Church (the Herne Hill United Reform Church), each church retaining its hall for its separate use.

In 1988 the United Reform Church Housing Association built Hilltops Houses next to the church hall, on land once occupied by the 1940 temporary hall. Many people in the community were involved in the project, as were members of the church. Hilltops Houses is now run by the English Churches Housing Association.

The original church hall was refurbished and modernised. It is not only used for church functions but is also hired to other societies, including the Herne Hill Society which holds its monthly meeting there.

THE SALVATION ARMY

Herne Hill's connection with the Salvation Army predates its foundation in 1865 in Whitechapel by the Revd William Booth (General Booth).

William Booth had undergone a religious conversion in a Wesleyan chapel in Nottingham in 1844. Some time later, on a Sunday morning, he preached at the Water Lane home of the Fosberys.

One of the regular worshippers at the cottage meetings was a young woman who lived in Russell Street, now Hillyard Street in Brixton. Her name was Catherine Mumford. It was pouring with rain at the end of the meeting and Catherine's carriage had not arrived. William Booth was asked if he could take her home. It was love at first sight and they married a short time later. There is a photograph of the Fosberys held at the Railton Road Methodist Church under which is written a statement testifying to the meeting and to the fact that William Booth had signed the 'pledge book'.

Many years later, the minister and a church worker visited Catherine Bramwell-Booth, a descendant of the general and his wife. She was then in her 100th year and was glad to hear news of the Railton Road Methodist Church, for she had heard much about it from her grandparents, William and Catherine Booth.

The Salvation Army entered Herne Hill through the 'Out Post' at Loughborough Junction in August 1881, from the Camberwell Corps (the Conquerors).

At one of the outdoor meetings held by the Salvation Army, two sergeants were 'run in' by the police following a complaint by an enraged citizen. The meetings attracted large crowds, especially at Easter time when the Brixton Corps sent their brass band to lead the marches. They had many converts, especially among the drinkers – one reported that his family wanted to know what was wrong when he arrived home sober!

Around About a Pound a Week by Maude Pember Reeves does much to enlighten the reader about the poverty of life in parts of Lambeth, Loughborough Junction and Camberwell. Hard liquor was easily bought at any number of public houses and longer opening hours meant that alcohol was available at most times. Within a short period the 'Out Post' had a become a 'Corps' and a hall ('the best in Loughborough Junction') was being hired for anniversary meetings. An officer from Eastbourne was assisting, officers were being appointed and editions of *War Cry* were a sell-out.

The Salvation Army remained at Loughborough Junction for many years. They moved their barracks and secured the 'finest hall in the neighbourhood' near the railway as a permanent home, remaining there until they were bombed out of the Junction during the Blitz. They moved to a hall in Wanless Road where they remained for many years. Although they have left Herne Hill they are still in evidence, for it is only a short walk through Ruskin Park to William Booth Training College in Champion Park and the recently-erected accommodation for students and staff. Who could miss the Gilbert Scott water tower?

BRIXTON SYNAGOGUE

Herne Hill did not have a synagogue but many people of Jewish faith attended the one in Brixton. Brixton's first synagogue was Rutland Hall in Effra Road, which no longer exists. From the beginning it was considered a temporary building, even though it had seating for at least 300 members and room for social purposes.

It was recognised as the Brixton Synagogue in 1912. During the First World War the community expanded as it became a refuge for many of those fleeing Europe. After the war, fund-raising for a new synagogue began in earnest and in May 1921 the foundation-stone was laid for a new place of worship. In 1924 a Rabbinical Diploma was conferred on the minister and two years later the new hall was consecrated by the Chief Rabbi. By 1931 it had a membership of over 400 and a class roll of 3,500.

The synagogue survived the Second World War bombing and gradually recovered its membership but by 1981 changing social conditions had reduced its numbers drastically. Many members had transferred to the synagogue in Streatham, where plans were being made to rebuild in Leigham

Court Road with money raised from the sale of the Brixton site.

Many business schemes were put forward and fell through until 1990 when a business centre was successfully launched. At the time of writing only the distinctive façade of the old synagogue is still intact, but a yew tree has been planted in its grounds, carrying on the Jewish tradition of warding off evil.

THE GERMAN CHURCH

Founded in a school in 1854, the German church in Windsor Road (later Walk) was built and maintained by private subscription. It was opened in 1855 and was the only church in the area in which services were conducted entirely in German. The minister had to be ordained by the German Protestant Church and was elected for life by the community. The affairs of the church were conducted by five elders, elected by subscribers for three years' service at annual meetings. The church was entirely independent and the members were usually respectable families of German descent. There were several such families living on Denmark and Herne Hills, including the Benecke family.

The church prospered until the First World War when circumstances could have made many of the families with German names change them for English alternatives.

The population in the surrounding area had changed entirely by the 1930s and was no longer as wealthy or prosperous. The church fell on hard times and was finally demolished in the 1970s following a fire and its illicit use as a witches' coven where sacrifices of fowl were made on the altar. It had been empty for years.

The land on which the church stood was encompassed within the departments of the Maudsley Hospital.

The German church, Windsor Walk, was the only local church where services were conducted in German. It opened in 1855 and was demolished in the 1970s.

Chapter 6

Parliamentary Representation

Before the Great Reform Act of 1832, Lambeth had no parliamentary representation except as part of Surrey. For nearly 50 years, attempts had been made to increase popular representation. Governments had fallen, riots had occurred, lives had been lost and responsible men had refused to pay taxes because they had no representation in Parliament.

However, the bill finally received royal assent and bonfires blazed throughout the land. A number of boroughs were established, each to elect two members to the House of Commons, and a parliamentary borough was created from the parishes of Lambeth and Camberwell. This was divided into three parts for purposes of administration: Lambeth, Camberwell and Newington. A report was published in *The Times* listing the character qualifications desirable for Members of Parliament: an 'unsullied reputation of high moral worth and abilities fitting for a legislator.'

To stand for Parliament one needed to be 'well-to-do' or financially supported by others. There was no salary and no expenses were paid. Today strict checks are kept on election expenses, but before the privacy of the ballot box it was easy to run the risk of the charge of bribery and corruption, especially when the hustings were often held at public houses.

There was always great excitement during election periods. Many more people attended meetings than were entitled to vote and gatherings were often rowdy and disorderly with too few officers in attendance to keep order. Mounted messengers would collect results and gallop to the central committee rooms every 30 minutes.

At the first election Lambeth had less than 5,000 voters. Meetings were held at the Father Redcap in Camberwell Green, the Hour Glass in Walworth Common and the Horns in Kennington, and large numbers of people attended, flying flags and waving banners. There were four candidates. Mr Charles Tennyson and Mr Benjamin Hawes were declared elected on a show of hands (voting was a very public affair) but a proper poll was demanded with allegations of bribery and corruption. Two more polls gave the same result and Lambeth's first two MPs were declared 'duly elected'.

Speeches given after the declaration made

Lambeth election, the hustings, Kennington Green, 1875; a typical scene at election time. Many more people attended the proceedings than were entitled to vote and counting was by 'a show of hands'.

mention of reform of the established Church and the House of Lords. Then the triumphant pair climbed into their carriages and drove to the Elephant and Castle where huge crowds had gathered to greet them.

In the same year the Reform Bill became law and another Act was passed which defined the boundaries of the counties. They also returned two Members of Parliament each.

The 1867 Reform Act saw a redistribution of seats countrywide and an increase in the voting franchise: for occupants of houses with a rateable value of £12 or more; for those in leased properties; for men in boroughs with at least one year's residence; and for lodgers paying £10 or more in rent a year. The Act should have doubled the number of people entitled to vote but many found it difficult to enrol because of the inefficiency of those controlling registration.

Obstacles were put in their way by those who supported different political allegiances and limitations were caused by working hours. However, the 1872 Secret Ballot Act made men more anxious to vote because for the first time they were free of the fear of reprisals from employers and landlords.

In 1884 a further Reform Bill was passed providing another increase in the franchise and a redistribution of seats and single member constituencies.

Thus, in 1885, Herne Hill became part of the constituency of Norwood and able to elect its own Member of Parliament. Indeed, Norwood's first MP, Thomas Lynn Bristowe, was well known in Herne Hill for he lived at the top of Denmark Hill, near the present site of the United Reform Church. He was a sidesman at St Paul's, Herne Hill, and Sunday-school treats were held in his fields. At the time of Thomas Bristowe's residence, David Chadwick, MP for Macclesfield, lived at The Poplars at the top of Herne Hill. William H. Stone, former MP for Portsmouth, lived at Casina House.

The parliamentary legislation dealing with voting changes also applied to the municipal elections. Because of the increased responsibilities delegated to local Vestries, reform became necessary and county boroughs were set up nationwide. London, with a population of over four million, was considered a special case and in 1888 the Municipal Act created the directly elected London County Council, to which was added parts of Kent and Surrey. Thus Herne Hill became part of London. The population of the city continued to expand and within a few years the LCC was thought too unwieldy to govern the new London. A two-tiered system was introduced in 1899. Some 28 new metropolitan areas were created, one of them being Lambeth where the population had reached 302,000.

In 1855 the Metropolis Local Management Act had been passed. This replaced the old Poor Law Vestries, with Vestries served by 120 elected members. It was these huge unworkable Vestry systems that were replaced in 1900 by Borough Councils, with a mayor, aldermen and 60 councillors.

Thus, in 1900, Herne Hill was a constituent part of Norwood within the new borough of Lambeth and was part of London. The borough boundary still cut the area known as Herne Hill in two and Dulwich was considered a separate constituency and was still part of Surrey.

In *Ye Olde Parish of Camberwell* Blanche made it clear that the voters of Camberwell wished to be considered as a parliamentary borough in their own right, with the privilege of electing their own MP. They had a population of 125,000 and a high rateable value, which they considered enough to sever the parliamentary bond with Lambeth. They were able to do so in 1885. In this way Camberwell became a separate metropolitan borough and was also part of London.

It was not until 1918 that Dulwich was joined with the metropolitan borough of Camberwell and had to consider itself part of London, although still a parliamentary constituency in its own right.

Borough boundaries were altered again when the metropolitan boroughs of Camberwell and Southwark were joined and Lambeth was enlarged by the addition of parts of Wandsworth in 1968.

A review of parliamentary boundaries saw the two parts that make up Herne Hill joined together for the first time in history, at least in parliamentary terms. The parliamentary ward of Herne Hill (not all of which is thought by residents to be in Herne Hill, but actually considered to be in Brixton) and parts of the old constituencies of Dulwich and Norwood, made up the new parliamentary constituency of West Dulwich and Herne Hill. The 1997 election was the first to be held under the new election terms.

Right: *Meetings were held at the Horns Tavern in Kennington during the first Lambeth election.*

Chapter 7

ᥦᥩᥩᥬ

THE NAMING OF AREAS AND ROADWAYS

The district names of places within the area now known as London are often based upon historical memory and past languages and dialects and are sometimes the result of interpretation of old spellings.

The derivation of names of roads, streets and buildings are usually more recent and cover associations with past residents, their homes and estates. They are sometimes named after local physical features or even after famous people who often had nothing at all to do with the area.

The development of transport services allowed people to move out of the crowded centre of London to the new suburbs, causing them to grow at a phenomenal rate. Many of the new roads that were created were named at random, apparently by people who knew little of the area's past.

Locally, legend suggests that some roads were named by builders and developers who called upon their own experience, for example their birth places. Hinton and Alderton Roads, lying under the railway embankment in the northern part of Herne Hill, are said to be named after their developers' home parishes in Oxfordshire. Hollingbourne Road is named after a parish in Kent and Warmington Road after a parish in Warwickshire.

Lowden Road is thought to have derived its name from its low-lying position under the hill of Poplar Walk. Holmdene and Danecroft Roads are named after houses in the area.

Gubyon, Kestrel, Rollscourt and Woodquest Avenues are aptly named for they are tree-lined, but in some cases the naming of roads is a little fanciful. However, words like grove, crescent and gardens do avoid the repetitive use of road and street. The author has found through the course of research that roads were sometimes named before the construction of houses took place.

A number of roads have been straightened and widened and some of their names changed over the years: Red Post Hill was once Ashpole Hill; Denmark and Herne Hills were Holloway and then Dulwich Hill; Norwood Road was Nights Hill Lane and Norwood Lane; and Coldharbour Lane was known as Camberwell Lane.

London

The name London is of unknown origin, although it is possibly Celtic (as is the name Thames). In Roman times the city was named 'Londinium'; the Romans often based their names upon the 'native' origin. For hundreds of years the name London referred to the area we now call the City of London. With the growth of transport systems and the consequent spread of population, London covered a wider area. In the 1880s it became the County of London and included boroughs that had originally been in surrounding counties – in Lambeth's case, Surrey.

When Greater London came into being, enveloping many more outlying boroughs, it was a massive area of 700 square miles. Now that the GLC has disappeared, London as a geographical entity remains but boroughs have taken a more prominent role in London's government. The City of London is still separate.

Lambeth

The parish of St Mary at Lambeth stretched from the Thames to the parish of St Giles' in Camberwell, the borders being along Denmark and Herne Hills.

Lambhithe – an old name for Lambeth – could be the Saxon 'hithe' (a muddy bank of a river) or it could be named after a berth for the landing of lambs in the spring to feed on the grass of the marshlands, perhaps the result of the overflowing of the rivers running through the land to the Thames.

Camberwell (Camerwelle)

It is not known why Camberwell is so named, although the second part is obvious – no habitation is possible without a supply of water, in this case, springs and wells.

Left: *A view of St Paul's Church in Herne Hill. The cart has its wheels turned to prevent it from rolling.*

When these three photographs were taken the houses in Herne Hill were occupied by families, some with servants. At the time of writing the majority are

multi-occupied. Some of the trees remain, but many of the bushes have gone and most of the railings were contributed to the war effort. Gas has given way to electricity and the roadway has been tarmacked. The granite sets that once stood at the side road crossings have been covered over. There is a constant stream of motorised traffic and very few cyclists labour up the hill.

Left: Due to the leases lapsing at different times on either side of the hill, the houses on the left were built a little later than the houses on the right.

Below: Herne Hill with St Paul's Church. Again note the delivery cart with its wheels turned.

The Parish Church is dedicated to St Giles, the patron saint of cripples. It has been conjectured that the wells had medicinal virtues and that 'cam' meant crooked, thus 'crippled'.

At the time of the Domesday Book in 1086, the parish was called 'Cabrewelle'. So, however Camberwell came by its name, it is certainly at least 900 years old.

Southwark

The works opposite the City on the south bank of the Thames had little to do with Herne Hill until transport developments linked the suburbs with each other and London.

In 1965 the metropolitan boroughs of Southwark, Bermondsey and Camberwell were amalgamated to form the new borough of Southwark, which stretched from the Thames to Lambeth, part of its border being down the middle of Denmark and Herne Hills.

Given the number of past residents of some distinction, it is a little surprising that very few are commemorated in the names of roads. Too much would need to be altered in the way of maps and postal services if the roads were to be renamed but perhaps recognition could be made in another way – certainly plaques commemorating famous forebears are in short supply.

Herne Hill (the district)

At first Herne Hill referred to the hill itself but, after the coming of the railway when the station was given the name Hernehill, the wider area gradually acquired the name Herne Hill.

Herne Hill (from Red Post Hill to Half Moon Lane/Milkwood Road)

Noted as Dulwich Hill on old maps, the first mention of Herne Hill was in the latter part of the eighteenth century. There are several suggestions for its naming but none is certain. It is possible that it was named after a heronry in the valley but there is no mention of this and the author feels that John Ruskin, one of the greatest observers, would have noted it had it been there during his time of residence (1820–80) or if it had been mentioned to him as existing in the recent past. The area might be named after a field called Le Herne in Brixton, which is said to have adjoined the hill. It is possible that the name is derived from a family called Herne who are reputed to have had property in the area. They were city merchants and some were buried in the crypt of St Bride's, Fleet Street, next to John Blades of Brockwell Park.

A strange suggestion is that Herne is an Old English word for a 'crooked boundary'. The hill *was* winding and situated on a border but why, in the eighteenth century, suddenly call a roadway by an obsolete word?

One part of the name is certain: Hill, or Hyll, meaning an elevated piece of land.

Acland Crescent

This road is named after John Ruskin's great friend Dr Henry Acland, founder of the Oxford University School of Medicine. They met at university in Oxford and their friendship, which was markedly beneficial to Ruskin, was constant throughout their lives. The entrance to the grounds of the Ruskin home on Denmark Hill was almost opposite Acland Crescent.

Bicknell Road (from Cambria Road to the junction of Kemerton and Finsen Roads)

Bicknell Road was previously known as Anstey Road but the name was changed because of confusion with another road of the same name in a nearby area. It is not known why the road was named Bicknell but it is thought that when a change became necessary it was remembered that the public house on the corner of the road was previously named the Bicknell Arms.

It is not thought that the original naming of the public house had anything to do with the Bicknell family who had previously lived on Herne Hill, even though Elhanan Bicknell had been a master of the City Vintners' Company. He died in 1860 and the house was sold four years later, long before the public house was built.

The Blanchedowne estate (lying between Denmark Hill, Champion Hill, Green Dale and Sunray Avenue)

The following names on the estate are not connected in any way to previous establishments, such as the Bessemer estate, the Grange and the Ruskin estate:

Crossthwaite – a route that crosses the estate ('thwaite' meaning way).
Dylways – probably from the old spelling of Dulwich ('dyl' is a plant with a white flower, and 'wich' a damp meadow, a marsh, or a way).
Blanchedowne – to whiten, or 'blanche', and 'downe', meaning a hill.

It is said that the dyl, a white flower, was prolific in the Dulwich area and when flowering was noticeable from a distance.

During medieval times there was an area called Blanchdowne in the southern part of Dulwich, near the old coppice and Little Lordship.

Brantwood Road (from Poplar Walk to Fawnbrake Avenue)

Developed in the 1920s and '30s, Brantwood Road is named after Brantwood, the house and estate near Coniston in the Lake District which John Ruskin purchased in the 1870s. The area covered by

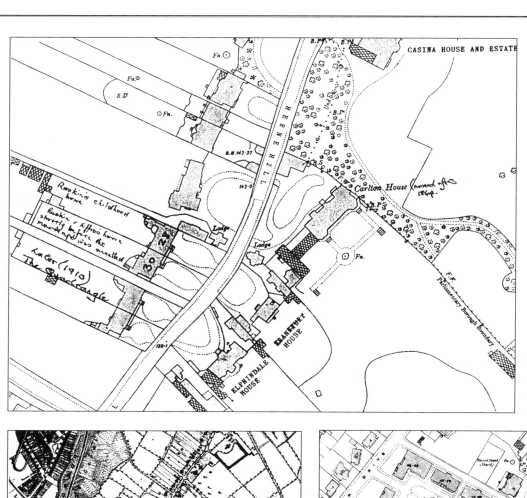

Left: *A map of the top of Herne Hill, 1890. Elphindale House and Frankfurt House are visible centre bottom and Casina House and estate top right.*

Below: *A map of the top of Herne Hill, 1939.*

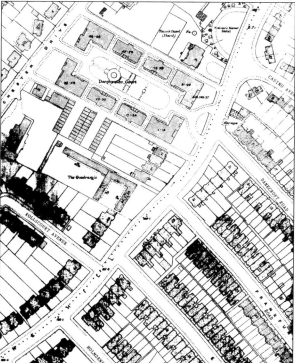

Left: *Streatham Detached, 1862. Part of the area of Herne Hill was completely detached from the manor of Leigham Court, purchased by Lord Thurlow in the 1780s when it was part farmland and part parkland. Lord Thurlow built a house in the grounds, but did not live there. On his death, the estate was sold and split up.*

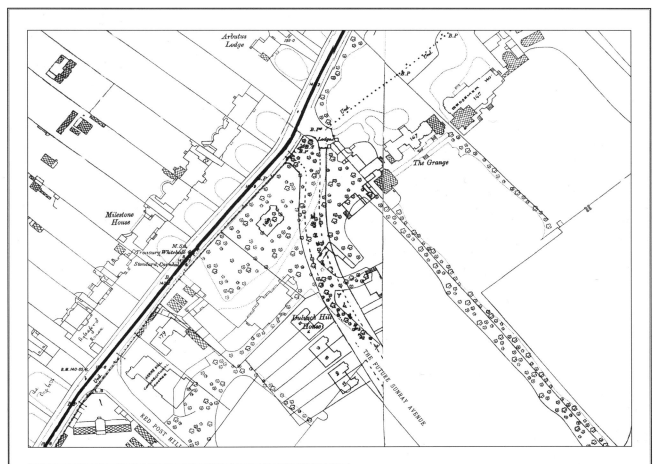

Above: *A map of upper Denmark Hill, 1894, when Sunray Avenue was being surveyed for later development. The Casina estate is in the bottom left corner and Arbutus Lodge in the centre at the top. All but one of the houses shown on this map have disappeared and there are numerous new roads. The milestone has also been removed.*

Left: *A map of the Herne Hill Road area, 1920s. The development of the Milkwood/Lowden Roads estate saw growth around the lower end of Herne Hill Road, much of it on land once owned by the Minet family. A church, St Saviour's, and a school for infants and girls was built into the plan and later Ruskin Park was formed. By the 1920s the two areas had merged and a Catholic church and library had been built. The local area was also served by a Post Office and numerous shops and pubs, as well as a good transport service. The Second World War saw some parts of the area altered beyond recognition.*

Brantwood Road was part of the Sanders estate and had nothing at all to do with Ruskin. The grounds of Ruskin's Herne Hill home did not reach the Brantwood Road area.

Brockwell Park

Once a common, Brockwell was named as a park after enclosure in 1810 and its subsequent purchase as an estate in 1813 by John Blades. An old house, Brockwell Hall standing by Norwood Lane was demolished and a new house of the same name was built upon one of the park's two hills; it is now referred to as the Mansion House.

Brock is an Old English word for badger as well as being the name for a stream. There are several springs within the park and evidence of a well in the Old English garden, once the kitchen garden of the estate. Park is the name given to the grounds of a manor-house and also an enclosed tract of land for hunting. As far as is known, there has never been any suggestion of hunting within the Brockwell Park area.

Burbage Road (from Half Moon Lane to Dulwich Village)

Only the first section of Burbage Road nearest to Half Moon Lane can be thought of as being in Herne Hill. It is named after Richard Burbage, the Elizabethan actor, theatre manager, friend and colleague of Shakespeare and Edward Alleyn.

The modern road is said to follow the line of an old pathway across the Severn Fields between the Old Greyhound public house in Dulwich Village and Herne Hill.

Cambria Road (from Coldharbour Lane to Bicknell Road)

Cambria Road is said to be named after the Cambria public house, itself named after a Thames barge, *The Cambria*. It is not known why the pub should be named after a barge but it could be a personal association of the original licensee.

Carlton House (on Herne Hill, lying next to the Casina Estate)

Whilst Elhanan Bicknell and his family lived on land next to the Casina estate the house had no name or number and the address was just Herne Hill. However, when Dr Edward Nicholson, a scientist who had premises (and worked) in the Elephant and Castle area, purchased the estate in the 1860s he named the house after South Carlton, Leicestershire, where he had lived as a child.

Carlton Parade (Herne Hill)

Carlton Parade is a row of shops with living accommodation above. It lies between Frankfurt and Elfindale Roads and was named after the nearby Carlton House.

The Carnegie Library (Herne Hill Road)

The library was named after Andrew Carnegie, a Scottish-American industrialist who considered that his family had sufficient money and that his fortune should therefore be used to fund educational and cultural projects.

The land the library stands on was purchased from the Sanders estate by the Minet Trust and given to the borough. According to the *Lambeth Official Guide of 1928* the Carnegie Library was named after 'the late Dr Carnegie' who was approached in 1901 by Mr Frank Burgoyne. Dr Carnegie eventually offered £12,500 and building commenced in 1904. At the time, the policy of the council was to have one library for every 40,000 people in Lambeth. It is the local authority's responsibility to keep the library stocked with books.

Carver Road (from Herne Hill to Half Moon Lane)

This road was named after the master of Dulwich College, Dr Alfred J. Carver, who, after the 1858 Act of Parliament, was appointed to 'modernise' and reorganise the educational system of the college after a long period of decline. He was one of the first masters of the college not to bear one of the derivations of the name Alleyn.

Casino Avenue (from Herne Hill to Red Post Hill)

Casino Avenue is named after the Casina estate, which faced onto Herne Hill at its junction with Red Post Hill. The Casina estate was purchased after the First World War under the 'Homes Fit for Heroes' policy and, with nearby land, was laid out and developed as the Casino estate.

The roadways making up the estate include the avenue, parts of Red Post Hill and Sunray Avenue, the latter two having already been partially developed prior to the new estate's layout. The houses on Herne Hill from Red Post Hill to the top of Casino Avenue by the petrol garage are also part of the development.

Champion Hill (from Denmark Hill to Green Dale)

Champion Hill is the most northerly part of the Dulwich estate on the boundary between the boroughs of Lambeth and Southwark. Once called Camberwell Hill, it was renamed after Champion De Crespigny, a member of a Huguenot family who came to England to escape persecution in the 1700s. The De Crespigny family prospered and owned a sizeable estate in Camberwell and were benefactors to the area.

De Crespigny Park and Champion Park are also named after the family. On old maps Champion Hill originally referred to an area on Denmark Hill which included the area that became Ruskin Park, the triangle of land between Denmark Hill and Champion Hill and the area to Grove Lane. Now it covers only Champion Hill itself.

Croxted Lane, 1860s. This is where John Ruskin walked as a young man and contemplated his literary works. The route later became the very busy Croxted Road from Norwood Road to Crystal Palace.

Coldharbour Lane (from Denmark Hill to Brixton Road)

Coldharbour Lane was originally called Camberwell Lane. The name is derived from an area that provided rest, but not shelter, along an ancient roadway, hence a cold harbour. Here travellers and drovers would also have found fodder and company, as distinguished from the warmth and food at an inn.

The lane is now a road on the northern border of the area of Herne Hill, above which runs the railway, forming a boundary between two areas.

Croxted Road (from Norwood Road to South Croxted Road and Park Hall Road)

Only part of Croxted Road lies within the Herne Hill area. It was known as Croxted Lane until the road was developed in the latter part of the nineteenth century. There are several explanations for the name:

Crokestrete – a crooked lane (it was winding).
Crox as a derivative of cross – a roadway along which pilgrims walked on their way to join the Pilgrims' Way to Canterbury.
A lane along which a branch of a river wound its way (one tributary of the Effra did flow along the road into Half Moon Lane).

An even stranger derivation would be from a jar or a pitcher, or an old horse or sheep.

It is said that pilgrims crossed the Thames near St Mary at Lambeth and made their way to Brixton via the roadway that became Acre Lane. From there they walked along Water Lane to either Half Moon Lane and on to Dulwich, or Croxted Lane and on to what is now Forest Hill, and from thence to join the Pilgrims' Way.

Deepdene Road (from Denmark Hill to Ferndene Road)

This road is possibly so named because the road slopes down to the valley (a dene). It runs almost parallel with Sunset Road and was laid out and partially developed just prior to the beginning of the First World War. Acland Crescent runs into the road, although it was laid out and developed at a much later date.

Deerdale Road, Oakbank Road, Haredale Road (from Herne Hill Road to Poplar Walk)

The clearance of trees from the lower part of Herne Hill during the Interregnum led to the area being used primarily for market gardening until the arrival of the railways and the housing development that followed. Many of the roads in the area have names that could be derived from the days when deer roamed the oak woods, and hares ran in the dales and on the banks.

Delawyck Close (Half Moon Lane)

Delawyck is an old spelling of Dulwich, derived from the white flower dyl and 'wyck' from 'wich' or 'wic', Anglo-Saxon for village. Another suggestion is 'wic' meaning a specialised farm. It is reputed that there was a knight during the reign of Henry III whose name was variously de la Wyk and de Dilewisse. The close was developed on the site of a dwelling called Delawyck House, originally part of the Dulwich estate, which could have been compulsorily purchased by the LCC.

Denmark Hill (from Camberwell Green to Herne Hill and Red Post Hill)

Denmark Hill is recorded as Dulwich Hill on John Rocques' map of 1762. It is thought to be named after the husband of Queen Anne, Prince George of Denmark, who is said to have had a hunting lodge on the hill and was thought to have kept a kennel of dogs in the area. Some think that it was his steward who had the lodge and kennel but that it was often used by Prince George. Dog Kennel Hill and The Fox Under the Hill are said to have derived their names from the same source, although the latter name could be because the Old Surrey Foxhounds were kennelled in the area before the hunt was moved to Shirley.

Right: *Ferndene Road just after the construction of the Carnegie Library in Herne Hill Road. The road was named Ferndene despite the fact that the first part of the road was named Dane Road after Dane House, a beautiful property on Denmark Hill.*

Left: *The junction of Herne Hill and Frankfurt Road. Local printers would often turn photographs into postcards and a loving aunt sent this picture to her nephew in hospital, it depicts his home.*

Right: *Elphindale Road, 1917. This is one of the side roads off Herne Hill leading to Half Moon Lane. The card was sent to a 'soldier at the Front'.*

Left: *Half Moon Lane, c.1905. This postcard was sent to Holland but carried no message as writing was not allowed on foreign mail. In 2003 the road is much busier but has not changed much physically.*

Dorchester Drive (from Poplar Walk to Brantwood Road)

Dorchester Drive was named after Dorchester House which was completed in 1935 on the site of Herne Hill Lodge. The house is now a Grade-II listed building.

The roadway was laid out in the 1920s but was not developed until the 1930s, allegedly due to the bankruptcy of the landlord. The private roadway of Dorchester Court, the frontage of which is on Herne Hill, leads into Dorchester Drive.

Dulwich Road (from Norwood Road to Brixton Water Lane)

The road that led from Norwood Lane to Brixton Hill was once called Water Lane because it followed part of the course of the River Effra. With the covering in of the River Effra and the subsequent construction of the railway embankment, the roadway was straightened. The section from Norwood Lane to the curve was renamed Dulwich Road and that from the curve to Brixton Hill was renamed Brixton Water Lane. The name Dulwich Road was simply chosen because it was the route to Dulwich.

Effra Road (from Water Lane to Brixton) and Effra Parade (from Dulwich Road at its junction with Water Lane to Railton Road)

Both Effra Road and Effra Parade are named after the river, the course of which flowed along parts of their locations.

Elmwood Road (from Half Moon Lane to its junction with Red Post Hill)

Elmwood Road could have been named to commemorate the elms that shaded the Long Pond before it was filled in or the elms that bordered the field on Half Moon Lane. One of the trees was the famous old elm at No. 50 Half Moon Lane that, according to legend, sheltered Queen Elizabeth I when she visited Dulwich and was caught in a rainstorm.

Ferndene Road (from Poplar Walk, crossing Herne Hill Road, to Denmark Hill)

This road was developed at different times over a long period. The first part, originally named Dane Avenue after Dane House on Denmark Hill, led from Denmark Hill through the Sanders estate. When the first part of Ruskin Park was created, the roadway wound around the park to join Dumbleton Road. That part of Dane Avenue was covered over following the second purchase of land and the creation of Ruskin Park as it is now.

Dane Avenue was extended to Herne Hill Road but was not fully laid out until after the First World War. The houses were built at different periods between the two wars on one side of the road. The building of some had to await the lapsing of the leases of houses on Denmark Hill and were built in the lower parts of the gardens of those homes. Construction was not completed until after the end of the Second World War.

Eventually the road was named Ferndene, adopting the name of the small road on the far side of

The houses on Ferndene Road were built as the leases expired on properties on Denmark Hill. The dwellings on the far left were built in the 1910s and the others during the 1930s at a time when it was customary for curtaining to be uniform, regardless of the different uses for each room.

Above: Half Moon Lane at its junction with Herne Hill and Milkwood Road, 1900. The decorations were in celebration of the new century.

Right: The Half Moon Inn. This is the third inn of the same name to be built on the site.

Half Moon Lane at its junction with Beckwith Road and Village Way, 1920s.

Herne Hill Road. The name is derived from 'dene', meaning valley, and ferns found in wooded areas. (Ferns became very popular during the Victorian period, after the production of plant cases enabled their importation from other climes.)

Finsen Road (from Herne Hill Road to Northway)

At the time of the purchase of the second part of Ruskin Park, Finsen Road was laid out on its northern border. The roadway was later curved round to include Dumbleton Road leading to Northway. The road is said to be named after Niels Finsen, a Danish physician and scientist who discovered the curative power of coloured rays. His lamp for concentrating violet rays was used in the treatment of lupus and other diseases.

Frankfurt Road (from Herne Hill to Elmwood Road) and Elphindale Road (from Herne Hill to Elmwood Road)

Both of these roads are named after the estates that lay next to each other on Herne Hill. The estates were part of the Dulwich House estate, their leases lapsing simultaneously. The roads were laid out and partially developed by 1910.

The grounds of Frankfurt House were next to Elhanan Bicknell's estate, the house of which was later called Carlton House. The terraces of shops between the two roadways form Carlton Parade.

Greendale (now from Champion Hill to East Dulwich Grove)

The name is derived from 'a country lane between two points' or 'a path leading to strip farming land'. The Dale (once called Green Lane) has experienced little development. It passes behind what is now Blanchedowne estate and emerges in East Dulwich Road near the James Allen School for Girls. It could be a survivor of an unmade road leading from the hamlet of Dulwich to St Giles', the Parish Church of Camberwell, which was used in the days before Dulwich had a church of its own. It is the only dirt road to have survived in the area.

Gubyon Avenue (from Herne Hill to Milkwood Road)

Gubyon Avenue is said to be named after a farm and its owner occupying the area. The first part of the road was originally called South Place. At that time there were only four large houses in the road.

Half Moon Lane (from the junction of old Norwood Lane, Herne Hill and Water Lane, to Dulwich)

Half Moon Lane is named after the inn that stood near the junction of Norwood and Water Lanes and Herne Hill, and the bridge that crossed the River Effra (Island Green).

Apart from the inn the most famous landmark was the ancient elm at No. 50 Half Moon Lane.

The Half Moon Inn

An inn with the sign of a Half Moon has stood in the vicinity since the beginning of the 1600s. It was part of the old coaching inn network, where travellers stopped for refreshment and rest. The inns were always positioned at a crossroads and the Horns in Kennington, the Father Red Cap in Camberwell Green and the Green Man at Loughborough Junction were similar establishments.

The Half Moon is no longer an inn on a coaching route, but a modern public house. The modern inn, dating from 1897, is the third of the same name.

Hawarden Road (from Croxted Road to Rosendale Road)

Developed during the first decade of the twentieth century, Hawarden Road is thought to be named after Hawarden Castle, Chester, the home of William Ewart Gladstone (1809–98), the Victorian politician who was Prime Minister on four occasions. The first home built in the road was Gladstone House. Its owner was an admirer of the politician and it is thought that he suggested the name of the road to the developer.

Herne Hill Road (from Coldharbour Lane to the junction of Herne and Denmark Hills)

Herne Hill Road originally ended by St Saviour's Church and it was not until the early 1900s that the Sanders estate sold land further up the hill, as far as the Carnegie Library, that that part of the road was laid out and developed.

The upper part was originally a pathway serving the large houses and gardens at the junction of Herne and Denmark Hills. When the leases on these properties lapsed, the road was laid out and the present houses were built during the 1920s and '30s. The road was obviously named after the hill but before it was officially established as a roadway the addresses used were the names of the rows of villas, terraces and cottages.

Heron Road (from Milkwood Road to Lowden Road)

Despite originally being part of the Archbishop of Canterbury's hunting grounds, there is no known information about herons or nesting sites at Herne Hill. Heron Road reinforces the myth of a heronry being situated here. This is one of the roads in the Milkwood/Lowden Roads development which now has houses on one side only, the other side having been bomb-damaged and then demolished.

Hinton Road (from Coldharbour Lane to Herne Hill Road)

The two railway bridges separate Hinton Road into distinct parts. The first part from the Loughborough Junction area consists of shops with housing accommodation above. It is now rather run down but was once part of the horse-drawn-tram route. The road is now thought of as part of the Milkwood/Lowden Roads estate but was actually laid out and partially built in 1865 before the larger development took place. Hinton Road is thought to have been named by a developer, after his parish of birth in Oxfordshire.

Howletts Road (from Half Moon Lane to Warmington Road)

Howletts Road was named after the meadow given for the 'use of the poor' in 1626 by Sir Edward Bowyer. It was sold by the parish in 1858. The old elm tree in Half Moon Lane was said to have stood on the boundary of the meadow.

Island Green

This is the meeting place of the branches of the River Effra (now the junction of Norwood, Dulwich and Railton Roads). In wet weather, before the course of the River Effra was bricked over, it often overflowed and caused an 'island of green'. There was also an Ireland Green at the junction of Ashpole Hill (Red Post Hill) and Half Moon Lane, which is visible on some old maps.

Kestrel Avenue (from Herne Hill to Fawnbrake Avenue)

The avenue is named after the kestrels that were said to nest in the spire of St Paul's Church on Herne Hill. The kestrels once hunted in the area behind the houses on the hill.

Loughborough Park/Junction

The junction and park were named after Loughborough House, the seventeenth-century home of Baron Loughborough (Henry Hastings), which stood in the vicinity. Loughborough Junction took its name from the nearby roadway and area, in the same way that Hernehill Station took its name from the nearby hill.

Meath House (a block of maisonettes facing onto Dulwich Road)

Meath House forms part of the Regent Road estate, built by the LCC during the postwar period to replace properties either destroyed or badly damaged during the bombing of London. It is named after the 12th Earl of Meath, Lord Brabazon, who was the first chairman of the LCC Parks Committee and Founder of the Metropolitan Public Gardens Association. Brockwell Park was purchased during his chairmanship.

Milkwood Road (from Herne Hill to Hinton Road)

Milkwood Road is named after the medieval manors of Milkwell and Wickwood. It was developed as the Milkwood/Lowden Roads estate in the 1870s, having previously been the site of market gardens.

Northway (from Cambria Road to Finsen Road and Ruskin Park)

Lying directly under the railway embankment, this roadway was named Northway because it is the most northerly road in the area.

Norwood Road (from Herne Hill to West Norwood, St Luke's Church)

This road was originally known as Norwood Lane because it was the route to Norwood, or the great North Wood, which stretched from Croydon to Norwood. Over the years the wood gradually lost its trees, particularly during the Cromwellian era, and by the 1800s the dome of St Paul's Cathedral could be seen from the windows of Norwood's first public house.

For centuries Norwood Lane was the main thoroughfare between Herne Hill, Norwood and Croydon. The only turning off the roadway was Croxted Lane. It was possible to walk along some country pathways to reach nearby areas.

The Peabody estate (off Rosendale Road, lying between two railway lines)

Built on the site of a disused brickfield, the estate is named after George Peabody, an American philanthropist who donated part of his great fortune to establishing a fund for the rehousing of London's poor. The Peabody estate was the first village-type settlement to be established. Until that time, all the association's housing had been built in the very limited areas available, which only allowed for blocks of flats.

Poets' Corner (between Dulwich and Railton Roads)

Poets' Corner is the name given to the complex of four roads lying in close proximity to each other. They are Chaucer, Spenser, Shakespeare and Milton Roads. None of these poets had any connection with Herne Hill.

These roads formed one of the first networks to be laid out in Herne Hill, years before the area was known by that name and before the railway embankment was built across the fields and market gardens. Shakespeare Road was later extended to Loughborough Junction.

Poplar Walk (from Herne Hill to Loughborough Junction)

The walk was shown on maps long before the area was developed but was not named as such. It could have been named after The Poplars on Herne Hill, which was so called due to the presence of poplar trees. There are relatively few houses along Poplar Walk and it is still mostly a pathway. It now lies between the back gardens of houses in Poplar Walk Road and the small roadways leading off Herne Hill Road.

Poplar Walk Road (from Milkwood Road to Lowden Road)

This road could have been named in memory of the past countryside but more likely takes its name from running parallel to Poplar Walk, its gardens backing onto the walk on one side of the road. There is no sign of any trees having been planted along its path and the road is now known as Poplar Road.

Railton Road (from Norwood Road to Atlantic Road, Brixton)

The naming of this road is uncertain. Different parts were laid out and named at various times, such as West Place and Commercial Place, and the whole length was not named until the 1890s. Suggestions are made that it was named after the railway or after the designer of Nelson's Column (although years had elapsed since), or perhaps after the second general of the Salvation Army, although the Army does not believe this to be the case.

Catherine Mumford met her husband William Booth in Herne Hill and there is a small street called Mumford Road off Railton Road. If named after her, she would not have been pleased to have a public house built on the corner of the road (it was burned down in the Brixton riots).

Herne Hill's first permanent Methodist church was built in Railton Road. There is the suggestion that the road was named after Gregory Railton who made an agreement in 1557 with two men, Henry Draper and John Bowyer, for the purchase of land. Herbert Railton (1859–1910), a draughtsman who abandoned architecture for book illustrations, is another possibility.

Red Post Hill (at the junction of Denmark Hill and Herne Hill, stretching down to Half Moon Lane)

Red Post Hill was originally called Ashpole Hill, after an ash tree adjacent to the post at the top of the hill. It could also have been named after the ass that was tied to the post, according to one source. The name of the hill was changed to Red Post Hill when the post was painted red to make it more prominent. In the days when many people were unable to read or write, a physical feature was often the main means of identification for an area, road or building.

Regent Road (from Dulwich Road to Railton Road)

This road was named after the public house on the corner of Dulwich and Regent Roads, the Prince Regent. The pub was named after George IV who was Regent whilst George III was unable to perform his royal duties.

The River Effra

The river is said to be named after the Celtic word for 'torrent' and, according to other sources, the Old English word for 'bank' of a river.

The Effra flows from Norwood to the Thames at Vauxhall. In earlier times it was a source of water for domestic purposes, but in mid-Victorian times the course was bricked over because the lower reaches had become contaminated and were thought to be a danger to health. At one time its course was known as the Shore, an old name for a sewer. One tributary flowed through the fields beside Croxted Lane, branching off to flow along what is now Winterbrook Road and Half Moon Lane, to rejoin the main river at Island Green and thence flow along Water Lane to Brixton.

Rosendale Road (from Norwood Road to Tritton Road, Norwood)

Only a small section of the road can be considered to be in the area of Herne Hill. It is said that the road owes its name to Rosendale Hall, a hunting lodge used by Charles II when chasing hounds in the area. The house survived until 1900.

Ruskin Park (Denmark Hill)

The park is named after John Ruskin who lived in the area of Herne and Denmark Hills for 50 years. It forms part of the original Sanders estate which consists of the grounds of eight houses. The park had nothing to do with John Ruskin but when the purchase of land to form a park was mooted, it was felt that contributions would be more easily attracted if the park was named after a well-known local personality. The assumption proved correct. Ruskin Park was extended in 1910 when further acres of the Sanders estate came onto the market.

Ruskin Walk (from Herne Hill to Half Moon Lane)

The walk was originally called Simpson's Alley, after a local benefactor instrumental in the foundation of the school that later became known as St Jude's. When Simpson's Alley was developed and the barriers that kept the roadway free of traffic were removed in the early 1900s, it was renamed after John Ruskin who was said to have walked there often.

Stradella Road (from Half Moon Lane to Burbage Road)

Stradella Road is said to be named after Allesabdo Stradella, an Italian composer who was murdered in 1645 and whose music was said to have been popular at the turn of the century. It is much more likely that the roadway was given a fancy name for a road in a 'dell', for it was developed beneath the high bank of the railway.

Sunray Avenue (from Denmark Hill to Red Post Hill)

Sunray Avenue was laid out during the Edwardian period and was not developed until after the First World War. It faces east for the rising sun and lies almost opposite Sunset Road.

Sunray Gardens

Sunray Gardens lie at the lower end of the old Casina estate, at the junction of Red Post Hill and Sunray Avenue, and make up Herne Hill's third and smallest park; the area was never formally set out or named as a park.

Sunset Road (from Denmark Hill to Ferndene Road)

Possibly named because it is in direct line with the setting sun (west), Sunset Road was laid out in 1911 but its development was delayed by the advent of the First World War.

Village Way (the link road between Half Moon Lane and Dulwich Village)

This was originally the site of a large pond but, when the railway line to North Dulwich Station was constructed, the pond was drained and a road was laid out. The bridge over the roadway is still the original iron bridge.

Wanless Road (between Hinton Road and Herne Hill Road) and Wingmore Road

There is no obvious reason for the naming of these two roads, unless 'more or less' has something to do with it. Wanless Road is divided into two by Herne Hill Road. The extension was developed under the high railway embankment and was the site of the disinfecting station, the mortuary and the bacteriological laboratories.

Water Lane (from Norwood Lane to Brixton Hill)

Water Lane derives its name from the River Effra that ran along the roadway. It is an ancient route along which pilgrims were said to walk on their way to Canterbury.

Winterbrook Road (from Half Moon Lane to Stradella Road)

In the past the River Effra had a tendency to flood the area around Winterbrook Road during the winter, which would explain the origin of the name. The problem was largely eliminated after the course of the river was bricked over.

SCHOOL NAMES

Bessemer Grange School

The school was named after the house built by Sir Henry Bessemer as a wedding present for his daughter which stood at the junction of Sunray Avenue and Denmark Hill.

The school was not built in the grounds of Bessemer Grange but on the site of the grotto in part of the original Bessemer estate. The buildings of both estates, together with those of the adjacent Ruskin estate, were demolished in 1947 and were replaced by the Blanchedowne estate.

Jessop Road School, Lowden Road

This school was named after the small road that originally lay between the school and Neville's Bakery and its housing. Both were built in the 1870s as part of the Milkwood/Lowden Roads estate. Jessop Road was built over and disappeared following the Second World War, and Jessop Road School was rebuilt.

St Jude's School (now in Regent Road)

The school was founded in 1832 for the 'infant poor'. It was built in West Place, later part of Railton Road, and became known as St Paul's School when the parish of St Paul's, Herne Hill, took responsibility for its religious teaching. When the building of the railway embankment isolated the school and surrounding area from St Paul's and the new parish of St Jude's was formed, that parish took responsibility for the school's religious teaching and it was renamed St Jude's. The new, enlarged and very modern St Jude's School was built as part of the postwar development in the place of considerably bomb-damaged property.

St Saviour's School (Herne Hill Road)

Built in the grounds of St Saviour's Church, the school opened in 1869 in response to the needs of the increasing number of children in the surrounding area who had no opportunity for any form of learning. Originally a girls' school, the premises were later extended to provide for infants. After the Second World War it became a mixed primary school which necessitated further additions.

Upper Herne Hill looking towards the Congregational church, before the trees and bushes were replaced by houses and traffic took over the quiet road.

Chapter 8

❦

EDUCATION IN HERNE HILL

THE HISTORY OF EDUCATION IN HERNE HILL

Foster's 1870 Education Act was one of the most significant legislative events of the second half of the Victorian period. It gave most children in England and Wales the opportunity to take the first step towards overcoming the handicap of illiteracy that held them within the poverty trap.

The Act was not intended to replace the various sectors which already provided education to a limited number of children, but rather to 'fill the gaps' in the system that was failing to reach so many, despite the good intentions of charitable organisations and the Church (Nonconformist, Anglican and Catholic).

The school boards established by the Act were charged with levying a rate to provide a basic education for the children of the poor. They had the power to waive school fees for those whose parents could not afford to pay.

Locally-elected boards conducted a census of all schools (including dame-schools with one attendant and as few as six to ten children) and a census of all the children attending elementary schools for fees not exceeding 9d. a week.

In Lambeth visitors were appointed to call upon all households in the area and register every child from the age of 3 to 13 years. The Act allowed elementary education to end at the age of 13. The name of the school was noted if children were already attending.

The findings revealed that throughout the borough thousands of children were receiving no form of education, despite various establishments run by voluntary bodies and private schools. Many children had only attended Sunday school, which in some cases was the sole education their parents received.

In an age when laissez-faire principles were the usual mode of thought, the London School Board acted with remarkable energy. Whilst plans for the construction of board schools went ahead, great efforts were made to ensure that all children had a school place. When schools were filled, additional premises were hired for those children who had not yet been allocated a position. Occasionally, parents were reluctant to send their children to school on a regular basis. Every effort was made to persuade them of the importance of attendance and meetings were arranged after working hours. In Lambeth, only if parents would not comply within six months were notices served upon them and very rarely was a child taken from home care.

By 1874 the first London board schools had opened. They were large, catering for anything from 800 to 1,000 pupils, often in classes of 50 to 80 children. The schools were commonly mixed, with separate sections for infants, girls and boys, each with their own entrance and concrete playgrounds.

In poorer areas, the schools were probably the cleanest places the children knew. The buildings were often three storeys high and the rooms large and well-ventilated, with big windows. Most had fireplaces, rows of desks and blackboards for instruction. Children had slates and chalk – cheaper by far than paper, pencil, pen and ink. There was usually a large assembly hall where morning prayers and important gatherings were held. The buildings were set in large playgrounds with shelters for wet weather and outside toilets.

EDUCATION BEFORE 1870

Prior to the introduction of the 1870 Education Act, many children from more affluent households were taught at home by tutors and governesses. The boys then often moved on to boarding-school.

Richard Fall, the son of a customs officer who lived on Herne Hill, was one such student. After a period of home tuition he attended an academy in Shrewsbury. He was a young friend of John Ruskin and during holidays they would study together.

John Ruskin's education had an unconventional start. He was initially taught at home by his mother who insisted that he read a chapter of the Bible each day; she had fond hopes of him becoming a clergyman, perhaps even a bishop. John's father was determined that his son should not endure the bully-ing that he himself had experienced in his Edinburgh school. None of John's education was full-time, not even when he attended Dr Dale's boys' school in Grove Lane, nor the school run by Dr Andrews of Beresford Chapel. In the early evenings he was tutored in mathematics and Latin by Mr Rowbotham of the Elephant and Castle, and in art by the artist Copley Fielding. John later briefly attended London University in order to gain a standard sufficiently high to enable his admission to Oxford University.

Day- and boarding-schools were often run by clergymen who, after all, had had the opportunity to receive some of the best education then available. Their experience contrasted markedly with the training many schoolteachers received, particularly those in dame, village and charity schools. Most, in the first instance, had assisted their own teachers as monitors.

Until the 1870s there was the Denmark Hill Grammar School and a number of schools and acad-emies for 'young gentlemen' in Grove Lane, the Walworth Road, and at the Elephant and Castle. For many years Wilson's Grammar School had stood next to St Giles' Parish Church, Camberwell, but it had fallen into disrepute. After a period of closure, it reopened in 1882 under a new Act. The school soon rebuilt its reputation and increased its numbers. Not many years later, the school received grants from the LCC in return for taking scholarship pupils from elementary schools.

There was the College of God's Gift in Dulwich, reformed under the Dulwich College Act of 1857, which boasted the famous Dr Carver. The college became one of the best-known schools in the south of England. In 1869 it moved into new premises, designed by Charles Barry, and in 1882 the lower school became a day-school, known as Alleyn's College. Both colleges continued to grow in reputa-tion and expanded their premises to accommodate the large increase in pupil numbers and the many subjects being taught. The colleges continue to prosper at the time of writing.

Education for girls was not normally considered a matter of such importance as that for boys. The girls of the Benecke and Bicknell households were particularly lucky in that family traditions expanded subjects taught to include the arts and sciences. Elhanan Bicknell believed that girls should have the same opportunity to learn as boys. His children all received an excellent education and, being Unitarians and therefore unable to attend Oxford or Cambridge, some of his sons attended foreign universities. His house on Herne Hill was a treasury of modern art, it had a very good library and many instruments of modern technology.

Frederick Benecke, a City banker, was born and educated in Germany. He understood the impor-tance of education and gave his children an excellent foundation of learning, quite apart from their fluency in languages. Both the Benecke and Bicknell families employed governesses whose names appeared in the census which was taken every ten years.

For many girls, home tuition accounted for their full education, but others went on to local day-schools. There were academies, seminaries and colleges in the Grove Park/Camberwell Green area, the most famous being the Pelican College just behind Denmark Hill. Some girls went on to boarding-school. Effie Gray, who married John Ruskin, visited the Ruskins when on her way to boarding-school from her home in Perth, Scotland. She was then 13 years old.

The teaching of social graces was often a large component of education in girls' school. Some pupils were lucky enough to gain more than this, although sometimes they were not able to put their attain-ments to full use. Achieving the highest standard often required something extra in character and family relationships, such as that possessed by Octavia Hill, a friend of John Ruskin, or Emma Cons of Old Vic and Morley College fame. Many young women became teachers, a respectable occupation, especially from mid-Victorian times when teacher-training colleges were founded.

In 1871, the Mary Datchelor School, a City of London charitable institution, which had been reduced to one pupil in its original foundation, opened in Grove Lane. It quickly became very suc-cessful and was probably the best school for girls in the area. A few years later a teacher-training college was added to the establishment. The school was selective in its intake and over the years developed a high educational standard.

Sadly, the school closed in the 1980s, a victim of the secondary school system that demanded entry by age, not by scholarship. The school management refused to accept this condition. As time passed there was a gradual decrease in the number of pupils as each grade reached the top form and departed. Now the school building is the headquarters for the Save the Children Fund.

Before the board schools were built, the biggest providers of elementary education for the poor were the National Society, the British and Foreign School Society and the Anglican National Society. The Anglican Schools were largely benefited by Government grants, whereas the Nonconformist schools were more dependent upon pupils' fees and money from supporters.

In the Herne Hill area, there were very few opportunities for schooling. The Unitarian school in Effra Road was founded in the 1830s, not long after the chapel was built. It was arguably of a higher teaching standard than many other voluntary schools. The Unitarians had a long history of teach-ing in difficult circumstances and sometimes of experiencing persecution. The school was founded by the local Unitarians and Elhanan Bicknell of Herne Hill was a contributor.

Almost opposite the Unitarian school in Church Road (now St Matthew's Road) was a National school. It was one of a large number of schools run by the National Society which was a union of Nonconformist and charitable bodies whose purpose was to provide schooling for poor children in their areas. They were one of the reasons why, by the 1870s, many people could at least sign their names on the marriage registers.

Both schools played a vital role in the education of a limited number of children living in the area between St Matthew's Church, Brixton, and Poets' Corner. After the large board schools were built in Effra Parade and Sussex Road, the roles of the two schools lessened. They were destroyed during the London bombing and neither was rebuilt. The Unitarians rebuilt their chapel and hall, from which they ran a Sunday school, but there is no trace at all of the National school.

There were National and British Foreign Society schools in the Camberwell area and the Green Coat School on Camberwell Green, but at that time few children in Herne Hill would have been sent to school at such a distance.

CHURCH OF ENGLAND SCHOOLS

The Church of England schools serving Herne Hill were founded by people who were concerned that so few educational opportunities existed for young children in the community. They saw that this restricted the children's means of bettering their way of life and becoming useful citizens.

There have been numerous changes in the field of education since the first small schools opened in the early 1830s. The schools have undergone structural alterations and changes in location. Two have survived and are flourishing. The third was destroyed during the Second World War and was never rebuilt.

There is no doubt that pupils had (and still have) a great affection for the small schools that put them on the road to learning.

St Matthew's School, Denmark Hill

In the early 1830s a severe epidemic of cholera spread to the south of the parish of Lambeth, causing many deaths. However, the people from the area around St Matthew's Chapel of Ease, Denmark Hill, were mercifully spared (probably because their water-supply was from a separate, uncontaminated source). As a thanksgiving offering for their deliverance, the congregation built a small school for girls which they named after their chapel. The school prospered and soon there were too many pupils for the available space. It was decided that a new school should be built in the Camberwell New Road which would include a section for infants.

At the time of the census following the passing of the 1870 Education Act, there were over 400 girls and infants attending the school. Boys had always had to leave St Matthew's after infancy and it was not until the late 1860s that a school was built in Denmark Road. This is still known as St Matthew's School for Boys in 2003.

Following the arrival of the railway in Camberwell and Denmark Hill and the spread of population south of Coldharbour Lane, a new church and parish, St Saviour's, was founded in the northern part of Herne Hill. A year later a Church school (again for girls) was opened in Herne Hill Road. This was quickly followed by the 1870 Education Act and the building of board schools in the vicinity.

When the LCC took over the educational responsibility, St Matthew's followed the policy of the council but kept its close association with the church. By then the chapel of ease had been replaced by St Matthew's Church and the parish of St Matthew's, Denmark Hill, had been established.

At the outbreak of the Second World War, children were evacuated to safer areas. Many pupils soon returned home and the two St Matthew's schools were reopened. The girls' school in Camberwell New Road shared its premises with the congregation of the church when St Matthew's was gutted by fire during the Blitz of September 1940. The school was destroyed. Neither was rebuilt and after the war a bus garage was built on the site of the school. Later, the School of Dentistry of King's College Hospital Medical School was built on the church site. The boys' school in Denmark Road is functioning at the time of writing.

St Saviour's School, Herne Hill Road

The arrival of railways in the Camberwell and Denmark Hill areas saw a rapid growth in population south of Coldharbour Lane. The fields and market gardens soon disappeared under roads and rows of small terraced houses. The parish of St Matthew's, Denmark Hill, could not cope with the increase, nor could the school cope with the demand for places. Its neighbouring parish, St Paul's, Herne Hill, was also expecting a huge increase in parishioner numbers as a result of the construction of the estate adjacent to the new railway embankment.

St Saviour's Church was built in Herne Hill Road on land given to the vicar of St Matthew's by James Minet. The provision of a school for children living in the new streets soon became an urgent concern.

St Saviour's School for Girls was opened in 1869, just a year before the Education Act was passed. The school was built in the church grounds and a small house was provided next to it for the appointed schoolmistress. It was not until the 1890s that pressure from parents resulted in the building of schoolrooms for infants. The population had doubled in the area around St Saviour's and the

1880s Act made it compulsory for children up to the age of 13 years to remain at school; previously it had been possible to leave school after the age of ten, if a certain standard had been reached. It was not until 1918 that the school leaving age was raised to 14 years and many years were to pass before, in 1944, a new Act raised it to 15 years.

Despite the construction of several London board schools in the Herne Hill vicinity and the fact that such schools had distinct advantages, Church schools were often the first preference of many parents when their children came to school age. For boys after infancy the choice was more limited and in most cases had to be the board schools.

In the 1890s the staff of St Saviour's were becoming concerned about the loss of play areas for the children as building continued on all the green areas in the district. The staff approached the trustees of the Sanders estate (which bordered upon Church property) and an agreement was reached for the use of a playing-field. When the second purchase of Ruskin Park land was made, a clause was incorporated in the agreement ensuring the school's use of the playing-field be continued – the agreement is honoured at the time of writing.

In 1904 the LCC took responsibility for educational matters in Church schools and this reinforced efforts to obtain scholarship places in grant-assisted grammar schools.

St Saviour's prospered and continued to be popular with the local people. Its teaching improved with the quality of staff appointed and its relationship with the church remained close.

Second World War bombing raids caused damage to the church and, despite repairs, the subsidence that was aggravated by the damage later made it unsafe. It was eventually demolished and the ground converted to play areas for the children.

After the war, changes in the educational system saw St Saviour's become a mixed school and boys no longer had to leave after infancy. The staff of the school also became mixed and a headmaster was appointed, breaking the tradition of a female head. However, on his retirement, the headship was again held by a woman, but sport remained a stronger feature than previously.

St Jude's School, Railton Road/Regent Road

Around the same time that St Matthew's School was founded, a group of people led by Mr and Mrs Simpson were becoming concerned for the well-being of young children in the area between Brixton and Herne Hill. A plot of land was purchased in West Place (later incorporated into Railton Road) and the small school for 'the Christian education of the infant poor' was opened in 'AD1834'. Gifts were made towards the running costs of the school (invested in 3 per cent Consuls) and the Lighting Association was a substantial contributor.

Looking remarkably like a church, the building had a schoolroom with lancet windows and a square castellated tower which was used by the Ordnance Map surveyors to view the district. The school and playground were surrounded by brick walls and railings and next to the school was a small house for the schoolmistress who was engaged to instruct the children in a single classroom. Later, monitors helped with the teaching and were usually tutored shortly before the lesson began. They then taught 'what they could remember' and some of them went on to become teachers themselves.

When, in 1844, St Paul's Church was built on Herne Hill and a new parish was formed, the 'Christian education of the infant poor' became the responsibility of the vicar and his parishioners. The school was called St Paul's until 1868 when St Jude's Church, Dulwich Road, was built and a new parish formed. The railway embankment, which virtually cut the Herne Hill area in two, necessitated boundary adjustments in both parishes. The newly-developing Milkwood/Lowden Roads estate became the responsibility of St Paul's and the small school was transferred to the care of the vicar and parishioners of St Jude's.

Following the passing of the 1870 Education Act, Her Majesty's Inspector of Schools recommended that infants and girls be taught separately, and so a new mistress was engaged for the youngest children.

In 1887, the parish hall of St Jude's was built in the garden next to the school and, from then onwards, morning assembly and special events were held there. This helped the problem of overcrowding suffered by the school, due to its great popularity in the district. A few years later the problem was so severe that a separate building for the girls was deemed necessary. In 1894 the schoolhouse was demolished and the schoolmistresses moved to a house in Railton Road. A year later the girls' school was completed and the old school building was renovated for the infants. However, the new premises were soon full and pupils were again being turned away.

In 1904 the LCC took responsibility for educational matters, but the physical structure of the buildings remained in the care of the school management.

With the introduction of secondary education grants, great efforts were made to gain as many scholarships and places within the central school system as possible. Over the years, steps for the well-being of the girls and infants were introduced, including the provision of medical and dental inspections and free milk for those most in need.

The evacuation of pupils during the Second World War was short-lived as many families could not bear to be separated. The school reopened soon after it had closed, but it and the adjacent parish hall

Left: *Jessop Road School, Lowdon Road, was built in the middle of the new Milkwood/ Lowden Roads estate in 1874. During the Second World War it became an Auxillary Fire Station. All signs of the trams have long since disappeared.*

were damaged by enemy action. On the cessation of hostilities, the education system changed significantly, with grammar and central schools being replaced by the mixed junior and secondary school system.

Although the damage suffered during the war was repaired, conditions were never satisfactory and the school was still too small. In 1973 St Jude's School moved to new, larger premises with spacious playgrounds in Regent Road. The number of classes increased, as did the number of pupils.

St Jude's School, as with other Church schools, has always been held in high regard and is still often the first choice for local parents in 2003. There are always more applications than available places.

The school has worked closely with the Parish Church and now has an even closer association. Every Sunday the school becomes a 'church'. The church and its membership are part of the school's management committee, as are the school staff, members of the community and representatives from the political parties. St Jude's Church was taken over by an office-furniture company.

LONDON BOARD SCHOOLS IN HERNE HILL

The formation of the London School Board coincided with the development of the Milkwood/Lowden Roads estate by the Suburban Village and General Dwellings Company, whose interest was building in areas that had direct contact with London through the railway system. The new estate lay next to the recently constructed railway embankment. Provision was made in the plans for a school in the centre of the estate and Jessop Road School opened its gates in 1874. It was one of the first to be built in the area.

St Saviour's and St Matthew's Schools were full to capacity and expanding, and the small St Jude's School could only be reached via the junction of Herne Hill Road, Half Moon Lane and Norwood Road. Jessop Road School was far bigger than the three Church schools. It had a capacity for over 800 children, including infants, girls and boys, with their own entrances and floors (infants on the ground floor, girls on the first and boys on the top floor). There was a shelter in the school grounds for use in wet weather and toilets in the playgrounds.

Not long after the opening of Jessop Road School, another board school was opened in Effra Parade which was larger than Jessop Road. It served children living in the developing Poets' Corner roads and those living in the area between Herne Hill and Brixton, south of St Matthew's Church, Brixton.

Simultaneously, a school was built in Sussex Road, off Coldharbour Lane. This is not strictly speaking in Herne Hill but it is known that some parents of boys who had attended St Jude's as infants preferred that their sons attended the Sussex Road School rather than the nearer school. Sussex Road School was considered 'less rough' and in time developed a very good educational reputation but the boys who had to 'run the gauntlet' to and from school four times a day rather wondered if it was really worth it.

All three board schools had their set backs and varying fortunes. Jessop Road School was loved by its pupils in pre-war days and was always full to capacity. During the Second World War, part of the school was used as an Auxiliary Fire Station. The surrounding area was damaged during the Blitz and the school received a direct hit with fatal casualties. After the war it was entirely rebuilt, no longer as an elementary school but instead as a junior school.

Many pupils had not returned from evacuation and some had grown up and served in the Armed Forces. Later, the lapsing of so many of the leases of the houses in the vicinity led to a further drop in pupil numbers, especially after the baby boom ceased and many of the families in the bomb-damaged areas had been relocated. Pupil numbers never really recovered, although a nursery school was built in the area of the original playground and the attending children usually transferred to the junior school.

The Effra Parade School suffered the same drop in numbers and also had the addition of a nursery school. Sussex Road School was declared redundant when the large estate surrounding it was demolished due to severe bomb damage. In the 1960s it was taken over by the Lambeth Polytechnic. However, a new estate built in the area of demolition resulted in the reopening of the junior school and the construction of an infant school a few yards away from the original school. All three board schools had a system of evening classes from the period before the First World War.

PRIVATE SCHOOLS IN HERNE HILL

As Herne Hill developed into a distinct suburb of London, a number of private schools opened. One of the most expensive was the Brockwell Park High School for Girls, a day-school which also took boarders. It had a kindergarten and a preparatory class for boys. It was held at The Cedars, one of the larger houses on Herne Hill, and taught English, maths, French, German, Latin, singing and the theory of music, needlework and calisthenics. Lessons in pianoforte, violin, singing and dancing were extra, as was 'drill', conducted by Sgt Major Wetherset. Close by there was the Fennella College for Young Ladies at No. 2 Shardcroft Avenue. It also had a preparatory class for boys and a kindergarten.

Mrs and the Misses Crouch of No. 62 Heron Road ran a 'Private School for Girls' with classes for young boys preparing for Dulwich College and other public schools. Advertised as giving 'a good education with individual attention', there were classes in singing, drawing, drill, music, French, German and English, and, at the end of term, concerts were given at St John's Church, Lowden Road, within a stone's throw of the school.

Another girls' school, Haydon House at No. 134 Milkwood Road, advertised preparatory classes for boys under ten years and private tuition in pianoforte and singing.

These, and all the other small private schools, disappeared without trace in the years leading up to the Second World War. They catered only for a small proportion of the child population of the area but probably gave to that handful of children a 'kinder' start than that enjoyed by those who attended the board schools.

SCHOOLS IN THE DULWICH AREA

The part of Herne Hill now in the borough of Southwark developed some years after the rest of the area. The leases of the big houses on the Dulwich side had lapsed some 25 years later than those on the other side and the parish of St Barnabas' was not formed until 50 years after that of St Paul's. Consequently, the need for board schools came a little later than for those in Lambeth.

At the turn of the century the grounds of the Dulwich House estate were sold and gradually laid out with terraces of small family houses. Many of the children occupying the new houses attended schools in the Dulwich area, one of which was the famous Dulwich Hamlet School.

The school had its origins in the old charity school that James Allen founded for the poor boys and girls of the hamlet, which met at the French Horn for over 100 years, then near the present Dulwich Park gates. After the 1857 Act, which had re-established Dulwich College, the Boys' Free School opened premises in Dulwich Village. When the London School Board was established, the boys' school was taken over by the board and became the Dulwich Hamlet School which was an elementary establishment.

This was the school which, in the early 1900s, gave to Richard Church 'three years of impossible happiness' and set him on the road to self education. At the time the school had an excellent headmaster who encouraged pupils to aspire to further education and whose school curriculum incorporated the teaching of the arts and an interest in sports. The Dulwich Hamlet School has retained the good opinion of the area. It has expanded in size, as well as in pupil numbers, and at the time of writing it is a mixed junior school.

Almost next to the Dulwich Hamlet School is another school. Built in the early 1900s, the board school catered for the children of the fast-developing roads around the hamlet and Croxted Road. When the Peabody Village estate was built and Rosendale Road grew apace, another board school was needed. The residents in the surrounding area objected to the building of yet another school and said it did not have any 'poor children'. This was the case at the time but when the area had fully developed there were poor children who needed providing for.

A school with the same charitable foundation as the Boys' Free School was the James Allen School for Girls (now known as JAGS by its old girls).

When the James Allen's charity school was moved to new premises, dividing boys from girls into different establishments, the girls transferred to a building near the boys' school in the High Street, which eventually became part of the Dulwich Hamlet School.

In 1881, provision was made for a girls' school to be built in East Dulwich Grove, on a three-acre site. The school and grounds were later greatly extended.

At the time when the girls' school was built in East Dulwich Grove, the infants, who previously shared premises with the older girls, were moved to a new school, next to the site of the James Allen school.

Over the years, many of Herne Hill's young people have attended all these schools; in Charles Booth's *Notebooks on The Streets of London*, mention is made in several instances of the new families moving into the area because 'good schools' were available for their children's education.

The London School Board's purpose was originally only to provide elementary education – it was thus rare for schools, other than those run privately or charitably, to go beyond primary teaching standards. But as time passed the board found it was compelled to follow the lead set by others and there were several notable examples.

Years before the passing of the 1870 Education Act, Frederick Maurice and his colleagues had founded the Working Men's College in Red Lion Square. Before the end of the first year, 174 pupils had enrolled and were attending. Insisting on basic standards in the three Rs, the college followed systematic courses, testing pupils and directing those who failed to meet the standards to preparatory courses.

All tutors gave their services free, among them John Ruskin, Dante Rossetti and Ford Madox Ford. Thomas Hughes, MP for Lambeth and author of *Tom Brown's Schooldays*, and Charles Kingsley, clergyman and author, were among the founders. John Ruskin often tutored his art-class pupils on Dulwich Common, afterwards providing them with a hefty meal at the Old Greyhound. And for those without he supplied an easel.

Even before the opening of the Working Men's College, Frederick Maurice had founded Queen's College in Harley Street for young women. Both foundations are active in 2003, although many conditions are no longer applicable, such as that which made it necessary for young women to be chaperoned when attending Queen's College.

Closer to Herne Hill the Lower Norwood Working Men's Institute was founded by Arthur Anderson of the Peninsular Steam Navigation Company, on land leased for 80 years from the Society of Friends of Foreigners in Distress.

The institute's purpose was to promote 'moral, intellectual and social improvement' of people living within a five-mile catchment area. Herne Hill was well within that distance and there was a well-trodden roadway between Herne Hill and Lower Norwood.

The institute again answered the pressing need for further education of poorer people. It ran classes in the three Rs, as well as lecture and debating courses. Many classes and events were held in the evening – how else could working men attend? To augment the funding, the building was hired out to dramatic and other societies and it is said that Mrs Patrick Campbell gave one of her first performances on the stage of the hall.

However, hiring the hall out was not enough and more funding was needed to ensure the institute's continuation. Help came in 1895 when evening classes were inaugurated and the Branch Polytechnic Institute, as part of the Borough Polytechnic, was funded by the Technical Education Board.

Over the years there were many changes and additions to the old building. Its name was changed and some of the subjects taught in the evenings had little to do with technology. Eventually the institute was concerned for the most part with the further education structure of school leavers.

The institute was closed in 1998, the local council considering it too expensive to maintain. Its facilities and the pupils were transferred to the Brixton Technical Institute.

The Lambeth Polytechnic School was founded in premises which previously housed the Surrey County Club. In 1897 the LCC decided to found a 'technical school for the building industry' and, in 1904, the Brixton School of Building was opened. Five years later, a School of Architecture was added – its director was Professor Beresford Pite who designed St Saviour's parish hall. At the same time, a junior day-school was opened for boys of 13 years and over and in 1912 a senior day-school opened, which later provided three-year courses in the main aspects of building. There was always emphasis on evening classes. In the 1960s, the former Sussex Road School was taken over by the Building Trades Department; some of the courses were conducted there, but when the Brixton school merged with the polytechnic of the South Bank and the Vauxhall Technical College, facilities were conducted in these colleges and Sussex Road School returned to its primary-school function. A new estate had been built in the surrounding area, which brought new families into the houses and blocks of flats.

A Working Men's Institute was founded in Dulwich Village and had a substantial library of over 800 books. It was supported by 'the gentlemen of position' in the hamlet who considered it a very worthy cause and thought it filled one of the gaps in many people's educational experience. Once a year, the institute held an entirely pleasurable event, a 'cottagers' flower show', a great attraction to people in the surrounding area.

In 1882, Quinton Hogg bought the Regent Street premises of the old Royal Polytechnic Institute. With many alterations, and supported by such men as Charles Woolley, the Regent Street Polytechnic opened. Charles Woolley was a life-long resident of Lambeth, living in Brixton and Dulwich Road, Herne Hill. He was a Lambeth councillor and one of its first aldermen. A variety of evening classes were held at the polytechnic, allied to all the activities of the Young Men's Christian Association.

The project proved so successful that an Act of Parliament was passed in 1889 aimed at providing technical education in polytechnics in London and the provinces. The movement was assisted by the City of London Parochial Charities Act of 1883, which enabled surplus funds to be directed to the establishment and upkeep of polytechnics in London.

In 1861, Stockwell College in Brixton was opened by the British and Foreign School Society, for the training of Nonconformist schoolmistresses. A little later Stockwell College School was built next to the college, enabling trainee teachers to gain experience in teaching. In 1895, a cookery school was instituted and some of the pupils were resident. In 1935 the school moved to Bromley and the site became a housing estate.

At the beginning of the century, St Gabriel's College was founded for the training of Church of England female teachers. In the 1980s it was amalgamated with Goldsmiths College, New Cross.

Over the years, the college underwent many changes. During the First World War, it was commandeered by the War Office and became known as the 1st London General Hospital, caring for the wounded. It reverted to teacher training when peace was declared but soon its original purposes gave way to ordinary college work. It subsequently became an evening institute and meeting place and was eventually converted into flats.

In 1891, the school board was enabled to remit all fees for elementary education. Another advance was made in 1902 when an Act was passed which provided for the setting up of a system of secondary school education with grants to established grammar schools in exchange for 25 per cent of places allocated free to elementary pupils who passed a qualifying examination. Later, new schools were built which admitted children at the age of 11 and provided grammar-school education for those who qualified by examination; this was known by the students as 'sitting the scholarship'. The scholarship system only created a few places at grammar schools, about four to six passes out of a possible 100 applicants from each school. Obviously there were many more who could have benefited from further education and some of these were directed to the central schools.

One of the disadvantages of the late development of a suburb is that it is necessary to cross borders to utilise some essential facilities. Herne Hill has been extremely fortunate in its Church and board schools but for more advanced education it has always been necessary to move further afield.

The postwar reorganisation of systems of education coincided with the 1947 development of the LCC Blanchedowne estate on Denmark Hill, on the site of the old Ruskin and Bessemer estates. It was recognised that extra school accommodation was necessary to cater for the children of arriving families.

A junior school called Bessemer Grange School was established within the estate and, a little later in lower Red Post Hill, a large comprehensive was built called the William Penn School for Boys. Initially there were 1,600 boys on the register. Many pupils came from Peckham, where the school had originally been founded, others from the new estate and surrounding areas. The Lambeth side of Herne Hill only had junior schools.

Attendance at the school rose and fell according to the surrounding movement of population but, by the early 1990s, the school roll had fallen to 400. The school finally closed and was relaunched under a new name: the Dulwich High School for Boys. This school concentrated on firmer discipline and school governors resolved to put great effort into its reformation, but to no avail. The school closed in August 1999 having been declared 'a failing school', despite opposition from staff and governors. It is planned to reopen as a mixed school, The Charter School, taking in 150 Year 7 children.

Many boys from Herne Hill have attended other schools in Tulse Hill, Norwood and Croydon. Girls have also had to travel further on reaching senior school age.

One such school, St Martin's in the Field School for Girls, was originally a charitable foundation attached to the famous church. It moved into more spacious accommodation in Tulse Hill and for a few years maintained its educational form. In the late 1970s, parents opted for comprehensive status in a ballot.

During the postwar period a number of private nursery and preparatory schools flourished in Herne Hill and adjacent areas. Many Victorian and Edwardian houses lent themselves well to conversion into school premises.

In 1976 the Herne Hill School was opened at the vicarage and hall of St Paul's Church. It was a nursery facility for 16 children and was started by Phyll Bennett, then the vicar's wife. The school proved so popular that soon the age range was expanded from three to seven-and-a-half years and it became necessary to find new premises to accommodate the increasing number of infants.

Premises at the upper part of Ruskin Walk were purchased and the school population continued to expand. Eventually the Ruskin Walk premises were transferred to St Paul's to accommodate the curate of the church and the new vicar of St Paul's moved to the modern vicarage of St Saviour's. The Herne Hill School took over the vicarage of St Paul's.

At the time of writing the small school has expanded to serve more than 200 children. It continues to give a kindly introduction to the world of learning and in understanding relationships with the outside community.

Chapter 9

Chapter 9

SOCIAL CONDITIONS AND
MEDICAL CARE

Social conditions and the provision of medical care have altered beyond all recognition over the last 100 years. Life expectancy has increased considerably and children do not normally experience the loss of a family member until much later in life. Many factors contributed to these changes in Herne Hill, but the provision of an effective sewage and drainage system and the supply of clean, safe water to all households were among the most important elements.

These advances were not made without delays. Acts of Parliament were not being enforced and a medical officer from Wandsworth said that he doubted if any Act had been so ignored as the 1871 Metropolis Water Act. In the 1890s the Llandaff Commission was appointed to investigate London's water-supply and drainage and sewage disposal. The commission found limitations and much incompetence and, as a result, in 1902 the Metropolitan Water Board was created and all areas of London were included in its control. The board bought private companies, built massive reservoirs, set up waterworks and undertook the provision of a network of drainage and sewage systems. When boroughs accepted responsibility for the collection and disposal of household refuse and street waste, the lives and health of the people of London were further improved.

In the early 1870s, it was reported that a little over one half of London's households had a constant water-supply. Being a relatively new suburb, Herne Hill was more fortunate than some longer established areas.

When the Milkwood/Lowden Roads estate was developed, both a clean water-supply and an efficient sewage and drainage system were laid out before any houses were built. Bathing facilities were not always 'on tap' and outside toilets were built against the back extensions, but a constant supply of clean water was piped into each kitchen.

As other sites developed, it was accepted that such facilities were to be included in the housing. When the Dulwich House estate was developed during the Edwardian period it was taken for granted that houses had 'modern facilities'. In many cases this included water piped to the upper floor for baths and toilets. Households with separate facilities were considered an essential means of preventing the spread of infection. When the Peabody Village estate was built off Rosendale Road, each small cottage had its own 'water closet' and 'scullery' and each flat had separate conveniences and constant running water.

The larger houses and estates in the Herne Hill area had benefitted from their own water-supplies and wells before they appeared in other homes. Many had water features in the gardens and grounds and lakes and fountains are visible on maps.

After the 1850s, when the Kingston Water Company began to supply water to Herne Hill, some households had both piped water and wells. It was essential to keep the two supplies for water was only piped at certain times. The wells were covered over when Herne Hill was rebuilt in the 1870s and '80s and are occasionally rediscovered during garden improvements. No. 30 Herne Hill, the marital home of John and Effie Ruskin in 1852, had water piped into the front of the house and its own well from which water was supplied to the kitchen. Most people collected water for their kitchen garden and plants in water-butts. Each household endeavoured to grow as much as possible in these gardens, storing any surplus produce for use in the winter.

DOCTORS AND DISPENSARIES

There have been significant changes in health care over the last century, but none greater than the role of the local doctor in the community. As suburbs spread, so more doctors moved into the new areas where they either practised alone or joined another doctor, often working from their own homes.

Brixton Provident Dispensary in Water Lane. For a small monthly payment basic care was provided for working men and their families. Contributors from Brixton and the area around Water Lane were able to apply for medical and, sometimes, nursing care. The dispensary was a lifeline for families in the days before general practices were easily available.

In the past the doctor would have made up his medicines. There would have been few aids to assist in diagnosis and treatment and patient visits would have been made on foot, horseback or by carriage. At the time of writing residents of the suburbs are registered with a doctor within a multi-general practice and the surgery is almost always full. Cars, telephones and modern technology have allowed for instant communication and assistance in the diagnosis and treatment of illnesses. Local chemists can provide antibiotics and countless other drugs.

In more affluent areas such as Herne Hill, doctors would once have had 'private patients', but in poorer areas many people only saw a doctor in an emergency. Those lucky enough to belong to dispensaries in the late 1800s were sometimes seen in their own homes, but more often at the dispensary premises.

Before the institution of the National Health Service, many 'panel patients' were registered with general practitioners. This was an entitlement of working people who had had a small sum deducted from their wages in case of sickness or unemployment.

There are now a number of multiple general practices catering for the health of the people in Herne Hill. Many people choose the doctor closest to home

and others attend the doctor they like the most or with the best reputation. A patient's acceptance sometimes depends on the distance between surgery and home and the size of the established practice.

The problems experienced by the poor encouraged the establishment of the Provident Dispensaries and saw King's College Hospital refounded on Denmark Hill in Edwardian times. It was the first London teaching hospital to move to the suburbs.

Although Herne Hill and Denmark Hill were generally considered to be wealthy, the areas south of Loughborough Junction and Brixton and spreading up from Camberwell were more thickly populated, considerably poorer and required greater help.

In many such areas Provident Dispensaries were formed to provide care for the families of working men who paid a small monthly sum in return for basic medical and nursing care. Some people living in the Milkwood/Lowden Roads estate joined the Camberwell Provident Dispensary and those living in Brixton and the vicinity of Water Lane, where the dispensary was situated, could join the Brixton Provident Dispensary. There is a plaque to that effect on the front of the building.

The Camberwell Provident Dispensary was founded in 1862 and provided for working people living within a radius of one-and-a-quarter miles of the Parish Church of St Giles. Its premises were near the corner of Camberwell Green and Camberwell New Road on the site of the old flower shop that lay behind the National Westminster Bank. Until 1898 the bank site was occupied by the old Police Station.

According to Blanche in *Ye Olde Parish of Camberwell*, in 1873 there were 6,000 members registered with the dispensary who between them contributed £600 a month in subscriptions. Some 7,000 visits were made to patients in their homes and more than twice that number were seen at the dispensary. Among the patients were 156 married women who had babies, and about 320 dental operations were carried out by 'Mr Thomas of Denmark Hill'. There were six doctors working at the dispensary.

In 1896, St Saviour's Church, Herne Hill Road, formed a Provident Society 'for the working persons of the Parish, their wives and children, whose total earnings did not exceed 30s. per week.' Drs Durno and Simpson, whose practice was in Coldharbour Lane, were the dispensary doctors.

Dispensary members usually paid 2d. to 8d. a month: 2d. for themselves and their wives, 1d. each for the first four children, the rest of the children being treated without charge.

Dulwich's Benevolent Society, the Dulwich Amicable Friendly Society, was supported by the well-to-do of the area and paid sickness and invalid allowances to members.

FROM WORKHOUSE TO GENERAL HOSPITAL

In 1884 the parish of St Saviour's, Southwark, which had benefited from the Alleyn Trust Fund, built an infirmary at the far end of East Dulwich Grove for the care of its parishioners. St Saviour's Infirmary was built next to the railway because land was always cheaper in such areas. Many of the admissions were from the various workhouses by order of the relieving officer or the district medical officer. On rarer occasions, admissions were authorised by the medical superintendent of the hospital. When adopted by the LCC in 1930, it became a 'general hospital' with a wider catchment area, including Herne Hill.

On the other side of the railway lines was one of Camberwell's workhouses, a Vestry institution for the indigent who had nowhere else to go. The workhouse was also taken over by the LCC and became St Francis' Hospital, eventually to be used for geriatric patients. There was a tunnel under the railway lines between the hospitals.

When the LCC took responsibility for the institutions previously run by the Guardians and Metropolitan Asylums Board, the undertaking of modernisation was massive. Among the tasks was the rationalisation of the many grades of staff. Within a short time, the grades of 10,000 nursing staff had been arranged and schools of nursing had been set up, enabling many young people to begin careers in nursing with the prospect of state registration within three or four years.

Many of the LCC hospitals were originally workhouses or parish infirmaries that became general hospitals on adoption by the LCC. The name of a saint was often used.

There were also asylums, which were either institutions for the insane or places for less fortunate members of particular societies. The Licensed Victuallers Asylum was for the relief of the poor.

Some asylums for the insane were privately run and others were attached to parish institutions. Until the late-nineteenth and early-twentieth centuries, the availability of effective care for mental illness was very scarce. Fortunately, it was a period of scientific and medical advance and Florence Nightingale's dictates were still influencing nursing care in hospitals. The goodwill of conscientious men and women was having a political effect and conditions began to improve. A degree of efficient medical care was becoming more widely available to a greater number of people.

Herne Hill has always been dependent upon institutions across its borders when it comes to hospitals. There were few eminent hospitals south of the Thames and at some distance there was Guy's Hospital with the old St Thomas' Hospital opposite. The latter sold its grounds to railway developers in 1868. In 1871 St Thomas' Hospital reopened on a new site on the south bank of the Thames. It embodied all of Nightingale's principles and eventually became one of the biggest hospitals in London. As with other older hospitals, attendance often depended upon a letter of recommendation from governors or supporters.

Most areas in London had fever hospitals to which infectious patients were admitted. The area of Herne Hill was served by the South Eastern in New Cross and the South Western in Stockwell. Both were opened in the early 1870s. Due to their specific purpose, fever hospitals had a much larger catchment area than the average general hospital. However, improved sanitation, greater knowledge of the modes of transmission of diseases, the length of the various stages of infection and, above all, vaccination and inoculation, gradually eliminated the necessity for such hospitals.

During the Second World War the South Western was used as a casualty clearing hospital and the South Eastern as a preliminary training centre for junior nurses from hospitals in the surrounding area, including St Giles'. After the war's end and the institution of the National Health Service, such hospitals were merged with nearby teaching hospitals, such as Guy's and St Thomas'. The South Western

Above: *The new King's College Hospital, as visualised by William Alfred Pite. Pite remained the hospital's architect until 1937 when he retired to Eastbourne.*

Left: *William Alfred Pite, architect of King's College Hospital.*

Right: *The grounds of the third King's College Hospital were given by Lord Hambleton, who lived in De Crespigny Park. He was a member of the W.H. Smith family and later became chairman of the hospital board.*

King's College Hospital's foundation-stone was laid by Edward VII on 20 July 1909.

was partly demolished and the remains used for non-nursing purposes.

King's College Hospital

During the early-Edwardian period, the district around the second King's College Hospital in Portugal Street was demolished to make way for the Law Courts, the Aldwych and Kingsway. The population was dispersed and the facility, bereft of patients, determined to found a hospital in a London suburb with a surrounding population in need of medical care. This would also provide the necessary clinical experience for the hospital's medical students. Coincidentally, a site next to St Matthew's Church on Denmark Hill came onto the market and was purchased in 1904 by one of the hospital governors, William D. Smith, who lived in De Crespigny Park. The site was given to the governors of the old hospital. An Act of Parliament was passed which enabled a new King's College to be founded on Denmark Hill. Fund-raising began and a competition was launched to find the best architectural design for the new hospital.

The contest was won by William A. Pite, the son of the architect of the Milkwood/Lowden Roads estate, and the brother of Professor Beresford Pite of the Brixton School of Technology. William Pite was appointed Honorary Hospital Architect in 1905 and remained so until 1937. At the same time, a female almoner was engaged and became one of the first persons to be appointed in that capacity.

The hospital foundation-stone was laid by Edward VII and Queen Alexandra in 1909 and in 1913 King's College Hospital, Denmark Hill, was officially opened by George V and Queen Mary. The old hospital in Portugal Street was demolished and the site was taken by W.H. Smith and Sons.

The old system for admission and attendance as an out-patient was in practice when the hospital moved to Denmark Hill. This meant that life governors, donors who gave 10 guineas a year, and annual subscribers were able to recommend admission for one patient and two out-patients annually. The senior medical officer was responsible for the admission of patients to wards from the casualty department.

At the outbreak of the First World War, part of the new hospital was taken over by the War Office for treatment of expected casualties and became the 4th London General Hospital. The war extended into years and casualties were far greater than expected. To ease the pressure on hospital beds, huts for convalescent servicemen were constructed in Ruskin Park and a bridge was erected over the adjacent railway. At the end of the war no trace was left of the bridge or huts but local people who were young at the time remembered visiting convalescent soldiers.

Despite having the use of only part of the hospital throughout the First World War, development

King George V and Queen Mary officially opened the hospital in 1913. At the outbreak of the First World War it was taken over by the War Office and became the 4th London General.

continued and the medical school, the schools of massage and electrical treatment and of radiography were opened and the forerunner of the Friends of King's began.

After the war ended, female medical students were admitted for the first time and the departments of cardiology, orthopaedics and urology were established, as well as facilities for the treatment of venereal diseases. In 1924, a preliminary training school for nurses was founded. At the same time, the hospital's long association with the Medical Research Council began.

Development continued in the inter-war years despite considerable financial difficulties, which led to patients being considered for referral to other hospitals. The hospital continued to have royal patronage and was visited by the Lord Mayor of London. Appeals were made by figures such as Sir Malcolm Campbell and H.G. Wells and fund-raising events were held at the Crystal Palace and at the Camberwell Baths. The hospital began to charge private patients £5.5s. per week. The private patient wing was opened in 1937 and the new medical building was completed by the addition of an animal house.

On the declaration of the Second World War, the hospital was mobilised as part of the emergency services and prepared itself to be a casualty station. In common with all London hospitals, it evacuated

King's College Hospital, May 1916, then the 4th London General Hospital, Denmark Hill. This postcard was sent by a small child to her aunt, informing her that school 'was lovely'.

The front view of the Maudsley Hospital, Denmark Hill. Henry Maudsley founded the hospital believing that early intervention was the right course of treatment for psychiatric illness. The building was taken over by the War Office before it was completed and was used in conjunction with the new King's College Hospital for the treatment of war casualties.

moveable patients to less vulnerable areas, together with nursing and medical staff. King's also served as the local hospital where many casualties were treated.

At the cessation of hostilities, King's briefly returned to its voluntary status. In 1948 the National Health Service came into operation. The wards were still named after their benevolent donors, but the working structure of the hospital was transformed.

The Royal Eye Hospital, later to withdraw from the group, and the Belgrave Children's Hospital amalgamated with King's and it became the district teaching hospital. Later Dulwich, St Giles' and St Francis' Hospitals were also incorporated into the group. From then onwards there was continual change and development.

A dental hospital and school was built on the site of the old St Matthew's Church and a new pathology building was opened. In 1968 the Queen opened a new ward block next to the private patient building.

In 1974 the NHS was reorganised and the District Health Authority came into being; over time development continued and additions were made to almost every branch of medicine practised within the group. St Giles' opened a psychiatric day centre and St Francis', Hamlet House, provided residential accommodation for the disabled. The Normanby College for nurses was opened as well as the Lister Health Centre, a thrombosis unit, an extension to the cardiac unit, a liver centre, a chest unit and a sickle cell centre.

St Giles' in-patient service transferred to Dulwich Hospital, an amalgamation of St Francis' and Dulwich Hospitals. Both St Giles' and St Francis' Hospitals later closed and their sites became housing developments. The Belgrave Children's Hospital transferred from Clapham Road to specially constructed accommodation within King's and became the Variety Club Children's Hospital. New community centres opened in the surrounding area, among them the Railton Road Health Centre near the Methodist Church. In 1987 a CT scanner unit was opened. The Herne Hill community responded well to the £1m appeal, with carol singing, coffee mornings, Christmas street collections and an exhibition of the history of King's.

In 1992 King's and Dulwich Hospitals became the King's Healthcare Trust. At the time of writing services are concentrated in the two hospitals, one of which was built in the 1880s and the other in Edwardian times. The trust employs approximately 4,000 staff, has 900 beds and treats over 300,000 patients a year.

A programme of redevelopment is in progress at the time of writing, estimated eventually to cost £100m, and the area once occupied by two redundant schools in Bessemer Road is being included. It is planned for most high technology services be centred upon King's College and that Dulwich Hospital facilities will be used for less technical healthcare.

King's has a new pharmacy with 24-hour service, and at the time of writing is in the process of rebuilding the accident and emergency department. A Joint Education Centre for the School of Medicine and Dentistry is being constructed, incorporating the department of general practice and primary care, with a lecture theatre for hosting national conferences.

A new neuroscience centre for the South East was opened and the facilities of the neurosurgical unit at Maudsley Hospital and the Brook Hospital were transferred to King's. Paediatric neurosurgery was transferred to the Variety Club Children's Hospital. In 2003 the building which housed the neurosurgical unit and the neurology ward is known as Mapother House. There are three neurology wards, with therapy facilities where neurology outpatient clinics are held. The old neurosurgical operating theatre and X-ray department are being converted for neurophysiology services.

And so it continues. King's College Hospital has changed almost beyond recognition since 1913. The original staff would be astonished could they return. However, at the time of writing the main entrance portico remains much the same, despite overlooking the multi-storeyed dental school instead of a Victorian Gothic church. However, a visitor might realise that the large catalpa trees are the matured survivors of those planted during the late-Edwardian period.

The Maudsley Hospital

Opposite King's College Hospital on Denmark Hill is another hospital called the Maudsley. It was founded by a remarkable man, Henry Maudsley, who had 'walked the wards' of University Hospital for five years, during which time he had gained ten gold medals, before qualifying in 1855. His first choice of medicine was surgery, not psychiatry, but, missing the opportunity of a surgical post by chance, he took a short-term position at the Wakefield Asylum, and the die was cast. At the young age of 23, he became medical superintendent of the Cheadle Asylum, Manchester. He returned to London after three years and as the result of one of his medical articles, he met his wife and her father, the superintendent of a private asylum in Hanwell. When his father-in-law died, Henry Maudsley became superintendent in his stead.

His experience over the years convinced him that early treatment of mental illness could obviate the need for long-term, if not lifelong, treatment in large institutions. In the early 1900s he donated £30,000 to the LCC for the building of a hospital within four miles of Charing Cross for the early treatment of patients with mental illness. There were so many delays and arguments that Henry Maudsley threatened to withdraw his gift and to write to the press giving his reasons for doing so. A site was instantly found on Denmark Hill and building began in 1911. The hospital was not completed until 1915 when it was taken over by the War Office as an annex of the 4th London General Hospital. It was used for the treatment of soldiers suffering from shell-shock. At the war's end, the War Office retained the hospital for the continuing treatment of shocked soldiers. It was not until 1923, five years after Henry Maudsley's death, that the hospital opened for civilian care, with accommodation for 75–100 patients, an out-patient department and research facilities.

Henry Maudsley had previously consulted Dr Frederick Mott, an eminent scientist, who believed that psychiatry should be taught at a university level. He moved his laboratories to the uncompleted hospital in 1914. One year after the hospital was returned to civilian use, the standard of pathology and psychiatry was considered high enough to warrant recognition as a school of the University of London. As the facilities increased at the Maudsley, so its reputation grew and staff and students came from all over the world to work and study there. In 1934 the Rockefeller Foundation and Commonwealth Fund endowed fellowships and university chairs were created in the pathology of mental disease and psychiatry. A villa for patients who were a danger to themselves and others, a new out-patients and a children's department were founded, as well as an occupational therapy department. A private patients' block was built in De Crespigny Park and King's opened a ward for psychiatric patients. The Maudsley staff ran clinics in other hospitals.

At the outbreak of the Second World War, patients and staff were transferred to safe areas in the country, but the out-patients department and research continued.

After the creation of the National Health Service, a commission had recommended the establishment of a postgraduate medical federation and separate hospitals for different branches of medicine. The Maudsley Hospital was deemed to have a special place in psychiatric medicine and there was an urgent need for the teaching of psychiatry in Britain.

The federation assumed responsibility for the Maudsley Hospital Medical School and renamed it the Institute of Psychiatry. The Bethlem Royal Hospital in Beckenham joined with the Maudsley.

In 1952 the neurosurgical services of Guy's Hospital transferred to the old private patient block in De Crespigny Park – inevitably it became known as the Guy's-Maudsley Neurosurgical Unit. The unit rapidly became a centre of excellence. Out-patient clinics were held at Guy's and the Maudsley. In the mid-1960s, a neurosurgeon from Edinburgh via King's joined the staff. The unit became the Guy's-Maudsley-King's Neurological Unit and continued until the neurosurgical unit services transferred to a new neuro-science centre at King's, with neurosurgical services for children transferred to the Variety Club Children's Hospital.

In 1967 the Institute of Psychiatry, which had until then been situated within the confines of the Maudsley Hospital, transferred to a new building further along De Crespigny Park. The staff at both institutions cooperated well and were able to expand their work with greater ease.

In 1972 a University Department of Neurology was created at the Institute of Psychiatry and later a neurology ward, called Mapother Ward, was opened above the Neurosurgical Unit. Clinics were held at both the Maudsley Hospital and King's College Hospital. In 1996, when neurosurgical services were transferred to King's College, the De Crespigney Park building (known as Mapother House) was converted to in- and out-patient neurology care for both the Maudsley and King's College Hospital.

Henry Maudsley would be surprised by the developments that have taken place in the field of psychiatry since he made his gift in the Edwardian period. Those who carried the torch for him would be amazed at the changes wrought by scientific research, operative skills and the use of drugs in the treatment of psychiatric illness.

CLEANLINESS IS NEXT TO GODLINESS

Local authorities became responsible for the provision of bath- and wash-house facilities following an Act of Parliament. This played a very important part in the health of the community. The authorities were also responsible for providing 'conveniences' in public places – often hidden in clumps of trees and bushes in parks or placed underground. In 1883, Mr A. Ashwell of Herne Hill patented the vacant/engaged sign for lavatory doors.

On the Camberwell side of Herne Hill, baths were built in Church Street and in East Dulwich Road, near Goose Green. In Lambeth a very big bath- and wash-house complex was built at the junction of Lambeth and Kennington Roads – it was equipped with large sinks and drying racks, as well as the baths. The facilities were in the centre of a very populous area, where few houses would have had modern facilities. Brixton boasted wash-houses and swimming-baths.

Personal cleanliness played an important part in the improvement in health. Many years have passed since Messrs William Lever and Andrew Pears became aware of the effects of primitive soaps upon the skin and William Addis had the idea of cleaning his teeth with a horsehair and bone brush. He had the wisdom to design a toothbrush which he then sold in his London shop. These products were soon being purchased over the counters of chemists and grocery stores nationwide.

Laundry shops provided a service for those who could afford the luxury of having someone else to do their washing and ironing. It would be collected and returned by the laundry-boy. The shops were also useful for people who had nowhere to dry their larger items. In some more affluent households, women were employed to 'do the laundry' on a weekly basis.

During Edwardian times, many houses had a concrete and brick boiler in the corner of the scullery. This was used for the weekly wash and also to heat bath water, which had to be carried upstairs to the bathroom.

People had become conscious that 'cleanliness is next to godliness' and when winter was over, spring-cleaning commenced. This included 'white washing' – the washing of the winter's bedding for an entire household. In April 1905 a young local woman called Dora sent a postcard to a friend in Leeds, apologising for being unable to visit as promised. She wrote that she and her sister 'are up to our eyes in white washing, so cannot leave home.'

It is likely that before modern amenities were built into houses, many of the affluent inhabitants of Herne Hill would go away whilst the house was cleaned from top to bottom. The Ruskin family stayed at The Queen's Hotel, Norwood, for a couple of weeks each year when John was young to allow sufficient time for their domestic staff to thoroughly spring-clean. The house was also spring-cleaned during their Continental travels.

Local authorities took care of street sweeping and the collection of domestic rubbish, which eliminated the use of 'dust holes'. The huge increase in horse-drawn traffic saw the accumulation of horse droppings grow apace. It was thought to be a source of infection and also a danger when tram lines became blocked. Many young boys earned a 'subsidence living' keeping tram lines and crossings free from dirt and soil and were part of the street scene in H.E. Tidmarsh's London paintings. These boys became redundant when waste clearance was taken over by the local authorities.

As motorised vehicles replaced horse-drawn traffic, so the number of babies and young children suffering enteric infections fell; it was thought the reduction in the number of flies living on horse-droppings was the main reason, coupled with a growing awareness of hygiene. The cleanliness depicted in photographs of roadways, parks and open spaces during the Edwardian period illustrates how seriously local authorities took their responsibility.

THE CONTROL OF INFECTIONS

The late 1800s and early 1900s saw an increased understanding of the causes and transmission of disease and the introduction of a number of measures concerning the control and treatment of infections. The Notification Act of 1888 was one of the most significant.

Medical Officers of Health were appointed by London boroughs and support services were established. One such amenity was the public disinfection service. When the Medical Officer of Health verified a case of infection, such as diphtheria, scarlet fever or smallpox, the disinfector's van arrived at the home to clear all items of clothing, bedding, etc. from the sick room. They were then taken to be destroyed or 'made safe' in the disinfecting ovens. The stations also dealt with infestations of vermin.

The disinfecting station on the Lambeth side of Herne Hill was in Wanless Road, lying directly under the railway embankment. The bacteriological laboratories, where diagnosis was verified, and the mortuary, for the reception of dead bodies prior to burial or for the coroner's examination, were also situated in Wanless Road. For those on the Camberwell side of Herne Hill, the disinfecting and cleansing station were situated in Peckham Park Road.

In Herne Hill and its environs, diagnosis of diphtheria could also be confirmed in the Wellcome Physiological Research Laboratories in Brockwell Park where preliminary work on diphtheria anti-toxins was carried out. The antitoxins could be purchased from the labs or from local chemists and administered by the family doctor prior to the patient's admission to an isolation hospital. Research into other infectious diseases was also carried out and huge quantities of antitoxins and vaccines were produced for use by the Armed Forces during the First World War.

An Act of Parliament in 1893 made it the local authority's responsibility to provide hospitals for the isolation of patients with infectious diseases. Herne Hill's patients were sent to the South Eastern and South Western hospitals. The ambulances, which were also provided by the local authority, then had to be disinfected before being used for other patients.

The bacilli that caused infectious diseases were not discovered until the last few decades of the nineteenth century. However, the length of time the diseases lasted and how long a bacillus could live outside the body were not understood until well into the twentieth century. Isolation hospitals were thought to be the answer to these widespread problems. Undoubtedly they did help, but they also meant that many people remained in hospital far longer than was necessary for the control of infection.

The families of patients infected with more serious diseases were subjected to restrictions on movement and in the case of death a wake was forbidden under penalty of a £5 fine. This was a lot of money considering family incomes could be as little as £2 a week. The head of the household could be fined for allowing another person contact with an infected patient or for failing to notify the district's Medical Officer of Health of an infection. The family doctor often undertook this task.

If a schoolchild developed an infection, the parents of other pupils often found reason for keeping their child at home – sometimes demanding that a place be found at another establishment.

The introduction of diphtheria inoculations saw clinics being opened in many areas. Herne Hill residents were able to attend the Diphtheria Prevention Clinic in Sussex Road or Camberwell Road and family doctors could also inoculate their patients.

In 1939, a massive campaign took place to inoculate children of 12 years and under. This, along with the later campaign to inoculate young children from the age of 6–12 months, virtually eliminated diphtheria. The vaccine used in the 1939 campaign was supplied by the Wellcome Physiological Research Laboratories, which was then based at Beckenham, Kent.

Cases of smallpox at this time were rare and vaccination had been compulsory for years, with many people displaying several scars on their upper left arms. Later, when only one small scratch was necessary to achieve immunity, little scarring was visible. From time to time there would be a smallpox scare and those most likely to be in contact, nursing and medical staff, would be revaccinated. The worldwide elimination of the disease means that vaccination is no longer considered necessary.

Measles, mumps and chicken pox were not usually matters of extreme concern. It was expected that attendance at school would lead to catching one or other infection from another pupil and it was thought 'the sooner the better' as, once caught, the illness would not recur. Often family members would infect their siblings so that they could all be ill together. This attitude lasted until it became possible to inoculate children at one of the Infant Welfare Clinics prior to starting school.

The contraction of scarlet fever or diphtheria was considered disastrous, not only because the infections were more severe, the complications serious, and the effects lasting, but because patients were admitted to isolation hospitals for varying lengths of time. Visiting was often limited to seeing children through windows or waving from gateways.

THE GREATEST KILLER

During the nineteenth and early-twentieth centuries, the greatest killer of young people was tuberculosis. Until the foundation of Brompton Hospital in the 1840s there was no remedy for consumption and people suffering from the disease were not knowingly admitted to hospital. The forms of treatment thereafter were limited and in most cases the disease was not recognised until it was too late. When the bacillus was isolated in 1882, it was thought that if the disease was recognised at an early stage perhaps bedrest, fresh air and good food might help. This policy had been advocated by Dr Lettsom of Camberwell when he founded the Royal Sea Bathing Infirmary at Margate in the 1790s. In the 1840s Dr Bodington advocated fresh air, graduated exercise, good food, the occasional glass of wine and a sleeping pill to ensure a good night's rest. Dr Lettsom's efforts were ignored and Dr Bodington's scorned for several decades.

In response to changes in attitude, the construction of sanatoria began during the Edwardian period. More affluent people had been travelling to warmer climes for many years and to the Alps, for bedrest on the verandahs of sanatoria.

As a result of campaigns by The League Against Tuberculosis, voluntary tuberculosis dispensaries were established which provided information about the prevention of the disease, as well as the care of contacts and the treatment of infected patients. In the early 1920s Borough Councils took responsibility for the dispensaries. Herne Hill's inhabitants attended either the Camberwell Clinic in Brunswick Square or the Lambeth Clinic in Effra Road.

It was said that no person suspected of the disease should lack advice or treatment and that close contacts could be examined and advised on the precautions to take. Medical examination of schoolchildren sometimes revealed 'scrofula', swollen lymphatic glands, mostly of the neck. When it was recognised that this was often a manifestation of tuberculosis, removal and time spent in a sanatorium was the usual treatment. The LCC had its own children's sanatorium in Brentwood, Essex.

During the early 1950s, it was estimated that tuberculosis killed five million people worldwide each year. The tide was turned with the introduction of the antibiotic Streptomycine and, to a more limited extent, by the different forms of chest surgery.

Within a decade, the numbers suffering from TB fell dramatically and before long sanatoria began to close and chest hospitals were admitting patients suffering from other forms of heart and lung conditions. Locally, chest clinics closed as it was no longer considered necessary for former TB patients to attend for regular check-ups.

THE SOCIAL CARE OF SCHOOLCHILDREN

It had been a shock to Government when three out of five men volunteering to fight in the Boer War were found to be unfit for service, many with conditions directly attributable to childhood malnutrition.

Charles Booth's, and later Seebohm Rowntree's, reports confirmed that 30 per cent of the population of main towns were living below the poverty line. Some charities had already recognised the problems caused by poverty and malnutrition in the child population and its effects upon their schooling, and had attempted to rectify some of the serious deficiencies. The Ragged Schools movement gave meals to pupils, particularly in wintertime, and clothing was provided for the inadequately dressed. Sometimes washing and bathing facilities were available for pupils, particularly those found to be vermin-infested.

In 1870 the London School Board was instituted and large schools were constructed. The children who attended the new board schools were very fortunate as the classrooms were often the healthiest, airiest and cleanest places they knew. Physical exercise became part of the curriculum as a health measure. The playgrounds and the assembly halls were used for such activities. Conditions in Herne Hill were a little better than in the surrounding areas of Lambeth and Camberwell. Jessop Road School, built within the Milkwood/Lowden Roads estate, had large classrooms with long windows and playgrounds, as did the Effra Parade and Sussex Road schools. Classes were large, with anything from 50 to 80 pupils, but conditions were better than those in some poorer areas.

In 1904 the LCC took full responsibility for the schools of the London Board and those run by such bodies as the National Society and the Ragged Schools. It took only the educational responsibility for Church schools. At the time, Church schools like St Jude's and St Saviour's rarely had such spacious conditions as the new board schools.

An enquiry discovered that many pupils were undernourished and recommended that school meals be provided for poor children. The response to this was patchy, but in 1914 the local authorities were compelled to feed the most needy children. Shortages during the First World War made this provision even more essential. The same enquiry also recommended that a Schools Medical Service be introduced. School medical inspections had begun in 1907. They took place in the presence of a parent and chests were examined and eyes tested. Children were referred to opticians and, if necessary, glasses were provided. Many children had their tonsils and adenoids removed and swollen glands were often found in the neck. This problem gradually disappeared when pasteurisation of milk was enforced.

A dental service with yearly examinations was introduced in 1911 – if caries were found, treatment was recommended. By 1912 the LCC had hospitals and treatment centres in the capital which cared for 54,000 children each year.

Not long after the Schools Medical Inspection Service began, a Schools Nursing Service was formed to work in conjunction with both the medical and dental services. Except when attending clinics, the average pupil's main contact was when a nurse visited the classroom for regular inspection of heads for lice and nits.

The development of the School Medical Services slowed during the First World War but regained momentum at the war's end. Church schools did not benefit from the services as quickly as board schools. In 1928, at the time of the 60th anniversary of the founding of St Jude's, the headmistress, Miss Higgins, wrote of the work which had developed in 'recent years' when she referred to 'the medical and dental inspections which should secure for present and future pupils a better state of health than their forebears enjoyed.'

In the 1930s free milk was provided for needy children and provision was made for milk ($1/3$ pint for a halfpenny) to be given to all children who wanted it during the morning school break. Open-air schools were founded for pupils with heart and lung complaints and convalescent homes developed at seaside and country locations.

Before the Government became concerned about the health of the nation, many public-spirited citizens had noted the rapid expansion of suburbia and the consequent loss of open spaces and recreational facilities, especially for children. In most cases it was they who campaigned and alerted local authorities when opportunities arose to purchase land, often private estates, suitable for conversion to parkland. Brockwell and Ruskin Parks were two such areas. It was rare for land to be given to a local authority by trustees, as in the case of the nearby Dulwich Park. All three parks proved to be 'lungs' by which South East Londoners breathed, relaxed and participated in games and sporting activities. In Brockwell Park they could swim in the lake. In 1936 an open-air swimming bath was built adjacent to the park and swimming in the lake, thought to be a health hazard, ceased.

By the 1890s, the people of St Saviour's parish were becoming anxious about the rapid disappearance of open fields under a sea of small terraced houses. The doubling of the population in the previous 20 years left nowhere for children to play and exercise. A committee, led by the parish vicar and the headmistress of the Church school, negotiated with the trustees of the Sanders estate to allow school games and sports to take place on land adjoining the church and school. When Ruskin Park was opened, this concession was written into the agreement and still applies at the time of writing.

The people of Herne Hill are very fortunate in that their forebears had the vision to realise how essential the parks would be. The headmaster of Effra Parade School had his pupils' needs in mind and the MP for Norwood, Thomas Bristowe, was prepared to stake a considerable amount of his own money to keep options open when all seemed lost. It is to such people that Herne Hill owes its history of better health than that enjoyed by many other London suburbs. The late development of the area as a suburb and the consequent lack of some facilities proved to be a real blessing.

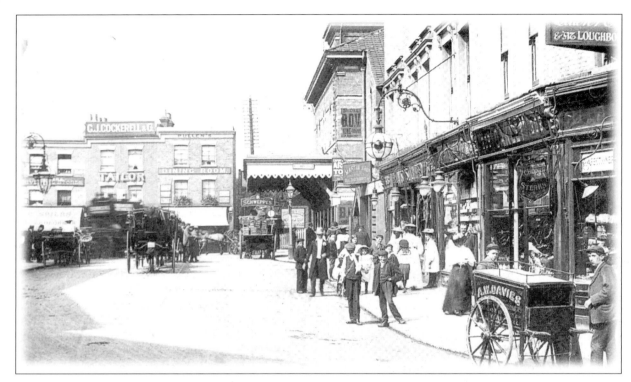

Above: *The Station Approach, Railton Road, on an Edwardian Saturday morning. The carriages are awaiting passengers from the trains. The railway line that ran through Herne Hill was part of the London, Chatham and Dover line.*

Right: *Lower Hinton Road, Loughborough Junction. This was part of the original path for horse trams from Loughborough Junction to Herne Hill. The route later changed because the 'arms' of the electric trams were too high to pass under the second bridge.*

Left: *One of the first 'official' trams stops at the junction of Dulwich, Railton and Norwood Roads.*

Chapter 10

❧⊙❧

THE TRANSPORT SERVICE

The growth of suburbs south of the River Thames led to the need for an adequate transport system. Stagecoach travel came first, but only the wealthy could afford to use coaches on a regular basis. The services were also infrequent and limited in destination. Coaches arrived at their termini long after the working man's day began and they departed long before his working day ended. Because of the lack of affordable and convenient transport, many people walked to and from work using short cuts, sometimes called 'ha'penny hatches'.

Several coach companies operated from Peckham, Camberwell and Dulwich and catered for those travelling to and from the City and Westminster. Coaches left in the morning and returned at midday or early afternoon. A few companies ran additional coaches in the later morning or early afternoon.

The companies did not welcome the arrival of the omnibus with its lower fares. The duty on horses, vehicles and mileage had been lowered or repealed, and omnibuses could carry many more passengers than coaches. Schedules were more frequent and there were no prolonged stops at points along the routes; one coach service had regularly waited 20 minutes at the Father Red Cap during each journey.

Despite their initial reluctance, coach companies were soon compelled to become omnibus operators. The most famous of the local operators, Thomas Tilling, started with a one-horse coach in the Walworth Road area and became one of the most important omnibus operators in London. With his main depot in Peckham, he was a major employer of men and his horses consumed thousands of tons of fodder annually. He recognised advances in

The Station Approach, early 1900s. This was one of the very few official horse-tram stops, at the junction of Norwood, Dulwich and Railton Roads.

The George Canning public house, Effra Road/Water Lane. Public houses were very convenient termini for horse buses; they frequently had front yards where horses and drivers could rest and seek refreshment. Buses came from as far away as the City, Westminster and Norwood. When the mode of transport changed and bus-stops came into being, a one-way system was introduced; one route passed through streets to Dulwich Road and the other along Water Lane, turning into Effra Road.

Lower Herne Hill Road as it was before the trams were re-routed. The Hinton Road journey had been more convenient and well suited to horse trams. Many of the properties shown in this photograph still stand at the time of writing, but several shops and St Saviour's Church were lost during the Second World War.

commerce and was able to adapt to modern circumstances. Tilling was the first to introduce the double-decker motor bus to Central London in 1904, although horse buses did not disappear altogether until 1915.

SHANKS'S PONY AND HORSE-DRAWN TRANSPORT

Before the introduction of motorised traffic, the horse was of prime importance in transportation. With the advent of the omnibus and tram, the horse population increased enormously, particularly as each vehicle required several horse changes to operate efficiently. The thousands of tons of corn, hay and maize consumed were the equivalent of today's petrol. The large stables were the garages and the blacksmiths and the stableman the garage mechanics and attendants. However, for thousands of people walking remained the usual mode of travel – it is interesting to note that a common expression for walking was 'to go by shanks's pony'.

In Herne Hill the delivery of goods to suppliers and consumers by carriers' horses was current until the beginning of the Second World War, particularly dairy goods, bakery items and greengroceries.

A rank with horse cabs was visible outside every railway station or sometimes within the station courtyard. Herne Hill had an outside rank in Commercial Place where the cabs and horses stood on specially laid granite sets.

Many people living on the hills and along Half Moon Lane kept carriages and horses, often using them to travel to their city businesses. Some continued to use their own transport after coach services had started to run from Camberwell and Dulwich. A few businessmen did not own a carriage and walked over the hill to Camberwell to travel by coach. John Ruskin was scathing about his neighbours who owned 'carriages driven by coachmen in wigs', but when the family moved to Denmark Hill and a carriage occupied their stables he changed his mind, even to the extent of designing a carriage to be made by a Camberwell coach builder. For years the family had hired coaches from a Camberwell livery stable for their travels around the countryside and on the Continent.

Most areas had livery stables and Herne Hill was no exception. There was a livery stable near the station from which horses could be hired for riding or coaching. This also enabled people to keep their horses nearby if they did not have stabling at home.

It was not unusual for riders to dismount and leave their horses on the roadside, whilst they conducted their business in shops or offices.

Hundreds of horse troughs were erected by the Metropolitan Drinking Fountain and Cattle Trough Association during the Victorian era. The association was appalled that the cruelty endured by thousands of horses was intensified by the thirst they suffered. Herne Hill had a trough at the curve of Dulwich Road. They were also extant in Camberwell and Dulwich and inns often provided water for their clients' horses, as long as they also bought a drink.

When trams were electrified, the horses were sold on or destroyed. Later, when buses were motorised, the difficulty caused by excessive piles of manure largely disappeared and the remaining problem was often removed by keen gardeners who collected the droppings from the carters' horses.

Motor cars and tractors almost eliminated the horse from our society. However, horse riding and carriage driving remain very popular country show events at the time of writing. At the Brockwell Park Country Show the exhibition of shire-horses and the horse-riding events are always well patronised and receive much applause. Police have long exercised horses in the lower reaches of Brockwell Park.

THE LIFE AND DEMISE OF THE TRAM

For years, coaches and subsequently horse buses, had plodded along the ancient roadway of Coldharbour Lane between the villages of Brixton and Camberwell. The development of the Milkwood/Lowden Roads estate in the 1870s and the housing that grew up around St Saviour's Church saw horse omnibuses travelling the area to Herne Hill from Coldharbour Lane. The later provision of trams brought a more regular service. Initially, trams were pulled along Hinton Road to Milkwood Road, but when electrification was introduced in 1909 the route was changed to Herne Hill Road where the bridges did not obstruct 'the arm' of the new-style trams. The change meant that there were two sharp curves to reach Milkwood Road in and out of Wanless Road.

Because of the nature of the housing and the limitation of road space, a one-way system or loop operated on part of the route, via Poplar Walk Road and Lowden Road into Milkwood Road with the return along the length of Milkwood Road.

Further along the route, the tramlines were laid close to the pavement south of Brockwell Park, thus ensuring double lines at the Norwood Road Junction with Dulwich Road where the trams to Brixton turned north. A pointsman was stationed near the park gates in order to operate the electrical points and direct the trams into their proper lines.

For many years the No. 80 tram (and then the No. 48 tram) operated from Southwark Bridge via Camberwell Green and Coldharbour Lane to West Norwood, with the crossover from Coldharbour Lane near Loughborough Junction. It initially provided a crucial service for the residents in roads between Herne Hill and Loughborough Junction

Stations, but following the war and the lapsing of leases on the Milkwood/Lowden Roads estate, the need diminished. For a short period a bus service was provided after the last No. 48 tram ran in 1951, but this was later withdrawn. A single-decker bus was introduced between Streatham, Dulwich and Brixton via Herne Hill Road. This runs in the day-time during the week and by no means compensates for the loss of the No. 48 tram service.

A route for buses (horse and then motor buses) had run between Kennington and Brixton for years, terminating at the George Canning public house on the corner of Effra Road and Water Lane. The George Canning had also previously been a stopover for long-distance coaches.

When the electrification of trams occurred, a route was planned through Herne Hill to Tulse Hill and West Norwood. It was thought impractical to use the George Canning as a tram stop, so a one-way loop was constructed between Effra Road and Dulwich Road via Morval and Dalberg Roads, with the return along Water Lane, past the George Canning into Effra Road. Buses now follow the same route.

The No. 78 tram traversed the route from Victoria Station via Vauxhall Bridge, Stockwell and Brixton to West Norwood, terminating just above the Thurlow Arms. The service was frequent, convenient for shopping and entertainment and connected with the several train services along the route.

The No. 33 tram also passed through Herne Hill. It ran between West Norwood and Kingsway Subway (eventually to Finsbury Park) via Brixton, Kennington and Westminster Bridge. On its return journey it followed the same route from Brixton to West Norwood as that of the No. 78. Its first tram left West Norwood at 4.57a.m. to enable the purchase of workmen's tickets.

All three trams began their journey from the tram depot at West Norwood, next to what later became the Fire Station in Norwood Road. Sunday services for both the No. 33 and No. 48 commenced nearly four hours later than on a weekday and the No. 78 ran only during the week. On reaching Brockwell Park, the No. 33 and No. 78 trams turned into Dulwich Road. The No. 48 tram continued under the railway bridge to Milkwood Road where a warning notice to pedestrians instructed 'Don't Dash Across'.

There were also a number of trams passing within walking distance of Herne Hill in Brixton, Coldharbour Lane, Denmark Hill and Camberwell Green. These gave people a wide choice of routes to and from their place of work. In their spare time people could travel into the outer suburbs and beyond, as well as into London.

Unfortunately, in the early 1950s buses began to replace the London trams. The last trams ran in Herne Hill in May 1951 and before long all physical signs of their history had been removed. In 2003, only the occasional tarmac of a roadway shows where the trams ran. Most people who grew up in the time of the trams remember them with nostalgia and regret their passing.

The last London tram was ceremonially burned in Chatham in 1953 and the tramlines all over London were dug up and sold as scrap iron.

COMPETITION BETWEEN TRAM AND BUS

Trams entered London's transport system in the early 1860s, but were initially a failure because the rails projected a little above the road surface. When this fault was rectified they rapidly became a popular means of transport for the man in the street, at first as single-deckers and then as double-deckers with an iron ladder outside.

Trams were longer than omnibuses and were able to carry more passengers for lower fares. According to Blanche in *Ye Olde Parish of Camberwell*, tramway companies were responsible for the repair of the roads they traversed and also had to pay rates per mile. It is therefore surprising that fares were low. Blanche considered that the companies saved ratepayers thousands of pounds each year.

London transport was a noisy affair and vehicles, including omnibuses, had iron tyres. It was years before solid rubber tyres replaced iron and not until 1923 that pneumatic tyres replaced the solid rubber tyres for all vehicles. The granite sets of many roads heightened the noise of traffic. Trams, moving in the grooves of their permanent tracks, were considerably quieter.

The great disadvantage of trams was that they were not allowed to enter Central London and were only able to run to the fringes, from where passengers walked to their destinations. Later, there were some exceptions and a loop passed over Westminster Bridge, along the Embankment and back over Blackfriars. Another line diverted north of Waterloo Bridge to the Kingsway subway and one ran from Vauxhall Bridge to Victoria.

A First World War pocket guide to London stated that trams were chiefly used to convey some of the 'countless throng' which poured into central districts of London each morning, but as they could not enter the City or the West End they were 'of little use to visitors' unless they wished to get to some of the suburban districts. However, 'omnibuses traversed London in all directions from early morning to past midnight.'

The direction of trams was dictated by their lines and their speed by legislation, initially ten miles per hour. However, omnibuses could weave in and out of traffic and use any route they wished, often traversing the same routes as trams. Thus, overall, they carried twice as many passengers as trams did. Their disadvantage was that for many years they were not covered in – a particular drawback in cold or wet weather and in the dark. In warm weather, however, nothing could be more pleasant for the sightseer. Most trams had been covered since 1905, five years after electrification had begun to replace horses.

Trams were considered safer than omnibuses because of the length of their two-way bogies and their four wheels at each end – a stabilising factor on road curves. They were also very cheap to run and needed little maintenance. Prior to the First World War, horse-drawn traffic (carriages, trams and omnibuses) had begun to give way to mechanised transport such as motor buses, electric trams and motor cars. Few people could afford the ownership of a motor car and many people still walked but, for a large number of those living a distance from their places of employment, trams and omnibuses were very important.

THE COMING OF THE RAILWAYS

The restrictions placed upon tramway companies in London meant that they could not afford to extend into areas without an established population. Railway companies had parliamentary support and forged their lines into open countryside. With the willing aid of speculative builders, the suburbs followed.

Although the structure of the railways was to have a drastic effect upon the countryside south of the Thames, the recognition of its impact was at first slow and localised. The railway was thought of more in terms of freight carriage, rather than as a commuter asset. Its significance began to dawn on the people south of the river when the London and Greenwich Railway reached London Bridge in 1836 and began to share its terminus with other companies, including the London & Croydon, the South Eastern and the London & Brighton.

The suburbanisation of South East London was intensified when railway bridges enabled the tracks to extend from south of the Thames to the northern bank. Blackfriars was built immediately adjacent to the existing road bridge to Ludgate. Cannon Street and Charing Cross followed. The latter entailed the dismantling of the beautiful Hungerford Bridge and the destruction of Hungerford market. Victoria was then extended from Battersea to Queen's Road.

Connections were built between London Bridge Station and Waterloo, and Charing Cross and Cannon Street. Eventually, it was possible to reach almost anywhere in Britain, albeit with changes of trains and connecting transport.

The construction of London's railways saw the destruction of homes on confiscated land. The displacement of residents created overcrowding in some areas and drove many people into the new suburbs. Benefits became apparent in time, including the movement of freight, the involvement of the General Post Office in the system, and the ability of many to travel widely. However, much of Greater London was permanently mutilated. Herne Hill and its neighbouring areas were scarred but the high embankment built across its open countryside was soon accepted as part of the landscape. Many people travelled by train to their places of work and used the bridges to cross the river. Indeed, when many of the roads, such as Stradella and Winterbrook, were developed, the houses were mostly occupied by City-going people.

The arrival of the railways gave the chief impetus for the development of the suburbs and changed the countryside of North Kent and Surrey beyond recognition. Land lying under railway embankments was often the first to be built upon, particularly when adjacent to existing main transport roads.

Left: *Herne Hill railway station and sidings, 1930s. The station remains much the same, but the sidings are no longer a prominent feature. The telegraph poles, which once carried numerous people's messages, have all but disappeared. The railway network was a prime target for bombs during the Second World War. Often this led to more damage in surrounding areas than on the lines.*

THE NEED FOR LOWER FARES

The railway line that turned Herne Hill from pleasant, prosperous countryside into a London suburb was the London, Chatham and Dover Railway. The company built a great bank through the fields and market gardens, a station near Island Green and a bridge over the crossroads. It cut Herne Hill in two. The line led from Penge, Sydenham Hill and West Dulwich and from Herne Hill to Brixton, Clapham and Battersea, eventually reaching the new Victoria Station. An extension was later built from Herne Hill to the Elephant and Castle, Blackfriars and Ludgate Hill, and so to Holborn. For this extension another bank was built between Herne Hill and Loughborough Junction, below which Shakespeare Road continued its development. A line passing through Denmark Hill had been built from Nunhead and Peckham Rye, connecting it with Loughborough Junction and East Brixton, and also Camberwell and the Elephant and Castle.

A spur connected Herne Hill to Tulse Hill and from there the line extended to West Norwood, Gypsy Hill and Crystal Palace. Thus, within a few years, the surrounding area was intersected by a network of railway lines and stations, ensuring that, in future, everyone could travel by rail.

It was necessary to ensure that the population could afford to use the various forms of transport. Parliamentary legislation encouraged rail and tram companies to lower fares for the workers. In 1864 special early-morning trains began to run into the central areas of London and trams to their termini, with workmen's tickets allowing return after 6p.m. This greatly benefited thousands of workers but sometimes meant that people arrived at work too early.

FREEDOM OF THE ROADS

Coinciding with the tram's entry into London's transport system in the 1860s came the first bicycle on which the rider sat high above the front wheel. It was followed by the penny farthing and the tricycle.

In the mid-1880s, penny farthing cycles were being raced in the grounds of Alexandra Palace. By the 1890s the cycle's front wheel had been reduced in size, the seat moved back and the pedals had been attached to the back wheel by a chain. When, shortly afterwards, John Dunlop's pneumatic tyres were fitted to the wheels, the modern bicycle was born and cycling fever began.

In his book, *Municipal Parks, Gardens and Open Spaces,* Lt-Col J.J. Sexby, who transformed the Brockwell estate and laid out Ruskin Park, wrote of the popularity of Battersea Park for cycling, especially with the ladies. He noted that 'roads which were formerly the nursery of cycling have developed into a fashionable promenade', and 'although Hyde Park had become involved in cycling... the cream of

society went to Battersea for the morning ride.' The park had been the first experiment in making cycling fashionable, but 'the age of experiment is over: cycling has become part of national life.'

As a very young boy, Richard Church remembered grooms wheeling bicycles into Battersea Park to await the arrival of carriages with the cyclists. He said 'the toffs' pedalled around the park for an hour or two before departing in their carriages, leaving their grooms to wheel the cycles home.

An Act of Parliament (1888) established the cyclist's right to use the roads and a clause made it compulsory for the cycle bell to be rung non-stop when in motion! Women insisted on taking part in the cycling craze and those who protested that it was indecorous for women to cycle were defeated by the split skirt (bloomers) introduced by an American cyclist called Amelia Bloomer.

By the 1870s, many cycling clubs had been founded and saw members cycling out into the countryside on a Sunday on their penny farthings or tricycles, often in uniforms of a cap, jacket and breaches. Tricycles were for one or two persons, if the latter the two were seated next to each other and the chain and pedals attached to the side wheels. The tandem, with one cyclist behind the other, came later.

Competitive cycling became popular, especially as it coincided with the enthusiasm for running. By the 1890s several large stadia had been built in the London area. In 1891 the Herne Hill Stadium was opened near Village Way. It combined an outer cycling track with a running track, a football pitch and a jump pit. Great cycling and athletic events took place there and were hugely popular, especially in the early days. Meetings were not confined to cycling and athletics – football matches were equally well-supported and events like donkey parades were very popular. Later, after the First World War, events were attended by as many as 15,000 people.

Sadly, popular motoring hastened the decline of interest in competitive cycling. The occupation of the stadium by the Forces during the Second World War left the grounds in need of repair and renovation.

Apart from a brief period during the 1948 London Olympics when Herne Hill Stadium was the venue for the cycling events, only the occasional competitive meeting has been held there. The popularity of competitive cycling decreased and London stadia closed. Only the Herne Hill Stadium remains.

CYCLING FOR THE MAN ON THE STREET

The arrival of the bicycle brought new freedom to the man on the London street. Once a cycle had been purchased, it cost the owner nothing to escape into the nearby countryside.

The activity was most popular with younger people who often became more widely travelled than their parents. Its success coincided with the realisation that activities such as cycling, running and swimming were very beneficial to health.

Richard Church considered that the half-share in a tandem given to him one Christmas was the passport to an unlimited freedom of the roads. Once he had mastered the technique of riding in tandem with his elder brother, the family was able to cycle to holiday destinations. When a move from Battersea was mooted, the family searched by cycle for a suitable home. The property they found was at the junction of Half Moon Lane/Warmington Road and Ruskin Walk (then Simpson's Alley). A little later, when a school was needed for Richard, the search was again made by cycle and Dulwich Hamlet School was soon discovered. The tandem was replaced by a cycle, which gave Richard even more freedom on the road. Years later, after his mother died and the family home had been broken up, he took his bicycle with him to rooms he shared with his brother in the Champion Hill area.

Richard Church's enjoyment in cycling continued throughout his active life. He bought his own children cycles and introduced them to the delights of the open road and they, in turn, passed their enthusiasm on to their children.

In the years before the First World War, the children of the Nevard family were also introduced to the freedom of cycling. One of the special requirements when the parents were seeking a new home was a side entrance into the back garden and a shed where the children could store their bikes. They had had enough of bicycles blocking the front porch and standing in the hallway!

The Nevards found just such a house near the junction of Trinity Rise and Norwood Road. Like the Church family, the Nevards retained their enthusiasm for cycling for many years. Beryl, the last Nevard in Herne Hill, lived in the family home until she died in the early 1980s – she had not cycled for years, but she often reminisced about its pleasures.

Cycling did have its drawbacks, however. On 31 July 1912, a young man sent a picture postcard of Brockwell Park Temple to a Miss Bentley in Worcester. He wrote:

Stuck it until 2pm – then train to Paddington. Did not half get wet and smothered with mud from the horse buses – not at all pleasant cycling across London in the rain... I'm all right now, though.

It cannot have been pleasant for the drivers of horse buses either who did not have wind shields to protect them from the elements.

During the interwar years, open road racing thrived and rallies were organised at Alexandra Palace and Crystal Palace. International cycling events were organised in various countries and cycling was introduced to the Olympic Games.

Cycle riding was immensely popular and remained so after the war. However, with the stated statistic of 'a car per household', the roads became more congested and cycling less pleasant. A car for each household was impractical, especially in areas built during Victorian and Edwardian times, where garage space was not available and street parking a nightmare, the fortunes of cycling have taken a slight turn for the better in the late 1900s.

In the twenty-first century many councils provide the occasional cycle lane along roadways and even in Brockwell Park certain paths are marked for cycling. For the experienced rider, there are occasional sponsored cycle rides to Brighton, ending where the 'Old Crocks' finish.

The cooperation of the police has seen safe bicycling being taught in several junior schools and Herne Hill Stadium is the venue for some evening and Saturday tuition.

BUS SERVICES AND BUS-STOPS

The area of Herne Hill served by omnibuses and, later, buses was wider than that covered by tram services. Horse buses had trundled up Herne Hill, along Half Moon Lane and Croxted Road to Camberwell, East Dulwich and Crystal Palace, before tramlines had appeared in Dulwich and Milkwood Roads. In his autobiography, *Over the Bridge*, Richard Church spoke of the 'hourly horse bus' that passed along Half Moon Lane in 1904. The terminus was at the Half Moon Hotel where the horse rested in the front yard before crossing the road to begin the return journey to East Dulwich and Peckham.

When Croxted Lane was laid out and became Croxted Road, buses (at first horse, then motor buses) began to traverse it to Crystal Palace on Sydenham Hill. From the time of its opening in 1854, Crystal Palace was the centre of all forms of entertainment for South East London. There were times when 'all roads led to Crystal Palace' and many thousands of people flocked there by all modes of transport available, including shanks's pony.

Buses and trams 'dropped down' and 'picked up' passengers as requested until bus-stops became a necessary requirement. Even so, there had always been points along the routes recognised as bus-stops and tram stops, such as that in Dulwich Road by Brockwell Park and on the island at the junction of Dulwich, Norwood and Railton Roads. Regular daily travellers were often picked up outside their homes along the routes. Mr Nevade, a manager at Covent Garden Fruit Market, travelled to work on the early-morning tram, which the driver would often halt outside Mr Nevade's house in Norwood Road. Until the outbreak of the Second World War, it was possible to dismount between bus-stops just by ringing the bell. Initially, the police opposed the marked stops, particularly for trams. They did not like crowds gathering and then moving out into the roadway, but eventually it was recognised that official stops were less dangerous than alighting and dismounting at will.

For many years now, Croxted Road has been part of the No. 3 bus service from Crystal Palace via Herne Hill, Brixton, Kennington, Lambeth Bridge and the West End to Camden Town.

Following the much-lamented demise of the trams, an extended network of ten bus routes served the area of Herne Hill, all passing through the junction at the bottom of the Hill: Nos. 2, 2a, 3, 37, 40, 42, 48, 68, 172 and 196. The distances covered extended far beyond the original bus routes serving the old Herne Hill.

The majority of buses which drove through Herne Hill crossed the Thames and passed through areas of high employment to destinations in the outer suburbs. There were many variations in services, with some extending their routes on certain days or during rush hours and others only running at weekends. It was necessary to learn the vagaries of the bus service or to own a good bus timetable.

At the time of writing some of the buses serving the area still run on the same routes. These include: No. 37 from Peckham to Richmond; No. 3 from Crystal Palace to Camden Town; No. 2 from Crystal Palace to Victoria and Golders Green. The route of the No. 68 from South Croydon to Chalk Farm has

been divided at Waterloo, the destination of the second section now being Hampstead Heath. The No. 196 bus no longer passes up Herne Hill to Camberwell and Waterloo, but diverts along Dulwich Road to Brixton.

Several bus routes, Nos. 40, 42 and 2a, No. 48 which traversed Milkwood Road and Camberwell, and No. 172, which passed along Dulwich Road to Brixton and eventually to Archway, have disappeared from Herne Hill altogether.

The old-style buses and the conductors have been replaced by larger, smoother-running buses, with a driver who sells tickets and inspects bus passes.

Traffic congestion is such that bus-stops are now standardised and it is no longer possible to ring a bell to alight anywhere on the route or to hail a passing bus between official bus-stops.

From time to time, new bus routes are introduced – some of these survive while others disappear. On certain days, buses with facilities for the disabled operate, usually between residential areas and shopping centres.

Due to traffic congestion, services rarely function on time. There are prolonged waits at bus-stops and often several buses with the same number and destination arrive within a minute or two of each other. It is necessary to allow extra time for one's journey.

Herne Hill Station Approach. Although at the time of writing the entrance to the station and the surrounding buildings appear very much as they were in the 1920s, the cinema no longer functions, the tramlines are gone and the street furniture and cars have changed. It is interesting to note that people are walking in the street without fear of busy traffic and that almost everybody is wearing a hat.

Chapter 11

WARTIME IN HERNE HILL

The outbreak of the Second World War and subsequent evacuation saw the number of people living in Herne Hill and the wider London area fall markedly. The drop in population was redressed in part when many people returned soon after, feeling that the threat of destruction by bombing had not and would not occur. Many of those who returned were women and children. Military service depleted the population further as the war progressed, and when bombing did commence rehousing became necessary.

Herne Hill suffered considerable damage during periods of enemy action. There were many casualties and more than 110 deaths, the majority of them at the site of explosions. Only a few streets escaped bomb damage from high explosives. There were also oil or fire bombs and exploding anti-aircraft shells – ack-ack shells – from the mobile units and those in parks and open spaces. Essential services were disrupted as gas and electricity lines, water mains and sewage systems ruptured and homes were temporarily evacuated because of unexploded bombs and ack-ack shells. Fire resulting from incendiary bombs and ruptured gas mains were also cause for evacuation.

Much of the property damage and the majority of casualties and deaths occurred during the Blitz between August 1940 and May 1941. The main targets of enemy bombs were the lines of communication, the railways, the stations and sidings and bridges. This was especially apparent in the Milkwood Road and Dulwich Road areas, in Croxted and Rosendale Roads and Half Moon Lane and their adjacent roads. Later, the damage suffered from 'flying bombs' was quite indiscriminate – it was estimated that each one destroyed 22 houses and 474 were damaged to a lesser degree. It was a blessing that only a few fell in Herne Hill.

Properties in Herne Place, Regent Road and Hurst Street were irreparably damaged and demolished. Two new estates and a school were built. The area adjacent to the Milkwood Road railway sidings altered beyond all recognition and most of the houses lying directly under the embankment were demolished and replaced by an industrial estate.

It was fortunate that each local area had its own fire-watchers, its ARP wardens' unit and Home Guards (attached to them were messenger boys, usually about 15 or 16 years old). First-aid posts and women's voluntary services were also arranged. Back-up civil defence, Auxiliary Fire Services, ambulance and police services responded quickly to emergencies. It was often the case that many more people turned up to help during emergencies than were 'on duty'.

Many houses had their own supplies of water and sand at their front doors to dampen down fires caused by incendiary bombs. Some had stirrup-pumps which were shared with others in the road. Most people knew how to use appliances and were conversant with the 'do's and don'ts' of dealing with emergencies. Above all, they trusted their neighbours, the vast majority of whom were prepared to help and support others in times of damage and injury. Often the homes of near strangers became the refuge of those in need.

It was also fortunate that not all high-explosive and incendiary bombs detonated and that fire-watchers and air-raid wardens were so vigilant.

During the early days of the war, air-raid shelters were deemed a good form of safety for civilians and thus many were built on vacant sites. One such shelter was built near the Norwood Road lodge in Brockwell Park. When the alarm sounded in the late afternoon of 15 September 1940, some people left their homes for the safety of the shelter and passers-by joined them. Shortly afterwards, the shelter received a direct hit. Six people were killed and others injured. For many local residents, this is the most remembered incident of the Blitz in Herne Hill.

Afterwards, the majority of people showed less inclination to leave what they felt was the comparative safety of their own homes for public shelters. Instead they moved downstairs and slept under the stairs, under tables or in Anderson shelters in the back garden. People became used to living 'below stairs' and in May 1941, when enemy planes suddenly ceased their raids, it took several nights of undisturbed sleep before people were sufficiently convinced that it was safe to return upstairs to their bedrooms.

Over the years, people became familiar with the sounds of the different aircraft – 'one of theirs, one of ours' – and the wail of the sirens which sounded over 1,200 times during the war, many more times than there were incidents in Herne Hill. Later, they would listen to hear if the V1s would continue or cut out above, in which case danger could be immediate. No warning was possible for the V2s – they were only heard after they had arrived.

There were further periods when it was necessary to sleep downstairs, either in the Morrison or Anderson shelters. In later years, many people remembered their Anderson shelters with affection, but few wished to retain their Morrison shelters which were big and heavy and almost impossible to move.

Local hospitals suffered a degree of damage during the war and St Giles' had to rebuild its operating theatre and kitchens. From then on, it worked with reduced ward space. Several bombs fell in the grounds of the Maudsley but no patients were in residence; only out-patient work and research took place. King's College Hospital cared for many casualties despite structural damage. Both Dulwich and St Francis' Hospitals were bomb damaged, but continued caring for patients, most of whom were evacuated when they could be moved.

Despite the war, all the hospitals, with the exception of St Francis' Hospital, continued their policy of training nurses to reach the state registration standard. Most nurses spent some time in country hospitals where they cared for evacuated patients. The nurses returned to their parent hospitals in their third year of training.

The majority of churches in the area suffered structural damage. St Matthew's, Denmark Hill, was fire-bombed in September 1940 – its spire stood for years, but its church was completely destroyed. St Saviour's Church never recovered from the blastings having had its foundations undermined. It was declared unsafe and eventually demolished.

St Paul's, Herne Hill, was luckier than most churches in the area. An incendiary bomb was quickly doused and later a nearby flying bomb incident resulted in some of the church windows being blown in. Its daughter church, St John's, Lowden Road, suffered from nearby bombing incidents but was repaired and continued functioning. It eventually suffered more from surrounding social conditions than from enemy action.

The Congregational church at the top of Red Post Hill suffered no direct damage, but its foundations were undermined by nearby incidents. Subsidence occurred and finally led to demolition

and rebuilding. A modern church stands in its place and is known as the United Reform Church.

The original St Faith's Church, Red Post Hill, received little blast damage. However, the Half Moon Methodist Church and halls were badly damaged and needed rebuilding. The church itself never recovered from the severe blast damage and was finally demolished. Wesley House, sheltered housing for the elderly, was built on the vacant site. The congregation joined with the people of St Faith's and finally moved to the United Reform Church.

St Jude's was severely bomb damaged and only the vestry could be used for church purposes. The church building was leased for commercial purposes. The parish is administered from the vicarage and church services are conducted at the newly-built St Jude's School, which was designed with this purpose in mind.

Holy Trinity Church, on the other side of Brockwell Park, had its foundations badly undermined and was declared unsafe. For years, services were held in its parish hall and then at St Matthew's in Brixton, until finally, nearly 50 years after the war ended, the church was thoroughly renovated and reopened with great celebration.

The Salvation Army outpost at the Loughborough Junction area was completely destroyed and for the next 40 years its home was in Wanless Road.

The Methodist church in Railton Road was severely damaged and finally, after several attempts at repair, it had to admit defeat. A fine modern church was opened in the 1960s. The Baptist church in Half Moon Lane was very fortunate in its avoidance of damage but the small Baptist church in Denmark Place was more seriously damaged. However, it was repaired and still functions.

Schools also suffered considerable structural damage. The parish school of St Jude's, Railton Road, eventually relocated in Regent Road. The new school was larger, with spacious classrooms and playgrounds. As a consequence its pupil numbers increased considerably.

Jessop Road School was used as an Auxiliary Fire Station throughout the war and was severely damaged. Eventually it was rebuilt and restructured as a junior school. The small road after which it was named disappeared entirely and its neighbour, Neville's Bakery, was also damaged. The bakery was sold and later demolished along with its surrounding housing, shops and the nearby Milkwood Road Tavern. Plans of the original bakery and its housing were found amongst the rubble and are now stored at Lambeth Archives, Minet Library.

St Saviour's School, Herne Hill Road, survived the nearby bombing and the demolition of the adjacent church. Damage was repaired and additional school premises were built, which considerably increased its pupil numbers over the following years. The Unitarian church and school in

Effra Road were both completely destroyed and all records lost. Half of them had been moved to another site to keep them safe but that was also destroyed. The Essex Street church and hall, The Strand, were also destroyed. Their records were lost, including those from many associated churches and schools.

The small National School, built opposite the Unitarian church in Effra Road, was also destroyed. Neither of the schools were rebuilt, but another very modern church was constructed on the Unitarian church site. The London Board Schools in Effra Parade and Sussex Street were bomb damaged, but both are still functioning.

Luckily, the Carnegie Library was hardly damaged by the incidents that occurred nearby. The library shared its premises with an ARP unit and one night the librarian on duty heard a strange noise. On investigation, she found a fractured radiator pipe was squirting water onto a bookcase. Her hand proving unequal to the task, she sat on the pipe, shouting for someone to turn off the water – she did not know where to look for it herself. She remained there for several hours before rescue came. The incident was caused by a high-explosive bomb hitting a nearby nursing home, which had occupied the wardens. All of the residents at the home had to be moved to a house on the corner of Rollscourt Avenue and Herne Hill.

The majority of incidents occurred on the Lambeth side of Herne Hill, probably because the area had a larger density of housing around the railways lines and sidings and less open space. Many bombing incidents in Herne Hill did not result in fatalities, but caused injuries that required hospital treatment. At the end of the war, the civilian fatalities resulting from enemy action were recorded by the War Graves Commission. The names, addresses, ages, family relationships, dates and places of incidents were recorded in books, copies of which are kept in Borough Archives at the Imperial War Museum and in the archives of Westminster Abbey. The Imperial War Museum also holds many of the 'incident' books kept by ARP and Civil Defence Posts, listing the incidents to which the wardens were called, the reason for the call and the result.

The first bombs that fell in the vicinity of Herne Hill in August 1940 did little damage. Some failed to explode and some landed in open spaces during the daytime. The most damaging incidents occurred in September when German planes began to concentrate on night attacks.

Herne Hill's first fatality occurred on 11 September 1940 and its last on 14 February 1945. There were terrible incidents when families, parents and children were killed, brothers on duty were killed and direct hits made on the Brockwell Park air-raid shelter and the Jessop Road Auxiliary Fire Station.

WARTIME CASUALTIES

Acland Crescent

Mavis Clark (23) at Acland Crescent	11.9.40

Brixton Water Lane

John Holt (41) at 2 Brixton Water Lane	5.7.44
died at King's College Hospital (KCH)	6.7.44
Mary S. Snazelle (78)	5.7.44
at 3 Brixton Water Lane	
Frederick Pearce (47)	5.7.44
at 6 Brixton Water Lane	
Henry Gilmore Pearce (53) as above	5.7.44
William J. Pearce (53) as above	5.7.44
died at King's College Hospital, same day	
Above three Home Guards	

Brockwell Park Shelter

All on 15.9.40 at Brockwell Park air-raid shelter

Dennis Allen (12)	149 Norwood Road
Grace Hagger (49)	121 Denmark Hill
Olive J. Kilsby (18)	52 Brockwell Park Gardens
Ivy Little (55)	16 Trinity Rise
Florence J. Reed (41)	30 Brockwell Park Gardens
Henry G.W. Reed (40)	30 Brockwell Park Gardens

Burbage Road

Elizabeth Feaver (59) at 9 Burbage Road	16.4.41
Frederick Feaver (56) as above	16.4.41
Joan B. Feaver (17) as above	16.4.41
Raymond Feaver (18) as above	16.4.41
Henry William Duck (63) at 108 Burbage Road	
Kate Duck (59) as above both on	22.6.44
Walter James Boutall, MC (55)	22.6.44
at 112 Burbage Road	

Cambria Road

Alfred Loten (52) of 1 Cambria Road	29.7.44
at 397 Norwood Road	

Carver Road

Joan M. Attwood (24) at 26 Carver Road	10.7.44

Coldharbour Lane

George W. Russ (33) at 361 Coldharbour Lane	
Florence R. Russ (30) as above	
Osbourne, mother and eight children,	
at 361 Coldharbour Lane all on	17.4.41

Dulwich Road

Gertrude Showell (64)	28.6.44
of 15 Dulwich Road at Acre Lane	
Arnold J. Yates (43) at 77a Dulwich Road	29.12.40
Beatrice P. Yates (43) as above	29.12.40
Colin Yates (6) as above	29.12.40
Miles Yates (14) as above	29.12.40
Patricia Yates (8) as above	29.12.40

Elmwood Road

William F. Andrews (38) at 20 Elmwood Road	
Arthur Probert (41) at 50 Elmwood Road	
Edward Probert (45) as above	
Frank Probert (36) as above all on	29.12.40

Fawnbrake Avenue

Albert E. Rawledge (46) (stretcher-bearer)	15.3.41
of 11 Fawnbrake Ave at police box, Grove Lane	

Gubyon Avenue
Ernest Boughton (31) of 30 Gubyon Avenue
at West Norwood – died KCH   4.7.44
Hawarden Road
William John Jackson (3)   5.11.40
  at 35 Hawarden Road
Half Moon Lane
Hertha Loebenstein (34)   12.9.40
  of 72 Half Moon Lane, died 13.9.40, Dulwich Hospital
Herne Hill
Helen Parkes (24) at 64 Herne Hill   1.11.40
Elizabeth J. Hall (62) at 62 Herne Hill   1.11.40
Henry F. Hall (58) as above   1.11.40
Eileen M. Hall (Dr) (28) as above   1.11.40
Claude L. Hart (28) of 13 Warmington Road,
  at 62 Herne Hill   (engaged couple)
Herne Hill Road
Charles Grantham (41) of 41 Herne Hill Road
Lena M. Harnett (48) as above (both died KCH 7.11.40)
Charles McDonald (48)   8.11.40
  of 41 Herne Hill Road – died at KCH
Francis G. Wood (57)   26.9.40
  at 76 Herne Hill Road
Heron Road
Reginald W. Cripps (15)   17.10.40
  of 41 Heron Road at Hinton Road
Hinton Road
Stanley G.D. Sandlin (44)   17.10.40
  at 31 Hinton Road
Joyce A. Hood (16) of 14 Upstall Road   17.10.40
  at Hinton Road/Loughborough Junction, died KCH
Thomas H.M. Greevy (63)   17.4.41
  of 46 Hinton Road at Loughborough Junction Stn
Hurst Street
Frederick W. Heath (4) at 25 Hurst Street 16.4.41
Elsie E. Henley (41) at 21 Hurst Street   16.4.41
Frederick Henley (48) as above   16.4.41
Vera Henley (22) as above   16.4.41
Martha Hobbs (68) as above   16.4.41
Jessop Road School House
All firemen at Jessop Road School House on 8.3.41
Percival H. Field (18)   Walter J. Spence (36)
Charles S. Yelland (47)
Kemerton Road
John H. Chapman (61)   17.4.41
  of 29 Kemerton Road at Hardness Road
Kestrel Avenue
Arthur J.S. Wells (56)   19.3.41
  of 43 Kestrel Avenue at Woodquest Avenue
Lowden Road
Monica Newton (63) of 43 Lowden Road   15.10.40
William Newton (65) as above (both at Pelier Street)
Mayall Road
Albert H. Petit (15) at 114 Mayall Road   17.4.41
Vera Maud Petit (3) as above   17.4.41
Lilian A. Tagg (57) at 118 Mayall Road   17.4.41
Arthur B.J. Watling (39)   22.1.46
  of 192 Mayall Road at Dulwich Hospital
  (of illness contracted in the National Fire Service)

Millbrook Road (Loughborough Junction)
Gladys E. Jebson (26) at 3 Millbrook Road 17.4.41
Richard J. Jebson (2) as above   17.4.41
Milkwood Road
George Bell (84) at 191 Milkwood Road   16.4.41
Selena Bell (85) as above (died KCH)   16.4.41
Florence Shucksfield (36) as above   16.4.41
William E. Shucksfield (35) as above   16.4.41
Martha A. Cropp (89)   16.4.41
  of 193 Milkwood Road (died KCH same day)
Elizabeth M. Field (31) as above   16.4.41
George F. Field (63) as above   16.4.41
Horace W. Smith (37)   27.9.40
  at 69 Milkwood Road
Barbara C. Wilkins (30)   16.4.41
  at 186 Milkwood Road
Albert E. Bevan (16)   10.6.41
  of 114 Milkwood Road at 51 Tiverton Road
George E. Morton (53)   27.9.40
  of 60 Somerleyton Road at 69 Milkwood Road
Percy E.W. Carnon (30)   12.7.44
  of 107 Milkwood Road at Mitcham, Surrey
  died at St Giles' Hospital on   20.7.44
Poplar Walk Road
Walter J. Handy of 78 Poplar Walk Road
  at Milkwood Road – died at KCH on   17.10.40
Railton Road
Hilda M. Smith (32) at 69 Railton Road   12.4.40
Peabody Estate and Rosendale Road
Georgiana Bryant (63) of Peabody estate   20.10.40
  at Rosendale Road
John S.C. Bryant (57) as above   20.10.40
Annie Wellington (7) of 50 The Cottages   4.11.40
  at Rosendale Road
Ernest Stanhope Follett (35)   29.12.40
  of 278 Rosendale Road outside Town Hall,
  Peckham Road – ARP ambulance driver
Spenser Road
Laura Ann Whitehead (67)   17.4.41
  at 63 Spenser Road
Stradella Road
Florence Smart (49) at 37 Stradella Road
  (WVS) died at Dulwich Hospital   11.8.44
Shakespeare Road
Thomas R. Alpin (53)   14.2.45
  of 19 Shakespeare Road at 112 Trafalgar Road
Mary M.S. Tyler (79)   29.9.40
  at 209 Shakespeare Road
Woodquest Road
Lionel Matthews (71) 1 Woodquest Road   19.3.41
  (ARP warden)
Florence H. Probert (48)   19.3.41
  at 4 Woodquest Road
Winifred A. Probert (41)   19.3.41
Richard Sadler (33)   19.3.41
  at 8 Woodquest Road
Alice Sadler (27) as above   19.3.41
Lilian Hall (34) at 8 Woodquest Road   19.3.41
  died in Dulwich Hospital on   20.3.41

Chapter 12

POSTWAR HERNE HILL

Many of the buildings on the Lambeth side of Herne Hill are late-Victorian and Edwardian, while those on the Southwark side are predominantly Edwardian. The disparity was largely due to the expiry of leases on the original estates. The development of housing that took place between the two world wars was also due to the leases having lapsed, but housing built in the first few decades after 1945 came about for a different reason.

A number of postwar houses were constructed on the sites of destroyed homes in Victorian and Edwardian roads. Estates and groups of flats also covered bomb-damaged areas and were for the most part built by councils. Due to the prevalent shortages and restrictions, private building was at times delayed, but eventually most of the empty spaces were filled.

Initially, priority was given to the repair of bomb-damaged houses and the provision of instant housing or 'pre-fabs'. Pre-fabs were meant to last up to ten years but in reality many were in use for longer periods because the shortage of housing was ongoing and many people liked living in the small cottage-like homes.

Pre-war vacant sites, such as Prynners Mead in Herne Hill, and those cleared of bomb-damaged properties, including Woodquest Avenue and Milkwood Road, were acquired and within a few years estates were laid out. In some cases the LCC acquired bomb-damaged sites, such as Regents Road, and built blocks of flats and small terraces of houses.

Due to the acute shortage of housing, many large dwellings were acquired and converted into flats, sometimes leading to injustices for the original owners. The subsequent population growth accompanied by the baby boom had a roll-on effect and increased the need for health and educational facilities. It was more noticeable on the Lambeth side of Herne Hill than on the Dulwich side, where there were fewer large houses. The roads had been laid out at a later date and the houses were often unsuitable for division. In any case, the land and properties were in the care of the major landlord, the Dulwich College estate, whose policies protected against over-development.

When the war damage had been repaired there were few areas left on which councils or private developers could build. At this point, older premises were demolished because either their original purpose had passed or they had become so dilapidated that only rebuilding was practical.

Vacant spaces were gradually filled on both sides of the borough boundaries. Maisonettes in the grounds of the Matlock Manor Hotel, on the corner of Herne Hill and Poplar Walk (demolished in the late 1940s), were ready for occupation in 1956. With gardens front and back, they stretched to the grounds of Dorchester Court and down Poplar Walk. The maisonettes had the letters a–d added to their numbers, to fit between the existing Herne Hill addresses.

Further down Herne Hill on the corner of Kestrel Avenue, a derelict property was cleared and a small complex of flats built in its place for residents needing a degree of care. Sheltered housing was built on the corner of Spenser Road and, next to it, standing back, a small block of flats.

In the 1980s, old dilapidated properties in Hinton Road were cleared. Two-storeyed blocks of flats for families were built and were occupied almost immediately.

The council built several family blocks of flats in the Southwark area, at the junction of Red Post Hill and Sunray Avenue and on the corner of Elmwood Road. Delawyck Crescent, built in the grounds of the demolished Delawyck House, Half Moon Lane, stands back from the road, and below the railway embankment there is a pleasant development of family houses with small gardens built around a winding roadway.

Close by, a three-storey complex of retirement homes was built in the grounds of two large houses – one of which was called Elm Lodge and had for years been the surgery of a medical practice. In the grounds of Elm Lodge stood 'the grand old elm – a sight ever to be remembered' which Blanche said, in the 1870s, 'must be several hundred years old'. It had 'a girth of 36 feet' and was 'perfectly hollow' in 'which as many as a dozen persons' could 'find sitting room'. Blanche felt 'no edict of Governors, or Act of Parliament, ought to be allowed to prevail against it.' In the event, time and natural decay prevailed against it and in the 1980s, when the old houses were demolished, there was nothing left but a few small saplings.

The new establishment is set in spacious gardens behind brick walls and wrought-iron gates, with plenty of room for tenants' car parking. The surgery was moved into purpose-built premises around the corner in Burbage Road, more convenient for doctors and patients alike. It lies under the railway embankment leading to North Dulwich Station and is part of a modern complex of housing.

The building of large Borough Council estates was a notable change in the postwar years. Massive estates had been constructed in the years between the wars, for the most part as slum clearance. By far the greater number had been built by the LCC. Some, in areas such as Downham, were the foundations of new suburbs.

Postwar Government money encouraged Borough Councils to enter the field in a big way. Herne Hill had few vacant sites for large estates. Blanchedowne, the biggest, was an LCC project and the Regent Road/Hurst Street development was a joint project between the LCC and Lambeth. On the whole, the small estates were considered reasonable and did not cause too much offence to the occupants of neighbouring housing.

HELP FROM HOUSING ASSOCIATIONS

The councils have been helped in their task of providing acceptable housing by the formation of housing associations. These took property into their care that had fallen on hard times and was not within the remit of the councils. The London Quadrant Association was one such association and the Milkwood/Lowden Roads estate just such an area. Bomb damage and the failure of many people to return to the area from war service and evacuation had led to a decline in conditions and, when the majority of the original leases lapsed in the 1970s, many residents found themselves tenants to a variety of landlords. The estate was rescued by the London Quadrant, who also took other groups of housing into their care, such as the terrace of dwellings opposite St Saviour's School and parish hall and individual houses, including one on the corner of Herne Hill and Rollscourt Avenue.

Another change, and one very beneficial to the community, was the recognition of the increased longevity of the population and the need to provide special housing for the elderly. Now known as sheltered housing, it is an extension of the almshouse principle, but not the workhouse ethos.

There are different conditions of acceptance and degrees of care in the various sheltered complexes in Herne Hill. Most are situated within reach of transport facilities. They are often in blocks of flats, such as at Wesley House on the site of the former Methodist church, Half Moon Lane, the Tudor Stacks in Dorchester Drive, run by the Anchor Housing, or Hilltops House on Red Post Hill, founded by the congregation of the United Reform Church and now run by the English Churches Association. In some cases the council built small bungalows for single people or married couples, such as those in Matlock Close, Poplar Walk.

At the time of writing most sheltered housing projects endeavour to involve residents in their running and in social events and extend invitations to the surrounding community. Many people respond and interest is maintained in the project and the people living within. There is usually a waiting list for sheltered accommodation.

Left: *After Aylesford House was demolished on the junction of Denmark Hill and Herne Hill Road, the site was vacant for many years. Sometimes fairs were held when caravans and tents arrived. Bunting blew in the wind and everybody had a good time. This ended when Herne Hill Road was extended above the Carnegie Library.*

Chapter 13

☘

THE DEVELOPMENT OF ESTATES

Throughout its history Herne Hill has undergone considerable development, often through the creation of estates. Until the Reformation the Church had been the biggest landowner. The land was initially sold to the highest bidders, but later, through a series of wills, marriages, division and sales, it was purchased by people who intended living on their estates. In time, the large estates were divided and each section developed individually. Development occurred as a result of the lapse of a lease or an estate being divided following the death of an owner. The coming of the railway and the two world wars also contributed to changes. Some estates were built as 'social experiments' or were the result of philanthropic concerns. Some were built by councils when the original purpose of the land had passed, or to replace properties destroyed by enemy action.

THE SANDERS AND MINET ESTATES

When Samuel Sanders purchased his estate on Denmark Hill in the 1770s, he could not have known how his deed would benefit future generations in the community. The estate stretched back through what is now Ruskin Park to Herne Hill Road and Fawnbrake Avenue, up Denmark Hill and down Herne Hill. The management of the land ensured that it did not fall into the hands of speculative builders and suffer the overdevelopment and gross overcrowding of some nearby areas. The estate had the added advantage of lying opposite land belonging to the Dulwich College estate, whose policy allowed only limited development.

Samuel Sanders recognised that the new bridges over the Thames would provide the impetus for wealthy merchants to escape overcrowded London. He granted long leases to the merchants and soon houses of variable size appeared on the Lambeth side of Denmark and Herne Hills. Each house had its own carriage entrance and garden stretching back to open fields, and later market gardens.

The new residents employed servants and, if children were part of the family, tutors, governesses or nurses. The majority also employed gardeners to manage the kitchen gardens, hothouses and conservatories. Not only did households endeavour to grow as much produce as possible but, during the later Victorian period in particular, there was great interest in cultivating plants and trees from other climes. The manufacture of new plant carriers and the increased speed at which steamships travelled, made it possible for people to grow exotic plants in their conservatories and gardens. There is evidence of this in Ruskin Park, an area which comprises the grounds of eight properties demolished during the early-Edwardian period, one being the original home of Samuel Sanders. Many of the features of these gardens were incorporated into the park, including magnolias, Judas and tulip trees, holm-oaks, Indian bean and the magnificent Turkey oak – now over 250 years old.

Improved coach services traversing Camberwell New Road, the Walworth Road and the age-old Coldharbour Lane, led to the construction of villas and terraces, leaving the fields and market gardens at the rear to their rural occupations. The new railway loop through lower Denmark Hill and Camberwell brought rapid changes. The area behind Denmark Hill and St Matthew's Church was soon laid out with terraces of small houses, and land south of the railway embankment leading to Loughborough Junction soon suffered the same fate. The only land spared from urban development was that within the Sanders estate.

The small roads of Wanless, Wingmore, Hinton and Alderton were laid out on land administered by the Minet family and, on the other side of Herne Hill Road, under the high embankment, Northway, Anstey and Kemerton Roads appeared. Soon they were lined with terraced houses. The properties in Hinton Road, near Coldharbour Lane, were three-storeyed shops with living accommodation above. The road continued under the two railway bridges to Alderton Road, where it met the old Poplar Walk. Later, at the bend, Hinton Road adjoined Milkwood Road, built under the embankment between Herne Hill and Loughborough Junction.

Above: *Chaucer Road, c.1916.*

Right: *Milton Road, c.1912.*

Left: *Shakespeare Road, c.1921.*

Below: *Spenser Road, c.1916.*

Within a few years the whole of the area south of Coldharbour Lane was intersected with roads lined with houses of varying sizes, and served by a variety of well-situated shops and two public houses. Trams and trains frequently ran through the area connecting it with local places and London. As well as Neville's Bakery in the centre of the Milkwood Road estate, there were small businesses which provided employment both in the vicinity and in Brixton.

In 1906 the Carnegie Library was built between Haredale and Ferndene Roads on land donated by the Minet Trust. The building was financed by the Carnegie Corporation.

The upper part of Herne Hill Road was originally a pathway serving the larger properties at the junction of Denmark and Herne Hills. In order to reach the hills, or Red Post Hill, it was necessary to walk up Poplar Walk. When the leases of the large properties lapsed, Herne Hill Road was extended and it became possible for pedestrians and traffic to reach the junction without recourse to the Poplar Walk detour.

The small streets on the library side of Herne Hill Road terminated at Poplar Walk and, for many decades, the walk led from Herne Hill to Coldharbour Lane. This is visible on a map dating from 1790. In the first half of the nineteenth century there were several kitchen gardens near the walk's junction with Herne Hill but these had disappeared by 1870.

Despite its length, the only houses on Poplar Walk are those above Lowden Road and, apart from the small cottages built to house the garden staff of the estates, no houses had been built before the Edwardian period.

Much of the lower part of Poplar Walk is a rather seedy lane, edged with the sides of houses and garden fences. It bears no resemblance to its original appearance and is rarely used as it once was. The Church of St Philip and St James stands on the corner of Lowden Road and Poplar Walk. It is the only Roman Catholic church in Herne Hill. Built in 1905, it is known as an Ellis Church after the benefactor, who built several churches in Lambeth at the time. Attached to the building is a very pleasant parish hall, where the Herne Hill Society held its monthly meetings for a number of years.

Matlock Manor Hotel stood at the corner of Herne Hill and Poplar Walk, its grounds stretching down to what is now Dorchester Drive. In the 1940s it was the last of the old Herne Hill properties to be demolished. Semi-detached houses were constructed in its place and, above them, modern maisonettes which stretch around the corner into Herne Hill. A small estate of sheltered housing has been built on the site of a demolished house on Poplar Walk. This is Matlock Close and consists of small, detached one-storey cottages standing in gardens. It has a community hall, and both residents and neighbours are encouraged to come together at various times.

POETS' CORNER, DULWICH AND RAILTON ROADS

It was natural that the improvements in roads and transport services would lead to the development of areas around coach termini. The George Canning Inn, at the corner of Effra Road and Water Lane, was one such terminus. Water Lane was lined with villas but the land beyond awaited the builders' attention. Following the death of a young landlord, his estate was sold to support his widow and children. Soon, the area known as Poets' Corner was laid out and, over the following decades, numerous houses were built. There was a variety of construction undertaken, including terraces of Georgian-type houses and two- or three-storeyed Victorian houses, some with basements. A number of the homes were detached and others semi-detached, depending on which style was fashionable. Each house had a small garden at the front and a larger one behind.

The construction of the railways saw 'the loveliness of South London' develop into suburbia. Within a couple of decades, as Walter Besant noted in his book *South London*, 'the country south of London' was 'covered with villas, roads, streets and shops' making it difficult 'to understand how wonderfully lovely it was before the builders seized upon it.' Maps depicting the area south and south-east of London showed a series of triangles, oblongs and squares, each edged with railway lines which would ensure that future inhabitants would have a railway station within easy reach of their homes. Most of the railway lines ran along high embankments and only occasionally through tunnels.

A station, Hernehill, appeared in the fields near the site of Island Green and a bridge was built over the roadway at the junction of Norwood Lane and Herne Hill. Half Moon Lane was straightened and the River Effra, which had meandered its way from Norwood along Half Moon Lane, Croxted Lane and Water Lane to Brixton, was 'bricked over'. Ruskin said that this occurred 'for the convenience of Mr Biffin, the chemist, and others.' For a time the old dry course could be seen along Half Moon Lane and parts of Dulwich Road. Within a few years of the arrival of the railway, large houses were being built opposite the Brockwell Park estate in Dulwich Road. By 1870, Regent Road, Herne Place, Hurst Street and Rymer Street had been laid out and partially developed.

In the late 1800s the roads at Poets' Corner terminated in fields below the railway embankment. Shakespeare Road had not yet been extended beneath another embankment leading to Loughborough Junction. A metropolitan drinking trough for the refreshment of horses and dogs stood on the corner of Water Lane and Dulwich Road. Further along Dulwich Road was the Prince Regent and, opposite Hernehill Station, the Herne Hill Tavern.

By the 1890s, Railton Road had been laid out. It included Commercial Place, adjacent to the railway station, and West Place, where the small Church school and its house were built. Railton Road later stretched to Atlantic Road and Brixton Market.

The streets between Dulwich Road and the railway embankment had reached Railton Road, behind which lay the long terraces of Mayall Road. Shakespeare Road was extended to Loughborough Junction, passing under a railway bridge. There were terraces of houses on one side of Shakespeare Road and the goods depot, the coal depot, and railway sidings on the high bank opposite.

Dulwich Road had also continued to develop, and shops, with accommodation above, stretched from the corner of Railton Road to Hurst Street.

The terraced houses in the side roads had gardens at the front and back. The houses in Hurst Street and Herne Place were generally larger and some were semi-detached with long back gardens. Between these two roads stood the Methodist Mission Hall, a branch of the Primitive sect, which was not politically in sympathy with other sects of the movement. There was a plant nursery with large glasshouses behind the hall; this was later converted into a garage.

The houses along Dulwich Road were all large with three storeys, many had basements and either stood as terraces or were semi-detached. Originally, the only buildings on the park side of Dulwich Road were St Jude's Church and vicarage and the two houses of Brockwell Terrace. However, by the 1890s

Map of the Milkwood/Lowden Roads estate, 1920s. The estate, built in the 1870s, added over 3,000 people to the population of the area. Most of the children attended Jessop Road School (in the middle of the estate) and many of the men were employed at Neville's Bakery.

large houses with three storeys and basements had been built between Water Lane and the church. After the demolition of the Brockwell Terrace houses, five dwellings were built between the Herne Hill park gates and the church. The occupants of these houses were well-to-do and warranted the colour red on Booth's 1899 map.

In the 1930s, the open-air lido and, later, community halls and a car park, were built on the site of the Brockwell Terrace houses. Apart from this addition, the park side of Dulwich Road has changed little since the early years of the twentieth century.

THE MILKWOOD ROAD ESTATE

The spread of the railway into the countryside spawned the growth of many building societies. These were formed to cater for a new type of housing for craftsmen and their families. Few of these societies still exist, but the Lambeth Building Society was formed from several such groups in the administrative area of the borough of Lambeth. One company, the Suburban Village and General Dwellings Company, was interested in building in areas that had direct railway connections with London, and aimed to provide 'as rapidly as possible' comfortable, healthy houses for 'the overcrowded population of the metropolis'. Herne Hill was just such an area.

Some 250 people subscribed to the Suburban Village and General Dwellings Company and the chairman applied to the Ecclesiastic Commission for a lease on land beside the railway. This had originally been part of the old manorial estate of Milkwell and Wickwood. The lease was granted but, unfortunately, the secretary of the company misspent the company funds. However, a journal called *The Builder*, in 1870, reported that a firm of architects, Habershon & Pite, had agreed to:

... build roads, sewers and between 480 to 650 houses — to be leased, sold outright, or in instalments over 21 years, each house to contain four to eight rooms, every domestic convenience and a piece of garden.

The foundation-stone of the estate was laid by Lord Shaftesbury and the construction of Milkwood, Lowden, Heron and Poplar Walk Roads began. Within a short time, the first of over 3,000 people who were to live on the estate had moved in and, on its completion, *The Builder* reported that the estate was a 'striking example of a new suburb'.

The construction of the estate coincided with the passing of the 1870 Education Act and the setting up of the London School Board. Jessop Road School was built in the middle of the estate.

Neville's built a large bakery next to the school, around which they provided pleasant homes and, on the railway side of Milkwood Road, a garden for the workers. Uniformed drivers delivered the bakery's bread; Neville's expected all employees and conveyances to be a credit to the company.

LOWER HERNE HILL

Occupying the lower part of Herne Hill, between what is now Milkwood Road and Gubyon Avenue, were two large properties. One was the Abbey, which did not have a religious foundation, but is thought to have resembled an abbey the owner knew. Slightly elevated, it stood well back from the road. The construction of the railway, which emphasised the triangular shape of the grounds, was said to have horrified the owner who no longer found the place to be tranquil. A little further up the hill, on the corner of South Place, was The Knoll, so called because it was built on high ground above the road. South Place had very few houses, the biggest being The Cedars. One of the last of the first generation of houses to be demolished, it had for several years been a girls' school with kindergarten and preparatory school for both girls and boys. South Place was later extended and became Gubyon Avenue.

Alfred R. Pite, the architect of the Milkwood/Lowden Roads estate.

It is difficult to utilise the space on triangular corners of roadways – they are often either left vacant as green spaces or, as at the angle of Herne Hill and Milkwood Road, are used for a mixture of residential and commercial purposes. In 1898, after the demolition of the Abbey, a branch of the London County and Westminster Bank was built. Later, it became the National Westminster Bank. Nobody could mistake the origin of the building, for it was typical of the style of most branches of the bank during that period. The company always endeavoured to build on corners, to make their banks immediately recognisable. Three flats were incorporated in the building, with their entrance in Milkwood Road. Two shops faced onto Herne Hill below the flats.

During the Edwardian period, the bank was extended, incorporating the shop adjacent to its premises. This probably took place when the original London County and Westminster Bank joined with Parr's Bank. The second shop was divided into two, one becoming a laundry. Both changed tenancies on several occasions over the years. Eventually, the wall between the two shops was partially demolished and the space came under one management, albeit with different functions. The bank closed in the 1990s and the building was converted into a restaurant.

A Post Office and sorting office was built next to the small shop in the early 1900s. Letters cost a penny to send and one could confidently expect a letter or card posted locally to be delivered to its destination within a few hours. The postcard industry was developing rapidly and there were at least three printers of cards in Herne Hill. The latest time of posting to connect with ships' departure times to other countries was advertised.

In time, the increasing workload at the Post Office led to rebuilding and the sorting office was removed to premises a little uphill from the old Post Office. Its activities continued to expand and, in the 1990s, there was great concern at the threat of closure. Fortunately, after much local protest, the sorting office was reprieved.

A Fire Station, known as sub-station No. E93, was built next to the original Post Office and began operating in July 1906. It was built by the LCC and opened on the same day as Brixton Station. At this time it was mandatory for the firemen to live on the premises and accommodation was provided above. The station was staffed by 'an officer, five firemen and a coachman'. There was a pair of horses, a horse escape and a hose cart. When the alarm sounded, pulleys dropped the harnesses onto the backs of the waiting horses. Girths were fastened, the engine attached and the doors opened to allow the coach to gallop away.

Initially firemen were on call for 14 days without a break, but in 1918 this period was reduced to 10 days. In 1920, a two-shift system was introduced, doubling the manpower, and it was no longer compulsory to live on the premises. Horse-drawn fire engines were replaced by motorised appliances. The Fire Station was closed just 14 years after its opening as engines could now cover a wider area. Since then the building has been variously a garage or car showroom. The accommodation above was converted into flats and part of the station below was rebuilt as a shop which at one time sold flowers.

There was originally a field next to the bank. It is said that a strong horse was kept there which helped loaded buses up Herne Hill, especially in wet and wintry weather. At the top of the hill, the horse was released to find its way back to the field and await the next bus. It is also said that, when the Fire Station equipment was horse-drawn, the horses were sometimes able to exercise and graze in the field. Much later, when the sorting office was built next to the old Fire Station, part of the field was converted into a garage which has since been modernised. In 2003 it has entrances in both Milkwood Road and Herne Hill.

Above: *The foot of Herne Hill in Edwardian times, showing the accommodation above the Fire Station, where firemen lived whilst on duty. The small field above the station was where horses grazed between shifts. The field was replaced by the sorting office and later by a petrol station.*

Above: *The old Natwest bank on the corner of Herne Hill and Milkwood Road became a restaurant. There is a Post Office, a sorting office, bus-stops and traffic lights. Opposite the small complex is Carver Road, developed in the 1920s.*

Above: *Cherry blossom in Kestrel Avenue on the corner of Rollscourt Avenue. This is one of the line drawings that Alison Roach undertook for the Herne Hill Society.*

Right: *No. 28 Herne Hill was the home of John Ruskin's family from 1823–43. John gave the lease to his cousin Joan when she married Arthur Severn. Two of the Severn children are pictured. On the expiry of the lease in the mid-1920s the house was demolished.*

During the late-Victorian period, the Herne Hill Mansions were built in part of the field. They were an unusual complex of two adjoining blocks of red-brick flats. They had four storeys and were considered 'desirable', despite the back windows overlooking the railway. In the Booth's inspector's notebook of 1899, they were described as 'newish' and the occupants 'comfortable and well-to-do'. The individual flats were later subdivided, with two or three on each floor. Over the years, the building and flats deteriorated and became dilapidated. They have been gutted and, at the time of writing, their future is unknown.

The Abbey Parade shops and the few houses next door were the only part of the Abbey grounds to be incorporated into the housing development of Milkwood Road. Hidden behind them was the Abbey Mansions, a small complex of flats bearing some resemblance to the Prince Consort's flats in Kennington Park.

Before the development of the Milkwood Road estate, none of the roadways that now connect the area to Herne Hill existed. Poplar Walk was a country lane and next to the railway sidings was a vestige of a roadway leading to market gardens. It passed the long gardens of the houses in South Place and the Abbey garden. There was a carriageway behind the gardens leading into South Place and thence to Herne Hill.

THE SECOND GENERATION, HERNE HILL

The original leases on the properties on Herne Hill began to lapse in the 1870s. The old homes were gradually demolished and new, late-Victorian-style houses built in their place. Some had basements and attics and two or three storeys. Most had gardens in front with low brick walls and attractive iron railings, and some had terracotta tiles patterning their upper walls and main doors with individual stained-glass inserts.

The houses were occupied by middle-class people who still employed servants and gardeners and, on Booth's poverty map, were signified as 'wealthy'.

By the beginning of the 1900s, most of the original properties on the Lambeth side of Herne Hill, as far as Rollscourt Avenue, had been replaced. Gubyon Avenue was lined with semi-detached and terraced housing, leading to the newly-developing Fawnbrake Avenue. Booth's inspector reported its houses as being occupied immediately after building was completed. Back extensions gave the dwellings 10 to 12 rooms and the inspector thought that they would let for £50 per annum.

Kestrel Avenue led from Herne Hill to Fawnbrake Avenue, and L-shaped Rollscourt and Cosbycote Avenues into Kestrel Avenue. Both Rollscourt and Cosbycote were lined with large detached and semi-detached houses. A member of the Bessemer family originally occupied the house on the bend of Cosbycote, where the garden was more extensive than the neighbours, and was laid out by Henry Bessemer's gardeners. In the 1980s there were still traces of the original layout. These three avenues are well-named as they are tree-lined; each spring they are a sight for the eye to behold, with their lovely trees laden with cherry blossom.

Like Gubyon Avenue, Kestrel Avenue had to await the demolition of the large properties on Herne Hill before the extensive gardens of those houses could be built upon. Thus, when the roads were fully developed, the older houses in both avenues had to be renumbered. This caused confusion at the time, and is a trap for researchers if unaware of the changes.

With the exception of three houses just above Rollscourt Avenue, the leases of properties as far as Poplar Walk lapsed at a later date than those in the lower part of Herne Hill. In early-Edwardian years, three large houses were built in place of those just demolished. They had three storeys and long back gardens; the sizeable front gardens later allowed for garage space.

In 1910 the properties then numbered 32 and 34 were demolished and The Quadrangle, a complex of 20 flatlets, built in their place. Constructed in mock-Tudor style, The Quadrangle was unique in that it followed the example of the Hampstead Garden Suburb by providing accommodation for single women. In 1926 a further 16 flats were built out into the long garden. They were slightly larger than the originals, but appeared to be in the same style. In the 1960s the communal bathing, laundry and visiting facilities were converted into flats, and all other flats were made self-contained. The grounds of The Quadrangle were divided into three gardens and tenants could have a small plot of their own.

The gardens of the large houses above Rollscourt, those of The Quadrangle and those of Rollscourt Avenue, formed a large open space which, for many years, supported a family of foxes, was a haven for hedgehogs and a sanctuary for birds. At night owls could be heard and in bad weather fieldfares sheltered there and wildfowl often dropped down on their flight between lakes.

The two houses that originally stood next to the site of The Quadrangle, Nos 28 and 30, had at various times been home to John Ruskin. No. 28 was his childhood home and No. 30, for a short while, his marital home. In 1871, he gave the lease of No. 28, which he had inherited from his father, to his distant cousin and her husband, Joan and Arthur Severn, on the occasion of their marriage. When the original lease expired, another was taken for 21 years.

When the two houses were demolished during the early 1920s, four more were built in their place – Nos. 26–32. A plaque commemorating Ruskin's residence was placed in the garden of No. 26. No. 32 was built at a later date in 1935. Differing in style, it

The Quadrangle, Herne Hill, was built in 1911. The complex comprised one-roomed flatlets, with communal bathing, laundry facilities, a visitors' room and a caretaker to make sure the tenants obeyed the regulations.

had a flat roof, which in time needed adjustment and special care. The house has always shared its side entrance with The Quadrangle, and at a later date with an electrical sub-station.

The large houses that occupied the four sites next to the Ruskin home were demolished in the early 1920s. Dorchester Court, a complex of 96 flats in eight blocks, considered 'the last word in modernity', was built in their place. At the time the homes were advertised as 'labour-saving flats', as were those at Rutland Court on Denmark Hill. The buildings in Dorchester Court were set around a large formal garden with a central fountain. The flats overlooking the centre gardens had substantial balconies, and these became gardens for their residents. Each block had four storeys, with either three or four flats on each floor. The middle blocks were smaller than the four corner blocks. Garages were provided for residents' cars behind the flats, on land that had been part of the long gardens of Nos 28 and 30 Herne Hill. At the time of writing, the plane trees facing onto Herne Hill, planted when the flats were new, are massive and appear as tall as the buildings.

The demolition of houses to make way for Dorchester Court coincided with several other building projects in the Herne Hill area. Although planned earlier, several were not completed until the 1930s because of the economic state of the country. Each was to bring many new families into the area.

The private road through the grounds of Dorchester Court led to the new roadways that would become Dorchester Drive and Brantwood Road. For many years, the open space between Fawnbrake Avenue and the gardens of the houses on Herne Hill had been part orchard and part meadow, and each year had hosted a summer fête, when 'the circus tent theatre came to town'. During the time of the last fête in 1925, the layout of the new roads and the services were already in place.

By 1927 many of the houses along Brantwood Road were receiving their first occupants. Semi-detached in the main and set back from the roadway,

each house had a small front garden which, again, later allowed for garage space. The ample back gardens adjoined those in Fawnbrake Avenue.

The houses on the opposite side of the road, whose back gardens would later adjoin the properties in Dorchester Drive, were a little larger in size. Some houses were detached and built at a later date – those on the bend leading into Fawnbrake Avenue were the last to be built.

Most of the houses in Dorchester Drive were built in the 1930s. It is said that the landlord of the properties wished each house to be different in style from its neighbour. With this in mind, he attended the Ideal Home Exhibition, but during the execution of his plan he became bankrupt. Development of the houses along the road was delayed but, eventually, each house was completed and was individual. There is a very modern house with a flat roof just opposite the private driveway of Dorchester Court. It is said to have been built for an ice-cream manufacturer, who requested that his architect design the house to his personal specifications. He wanted the house to reflect the source of his fortune. Whatever the truth of the matter, the house is definitely different and, inside, it is very comfortable.

The house that stood for years behind Matlock Manor Hotel was demolished on the death of its owner and, in the 1980s, was replaced by Tudor Stacks, an Anchor Housing Project for retired people. Herne Hill Lodge, the path to which ran beside the childhood home of John Ruskin, was demolished in the early 1930s and was replaced in 1936 by Dorchester House, No. 5 Dorchester Drive. It is now considered so typical of houses of the style and period, that it has been listed Grade II – one of the very few listed buildings in the Lambeth area. It lies in a garden behind The Quadrangle.

Next to Dorchester House, just before the road bends towards Brantwood Road, there are two maisonettes. Built in 1952, they are typical of the structures of that period and not entirely in keeping with the surrounding houses.

The trees that hid the houses in nearby roads from the sight of the occupants of Dorchester Drive were felled, despite strong objections. They were supposedly removed in preparation for development of new residences on the site but there seems to be no hurry for completion.

THE SECOND GENERATION, DENMARK HILL

The original leases of properties on the Lambeth side of Denmark Hill appear to have been renewed at some point, for the houses were not demolished until some time after those on Herne Hill, despite the leases being granted at an earlier date in the first instance.

The houses on Denmark Hill were known by name rather than number and included Aylesford, Milestone, Arbour Lodge, Fairfield, Elmwood and Chestnuts. Their grounds stretched back to the later Ferndene Road.

The grounds of the houses above what is now Ruskin Park were not as extensive as those a little higher up the hill. Here the gardens reached to Dane Avenue, which wound through the Sanders estate, and later formed the boundary of the first part of Ruskin Park.

The properties at the upper part of Denmark Hill had been demolished at the outbreak of the First World War and were not replaced until the mid-1920s. Doubtless, the economic conditions of the war and its aftermath were the main factors for the delay.

One dwelling, Aylesford House, on the corner of Herne Hill Road, was demolished years before the site was redeveloped and, for a considerable time, was used as part of the venue for the summer fête of the Congregational church on the opposite corner of Denmark Hill. Its near neighbour, Milestone House, named after the 'IV milestone from Cornhill and the Treasury, Whitehall' which stood opposite, was demolished in 1916. It was not until 1925 that two semi-detached houses replaced it.

Similar properties were built as far as Sunset Road. The houses, many more in number than the original few, had two storeys, good-sized back gardens and front areas that later allowed for garages or car-parking space.

Sunset Road and Deepdene had been laid out by 1914, but full development did not begin until some years after the end of the war. Both roads exhibit many different styles of housing and led to Dane Avenue, the country lane that ran behind the Denmark Hill properties. Several houses at the lower part of Deepdene Road were built in late-Edwardian style and a line of three-storey semi-detached houses were built on rising ground between Sunset Road and just beyond Deepdene Road.

Dane Avenue continued along the park's boundary to the main road and, strangely, later changed its name to that of the small side road on the opposite side of Herne Hill Road, Ferndene Road. It is not possible to say why the road was no longer named after the rather lovely Dane House that stood on Denmark Hill for nearly 100 years, for the first part of the road, before development, was called Dane Avenue.

Over the next 50 years, large houses were built on one side of Ferndene Road. The different designs and facilities built into the houses speak of the slow development of the road. The houses, in some instances, had to await the expiry of the leases of properties on Denmark Hill before building could commence. Most of the homes were built in what would have been the lower land of the original

gardens, probably where the kitchen gardens and stables were located.

Following the purchase of the extension to Ruskin Park, a new roadway was laid out on the north side of the park and a long terrace of Edwardian-type houses built. At the junction with Herne Hill Road stood the new parish hall of St Saviour's and the vicarage. The new road, Finsen Road, eventually extended around the corner to Northway. Originally this part of the road, which joined Dane Avenue, was named Dumbleton Road. The mid-Victorian terraced houses here had two storeys and, according to Booth's inspector, both Northway and Dumbleton Road were similar in style to the 'local type'. Some of those living in the roads were 'comfortable' and others 'poor'.

As in surrounding areas, the housing below Sunset Road developed as the leases lapsed on the original properties and economic conditions allowed.

The grounds of the first-generation properties were substantial, thus allowing for a greater number of new houses to be built in their place, and in the case of those just above Ruskin Park, for houses to be built in Ferndene Road. One older house remains, white and double fronted, similar to one built next to the United Reform Church at the top of Denmark

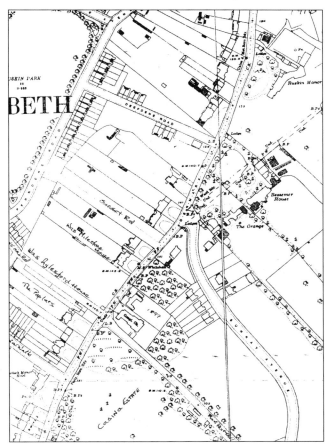

A map showing upper Denmark Hill, 1916. Sunray Avenue has been developed and Ruskin Manor is in the top-right corner. The Casina estate is bottom centre and Ruskin Park top left.

Above: *The Fox Under the Hill, on the corner of Champion Park and opposite the houses and gardens that later became Ruskin Park. The inn received a direct hit during the war and was later rebuilt as The Fox on the Hill on Denmark Hill at the Triangle.*

Right: *The Triangle, Denmark Hill, early 1900s, before the formation of Ruskin Park.*

Ruskin Manor, Denmark Hill, was sold by John Ruskin in the 1870s and was later combined with the Bessemers' home to form a hotel. After the Second World War it was compulsorily purchased by the LCC and became the Blanchedowne estate.

Hill. As with that house, the one in the lower area is now used for community purposes.

Just opposite the junction of Sunray Avenue and the Blanchedowne estate, is a relatively new complex of housing. Originally, the land was donated as a site for the rebuilding of St Philip and St James', the Roman Catholic church in Poplar Walk. However, it was found to be too narrow to accommodate a church, a residence, a parish hall and enough car park spaces. The ground was sold for housing and Porchester Close was built in the early 1980s. The close is a complex of maisonettes and flats, allowing for open space, flower-beds and car parking. The money from the sale of the land was used to refurbish the small church and to build an adjacent parish hall.

Next to Porchester Close is Rutland Court. Built in the 1930s, the accommodation was considered very modern. The two substantial blocks of flats are set in a long garden area with flower-beds and bushes.

Acland Crescent, winding from Denmark Hall to Deepdene Road, is lined with detached and semi-detached houses, each with garage space and ample back and front gardens. The road was laid out in the early 1930s and was gradually developed in the years prior to the Second World War. No. 34 was the site of the first bombing in Herne Hill, and also of its first fatality. The house was rebuilt after the war and the other vacant spaces in Acland Crescent were filled. It is a pleasant road, with well-tended gardens and flowering trees.

Denmark Hill

Before the construction of the Blanchedowne estate in 1948, there were far fewer residences on the Dulwich side of Denmark Hill than on the Lambeth side. In the late-eighteenth century, Denmark and Herne Hills were so sparsely occupied that highwaymen were said to be a problem and guards with firearms were stationed on the triangle of land between Denmark Hill and Champion Hill; said in popular mythology to be a 'plague pit', the small plot of land was, in fact, the boundary of the two parishes of Camberwell and Lambeth, and thus very difficult to build upon.

Prior to the building of The Fox On the Hill, the triangle was covered in trees and sloped uphill. At the time of writing it is levelled several feet above the pavements of both roads.

Mr Edwards, in the record of his 1789 journey to 'Brightenston', reported very few houses on either side of Denmark Hill. However, he did list a house belonging to Richard Lawrence Esq., which was built by Mr Blackburne and is now the site of the King's College Hospital modern ward block.

There were also eight other houses, among them the home of Samuel Sanders Esq., 'owner of the land on which the houses stood'. Edwards also noted

The Ruskin family moved from Herne Hill to a more spacious house with extensive grounds on Denmark Hill. Here they had plenty of room for their entertaining and art collection. There was a lodge at the entrance, to keep out unwanted guests and preserve their privacy.

another 'elegant' house being built for Mr Sanders and, further up the hill, 'Denmark Hall', which, although originally intended for public entertainment, had been divided into residences. Nearby were tearooms, kept by Mr Lightfoot, and the IV milestone.

Throughout most of the nineteenth century, there were three main estates above the triangle on the Dulwich side of Denmark Hill. The first residence uphill, situated in a seven-acre estate, was the home of the Ruskin family for 30 years. Several gardeners were required to look after the meadow, orchard, kitchen garden and blossoming trees, and the house, three-storeyed, with a basement and wings on either side of the porticoed entrance, needed at least six female servants to cater for the needs of the family and the building. There was also a lodge at the estate entrance which was at one time the home of John Ruskin's friend and publisher, George Allen, who had married a maid of the household. After the death of John's parents, the house and estate were sold, eventually becoming an hotel.

The much larger neighbouring estate was purchased in 1863 by Henry Bessemer. A modest house when the family moved in, the amazing inventor soon devoted much of his energy to improving and enlarging the property, and turning the grounds into a veritable wonderland and a repository for many of his ideas. When his daughter married, Henry Bessemer presented Bessemer Grange as a wedding present. The architect was a friend, Charles Barry junr, who had worked with him on numerous occasions.

As with Henry Bessemer's own house, there were conservatories, hothouses and glasshouses, but there was no paddock for deer, no herd of Alderney cattle,

The back of Henry Bessemer's house on Denmark Hill.

Right: *The conservatory adjoining the dining-room of the Bessemer house.*

Below: *The revolving platform and telescope designed by Henry Bessemer for use in his observatory. At the time of Bessemer's death the lens had not been refined. It was not completed and the telescope was never used.*

Right: *The observatory and pavilion in Henry Bessemer's garden on Denmark Hill. He designed the two buildings with the help of Charles Barry junr.*

The grotto in Henry Bessemer's garden was made from the materials extracted from the grounds when the lake was created.

and no observatory. Following Henry Bessemer's death in 1898, the estate was sold. It was eventually joined to the Ruskin estate to become one large hotel with a golf course, tennis courts and an extensive ballroom.

Next to the Bessemer estate was Dulwich Hill House, the home of Thomas Bristowe, Norwood's first MP. The grounds of the house stretched to the corner of Red Post Hill. About five years after the election of Thomas Bristowe in 1885, the estate was sold. The MP had found the journey to and from Westminster too time consuming, making it difficult to conduct his own business affairs. His move away from the area was regretted, for he had done much to help his constituents. He was particularly remembered for his chairmanship of the committee set up to secure the Brockwell Park estate for the people of South London and, later, for the advent of his sudden death at the park's opening ceremony.

In 1894, not long after Bristowe's death, the Red Post Hill Land Company leased land from the Dulwich College estate and agreed to develop a new road, Sunray Avenue, with 50 semi-detached houses valued at between £700 and £900 each. In the event, far fewer houses were built, all towards the Denmark Hill end. The land bordered the Bessemer estate and the new road wound its way down to meet Red Post Hill. A few years later, land on the corner of Red Post Hill was leased for 500 years from the Dulwich College estate for the building of the Herne Hill Congregational Church, now the United Reform Church.

A house had already been built adjacent to the church grounds in 1897, although its appearance is more Georgian than late-Victorian. Next to it was a coach-house, with accommodation above for the coachman. Later, both house and coach-house were converted into accommodation for the staff of King's College Hospital. The house was mentioned by one of Charles Booth's inspectors in 1899 as being one of the very few houses on the Dulwich side of Denmark Hill.

THE CASINO ESTATE

Casina House stood on the corner of Herne and Red Post Hills. It was reputedly built for the defence lawyer, Richard Shaw, from the proceeds of the protracted, abortive impeachment trial of Warren Hastings. The house was designed by John Nash and the grounds were laid out by Humphrey Repton.

Later, for a short time, it was the home of Joseph Bonaparte, uncle of Napoleon and ex-King of Naples. However, for the latter part of the nineteenth century, the estate was in the ownership of the previous MP for Portsmouth, W.H. Stone, who was, at the time of his residence with his family, Justice of the Peace for Surrey. A keen gardener, he arranged that the yearly Surrey Horticultural Show should be held in the grounds.

By the beginning of the Edwardian period, the house and estate were said to be 'ripe for development' although the building was still considered to be attractive. It wasn't until after the First World War that the estate grounds were purchased by the borough of Camberwell in response to the 'Homes Fit for Heroes' movement and the new Housing and Town Planning Act, with the promised aid of a government subsidy. At the same time, land below the Congregational church and hall on the other side of Red Post Hill, as well as land in Sunray Avenue that previously had been scheduled for development, was purchased.

By 1920, the Casino estate roads were laid out and the building of houses could begin. These were small, two-storeyed terraces and semi-detached houses, with tiled, sloping roofs, chimneys and casement windows. Each dwelling had a front and back garden edged with privet planted inside wooden fences. Except for those facing onto the main roads, the houses were set back behind grass verges and small green areas. The estate was completed in 1922 when a plaque to that effect was erected on the house next to St Faith's Church. The estate, one of the first of its kind, was considered exceptionally good, and

Herne Hill, 1930s. The Casino estate was built in response to the 'Homes Fit for Heroes' ethos after the First World War. The road layout has hardly changed, but the old-fashioned lampposts, the church spire and many of the trees and bushes have gone.

Above: *The extensive grounds of Elhanan Bicknell's house.*

Right: *A pass to view Elhanan Bicknell's house and grounds, and his large collection of contemporary art. Interest was so great that it was reported the line of carriages stretched for more than a mile from the house.*

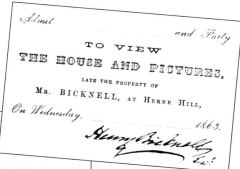

Left: *The Bicknell family house on Herne Hill, 1859. The house had been considerably extended by Elhanan Bicknell in order to accommodate his family and growing art collection. The grounds of the estate stretched from the Casina estate to the later Frankfurt Road, and down to Half Moon Lane. This photograph was taken by Elhanan's son, Sidney Bicknell.*

was visited by many people from housing authorities planning similar projects. The planners, of course, had no conception of the future growth of car ownership, nor the problems that car parking would cause.

During that period, there was an acute shortage of housing, particularly for working people who could not afford to buy. The Housing Act of 1919, and the promised government subsidies, triggered a great surge of municipal building in the new suburbs of London. The Act had placed the necessity of providing housing on municipal authorities, instead of giving them a choice of doing so, as had previously been the case.

As with Blanchedowne, the new estate had a number of built-in advantages. It was within easy distance of rail and road transport, as well as shopping areas, parks, libraries, schools and churches. The number of new families was not so large as to upset the established equilibrium of the area.

The Casino estate also had a unique feature. In the original plans an area of the estate had been set aside for the future development of parkland. The section chosen was at the lower part of the estate, including the lake and its surrounding land. Over the years, the open space gradually grew into a park called Sunray Gardens.

THE DISTINGUISHED
AND
ELEGANT RESIDENCE
AND IMPORTANT
FREEHOLD & LEASEHOLD ESTATES
Of the late ELHANAN BICKNELL, Esq.,
SITUATE AT
HERNE HILL AND DULWICH, SURREY,
For Sale by Auction, by
ELLIS & SON,
Auctioneers and Estate Agents,
63, FENCHURCH STREET,
1863.

The sale notice for the freehold and leasehold estates of Elhanan Bicknell in Herne Hill and Dulwich, 1863.

THE BLANCHEDOWNE ESTATE, DENMARK HILL

In 1947 the LCC demolished the hotel facilities in the grounds of the Ruskin and Bessemer estates and thus destroyed so much that was beautiful. The large Blanchedowne estate was built on the site and brought hundreds of new families to the area. The estate stretched from above The Fox on the Hill to Sunray Avenue and back from Denmark Hill to the properties on Champion Hill and what is now Green Dale. The wall of Henry Bessemer's estate once lined Green Dale, then Lane, behind which lay his observatory.

The Blanchedowne estate comprised small terraces of houses and blocks of flats several storeys high, some with balconies. Rumour had it that the plans of the estate were inadvertently turned around, meaning the flats were built in front of the small houses instead of behind.

The original plans provided the estate with a primary school called Bessemer Grange, which is said to have been built on the site of the grotto within the Bessemer estate. Nearby, on Red Post Hill, a secondary school, called the William Penn School for Boys, was later provided.

The Blanchedowne estate had easy access to railway stations and tram and bus routes ran along its borders. There were also four parks in the vicinity which provided sport and leisure activities. The LCC had chosen the site well. Shopping facilities increased nearby and in the Camberwell and Brixton areas there were markets and department stores.

The Parish Church of St Faith's was nearby in Red Post Hill and soon the parish included the whole of the estate within its boundaries. There were also churches of other denominations in the area.

Many people wished that the fine example of 1920s architecture found in the nearby Casino estate had been mirrored by the LCC planners some 30 years later. They regretted that small houses had been built instead of the blocks of flats on Denmark Hill, once a pleasant tree-lined road. There was a great outcry in response to news of the destruction of the Ruskin and Bessemer estates. The Bessemer grounds were considered 'wonderful' by the local people and, in particular, the felling of the trees was abhorred. It was agreed that the large chestnuts bordering Denmark Hill should remain but, on completion of the large blocks of flats, the tenants complained about the restricted lighting and the trees were subsequently felled.

TEN LARGE PROPERTIES ON HERNE HILL

During the last decade of the nineteenth century, the leases on ten large properties on the Dulwich side of Herne Hill lapsed. The lots were apparently sold as one, which ensured conformity of development. Known as the Dulwich House estate, the grounds of the properties stretched back to Half Moon Lane and, when fully developed, a network of roads covered the area bordered by Danecroft Road, Ruskin Walk, Ardberg Road and Half Moon Lane.

By 1897 the first of the roads, Hollingbourne and Holmdene, were laid out, and a few houses built in both. Charles Booth's inspector reported that in Holmdene, the houses at the south-east end were 'good class' and three-storeyed. Further up the road, the houses were newer, but he added, 'each taking in a lodger'. The houses in Hollingbourne were all new, two-storeyed, and with attics. They were 'comfortable' and their residents were 'City-going people'.

Ardberg Road had a few red-brick houses which were well built and occupied immediately upon completion. Beckwith Road was also incomplete, the two-storeyed houses had gabled attics and were all 'keeping a servant'.

As with many other streets in the area, the inspector spoke of 'many Germans' moving in, giving the

Two years after his death, Elhanan Bicknell's collection of Victorian art was auctioned by Christie and Manson's. The sale, which featured in the Illustrated London Times *in March 1863, lasted a week and achieved record-breaking amounts.*

proximity of easy travel to the City and 'good schools' for their children as a reason for the trend.

By 1910, the picture was entirely different. Houses had been built in all the roads and Simpson's Alley had become Ruskin Walk, with houses built in the lower parts. The aspen trees had been felled and the barriers that had prevented access to vehicles removed. Richard Church said his mother's hearse was the first vehicle to traverse the new road. The home of the Church family was on the corner of Warmington Road, an L-shaped road from Ruskin Walk to Half Moon Lane via Howlett's Road. It had been developed earlier, by a builder who erected a plaque on the side of the corner house.

The interior of the Church house was designed by a theatrical impresario, in a flamboyant manner – the drawing-room was painted gold and was set with mirrors that gave the impression that the room stretched on and on indefinitely.

Over the years following the demolition of the Dulwich House estate, houses were built lining the roads down to and including part of Half Moon Lane. The houses differed in design and size, according to the several contractors and dates of construction.

The large properties on Herne Hill above St Paul's Church were demolished, with the exception of Belle Vue. Its grounds stretched down both Ruskin Walk and Hollingbourne. It was not until the 1930s that the house was demolished and its grounds developed. Rows of modern houses appeared on the hill, and in upper Ruskin Walk and Hollingbourne Avenue. Belle Vue was remembered with affection by many residents; its large gardens and field had been the venue for many Sunday school treats. It was after Thomas Bristowe moved away from Dulwich Hill House that Belle Vue first opened its grounds to St Paul's for church functions. The

obligation was passed on through the family and it continued to open its grounds for nearly 40 years.

One of the largest houses on Herne Hill had been Carlton House, which was the home of the Bicknell family. In the 1860s the house was purchased by Edward Nicholson. With the first generation of houses on Herne Hill the dwellings were given names. When the area's population grew and the new houses were built, each residence was numbered and Carlton House became No. 5.

The grounds of Carlton House adjoined the Casina estate and stretched down to the later Elmwood Road. On Herne Hill itself, it adjoined the smaller Frankfurt House estate. The area of the lodge and entrance gate of Carlton House is now the site of a garage. Close by is a terrace of three-storeyed houses called Danecroft Gardens. Carlton Parade, a row of shops with living accommodation above, was erected on part of the site of Frankfurt and Elphindale estates, situated between the two roadways of those names.

As far as Hollingbourne Road, large three-storeyed houses with attics replaced the original homes; one had a look-out on its roof. The corner houses were larger and some had conservatories attached, which over the years became the pride and joy of their owners. Many trees were planted in the gardens and bloomed and fruited each year.

Below St Paul's Church and its vicarage there were four large houses. Each property had a substantial garden, two of which stretched down to Half Moon Lane. The leases of the four properties were held by Dulwich College estate. When they lapsed in the 1920s, plans were made for Carver Road and the construction of houses along Half Moon Lane to Ruskin Walk. Part of the land in Half Moon Lane was a 'few acres of meadow land' containing 'a real hedge and ponds', 'stretching to Herne Hill Station' which Richard Church could see from his bedroom window at No. 2 Warmington Road. The development of the area was speculative. Most of the houses built in Carver Road and Half Moon Lane were occupied by 1925/26 and remain an attractive 'modern' feature, in an otherwise almost exclusively Victorian/Edwardian area.

Only three houses were built in the grounds of the vacant properties at the lower part of Herne Hill but, after the Second World War, blocks of flats called Pynners Mead were built in the grounds of the properties next to the church. Flat roofs were then fashionable but the roofs of Pynners Mead began to leak and had to be replaced by a more conventional sloping design.

Just before the outbreak of the Second World War, the vicar of St Paul's had taken the opportunity to purchase a small portion of the vacant land adjoining the church grounds in order to build a parish hall. This project was postponed until hostilities ceased and the first flush of bomb-damaged properties had been repaired or rebuilt. The parish hall, very much a building of its time, was opened in 1958, and has since served as the centre for many activities and ongoing projects, not only for the church, but for local societies and private functions as well.

Fortunately, the large holm-oak planted in the neighbouring garden during the Victorian period survived all the upheaval that went on around it. It is one of the few to do so, in an area once so fortunate in its tree cover.

THE SPRINGFIELD ESTATE

In the early 1890s Springfield House was demolished and the estate sold, thus releasing a substantial area of land for development. The site lay between two high railway banks and Half Moon Lane, and close to means of travel, shops, schools, libraries, parks and open spaces.

In 1899, when Booth's inspector traversed the area, he reported that Burbage Road, as far as the railway bridge, had large detached houses on one side only, and Winterbrook Road had double-fronted new houses, faced with red brick, as did Stradella Road. In this area the residents were mainly City folk who had moved because of the proximity of good schools for their children and the railway station for their own travel.

By the end of the Edwardian period, Stradella Road was lined with substantial houses which had sold for £700–£900 each. The L-shaped street led from Half Moon Lane to Burbage Road where it was joined by Winterbrook Road just beyond the bend. Care had to be taken when developing it to avoid harming the bricked-over course of the branch of the River Effra which ran along Half Moon Lane and through the old Springfield estate. When the Baptist church was built at the junction with Half Moon Lane, special supports had been placed over the river's course.

Due to the substantial gardens of the large houses along the east side of Half Moon Lane, few houses were built below the railway bridge in Burbage Road. In 1899, Booth's inspector referred to the Half Moon Lane properties as 'old Houses'. It is said that the dwellings were originally built to prevent small houses for the less well-to-do being built in close proximity to the new Springfield Road estate.

It could not have pleased the estate governors when, later, a road construction depot was situated under the railway embankment in Burbage Road, although it was probably difficult to use the site for other purposes. Convoys of vehicles for road-making and repair, including steam-rollers and tar boilers, would depart early each morning with the convoys timed to reach their destination by dawn to avoid causing traffic jams.

Next to the Burbage Road junction with Half Moon Lane were several old houses, one of which was Delawyck. When these buildings were demolished during the postwar period, the grounds were redeveloped. A small council estate was built lying back from the main road and protected by a green area with large trees. Next to Delawyck, was a building that housed one of the King's College Laboratories.

The lease of the Half Moon Inn, the grounds of which adjoined the estate, lapsed at the same time as that of the Springfield estate. The old inn was demolished and a new Half Moon Hotel, without the gardens and stables, was built and opened in 1898. It was nearer the junction of the main roads than the previous inn and closer to the railway lines.

Over the years, the old inn had gradually changed from a coaching inn for travellers to a public house for local people. It was the terminus for the horse- and later the motorised bus that travelled hourly along Half Moon Lane to East Dulwich.

At the time of the opening of the new Half Moon Hotel, Booth's inspector spoke of it as 'an elaborate, florid, large, newly decorated public house' which had been sold for £64,000. His companion did not think it could possibly pay. He was wrong, of course. At the time of writing it is still a bus-stop and a landmark for travellers, with its painted sign of the half moon swinging in the wind. However, its front yard is no longer a stand for horses awaiting the return journey to East Dulwich.

Between the Half Moon Hotel and the new Stradella Road, a terrace of shops was built, each with two-storeyed living accommodation above, a back extension, and an area behind for the delivery of goods. Similar to those on the opposite side of the road, but slightly smaller, they filled the shopping gaps in the area, making Half Moon Lane almost self-sufficient.

Left: *Half Moon Lane. Over the years numerous photographs have been taken of this area, featuring the Half Moon Inn and the surrounding shops.*

Left: *Brockwell Hall was built between 1811 and 1813; the architect was D.R. Roper. There has been little change to the outer structure, but the inner areas have become a restaurant and, for a while, the upper parts were used as a house by the park keeper and his family.*

Above and below: *In 1823 plans to develop the Brockwell Park estate were discussed. Fortunately, the development did not take place, but later two houses were built in the parkland. The spacious Clarence House was built in the 1820s and stood in its own grounds within the park. When the lease expired 100 years later, the house was demolished and the grounds were incorporated into the parkland*

Above: *A survey instigated by Dr Thomas Edwards in the 1820s who suggested that John Blades should develop his parkland in conjunction with the doctor's own Tulse Hill estate. Fortunately, John Blades declined and Dr Edwards carried on with his own plans for the Tulse Hill area.*

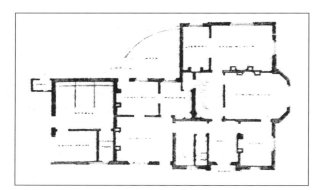

Right: *Brockwell House was built on land near the Herne Hill entrance to the park during the Victorian period. In the 1880s the house and its surrounding grounds were leased by Henry Wellcome for the physiological research laboratories. In early 1920, despite the move to open Brockwell House as a museum for Lambeth, the building was demolished soon after the death of the project's chief advocate, Charles Woolley.*

Chapter 14

❧❧❧

THE GROWTH OF PARKS

The Metropolis Management Act of 1855 enabled the Metropolitan Board of Works to apply to Parliament in order to benefit the public. When the LCC superseded the Metropolitan Board, one of its first steps was to enquire about the provision of recreational facilities. To remove any future argument, a clause ensuring that parks and open spaces would be available to the people of London was inserted into the 1855 Act.

Some London parks had already been created and, in 1887, Victoria, Battersea and Kennington Parks were transferred from Her Majesty's Office of Works to the Metropolitan Board of Works. Later came Ravenscoft and Clissold Parks, and Dulwich Park was given by the Dulwich College governors.

In 1889, the LCC was presented with Myatt's Fields by the Minet family and with Waterlow Park by Sir Sidney Waterlow.

Commons and Open Spaces

In 1868, a Parliamentary Select Committee was set up to enquire into the most appropriate means of protecting commons, forests and open spaces, many of them relics of the feudal past, in and around London.

The conclusion was that no further enclosure should take place within the metropolitan area and trustees were appointed to uphold this decision. The year 1866 saw the introduction of the Metropolitan Commons Act, which prescribed a practice under which commons in the neighbourhood of London would be secure.

BROCKWELL PARK

In 1800 the area now known as Brockwell Park was called Brockwell Common. The land comprising the park was once part of a large estate granted by the Crown to the monks of Bermondsey, the income from which was for the care of 'the sick poor' of St Thomas' Hospital, Southwark. At the Reformation, all Church property was confiscated by the Crown, and sold on to the highest bidders. Later, during the Interregnum, the land was acquired by the Tulse family.

The Blades-Blackburn estate, before it was Brockwell Park. The back portico of Mansion House is just behind the trees on the right.

Through a series of wills, divisions and sales, 60 acres of land on the southern part of the Tulse estate became available for sale and, in 1809, was bought by John Blades, a glass manufacturer of Ludgate Hill. Later, he was able to purchase more land to the north of his estate, stretching to what is now Water Lane in Brixton.

John Blades was a man of considerable substance, who became sheriff of the corporation of London and of the county of Middlesex. His wife had died at the age of 30, leaving him with a son and three daughters, one of whom might have had the condition we now call Down's Syndrome; certainly she was handicapped.

John Blades' first action was to demolish the old Brockwell Hall, which stood on Norwood Lane by the River Effra, and then build a substantial mansion, later known as the Mansion House, on the highest point in the park, the southernmost of two hills.

A family chapel was built in the style of a Greek temple a short distance from the mansion. Behind was a walled kitchen garden, which had its own water-supply. Small lodges were built at the two entrances to the estate.

In 1823, discussions took place with the owner of the adjoining land, who felt that it would be

The Dulwich
Society

Above: *Dulwich Park was given to the people of the area by the guardians of the Alleyn Trust, which was established by Edward Alleyn in the 1600s. The park is very close to the art gallery, the old College of God's Gift and the almshouses.*

Left: *The Dulwich Society works to maintain the local community.*

The temple, Brockwell Park, early 1900s. This was once the Blades-Blackburn family chapel. It subsequently became a shelter adjoining the outer wall of the old garden.

Left: *Brockwell Park Norwood entrance, 1907. The lodge that guarded the old estate still stands at the time of writing. For years it housed the gatekeeper and his family.*

Right: *The Norwood Road entrance to Brockwell Park is to the left of the photograph. The left-hand awning on the building reads 'Brockwell Park Café'.*

Brockwell Park on a hot day in the 1930s. Deck-chairs in the shade await those seeking protection from the sun.

advantageous to both estates if they were developed simultaneously. Fortunately, John Blades rejected the proposal, although shortly afterwards houses were built facing onto Water Lane. A short time previously Blades had bought the land on which the construction took place from the Tulse estate – it is thought the accommodation was built in order to house members of his staff. Clarence Lodge was built in the park and, in 1828, two semi-detached houses were also constructed, facing onto what is now Dulwich Road. They were designed by J.B. Papworth who was responsible for the furnishing of Brockwell Hall and much of the glassware manufactured by John Blades. A terrace of houses had been planned, but only two were completed before John Blades died in 1829.

The estate passed to Joshua Blades Blackburn, the son of his eldest daughter, as his own son had died in 1828. In John Blades' will he left a life interest in Clarence Lodge and the Brockwell Terrace houses to his daughter, Caroline, and to his eldest daughter, Elizabeth, he gave a life interest in Brockwell Hall. The year before his death, Blades had arranged a deed protecting the care of his third daughter, Laura, appointing Caroline and his brother-in-law as guardians.

Brockwell House was built to the south of Clarence Lodge in the 1860s and both houses had their own carriageways to the park entrance. The two dwellings had extended leases with the Blades-Blackburn estate, which caused some difficulty when the land was sold to create one of the premier parks of South East London.

In 1867, a small area of the land facing onto Dulwich Road was purchased by two men who recognised that a new church in the area had become necessary to cater for the needs of a growing population. They gave the land freely to the Ecclesiastical Commissioners and, in October 1869, a little over a year after the foundation-stone was laid, the new Church of St Jude's, Dulwich Road, was consecrated. The vicar and his family moved into the newly-completed parsonage.

By the 1880s the residents of the Herne Hill area were becoming concerned about the rapid encroachment of buildings upon the surrounding countryside. People in nearby communities were also worried and, as a result, Myatts Field Park and Dulwich Park were established. In addition, the Dulwich estate governors had ensured that many acres of land should be preserved for sports and playing-fields in the Dulwich area – provisions which exist at the time of writing.

Mr Harris, headmaster of Effra Parade School, was particularly worried about the loss of open spaces for his pupils and, when the 78 acres of the Blades-Blackburn estate came onto the market, he wrote to Norwood's MP, Thomas Lynn Bristowe. He suggested that the land was very suitable for a public park and that a fund be set up to buy the land for the people of South East London. A public meeting was called and many people attended. A committee was formed with Thomas Bristowe as chairman, the Revd Ransford, vicar of St Jude's Church, as deputy, and Evan Spicer, alderman of Lambeth and later chairman of the LCC, as a member.

However, there were complications. Due to mental illness and his confinement in an institution, Joshua Blackburn was not able to transfer land away from the estate. A previously-passed Act of Parliament for the conversion of the grounds of Raleigh House, Brixton, into a park, also complicated the proceedings. That estate was considerably smaller than Brockwell and, because of the provisions of the Rush Common Act, no building of any sort could be erected in the grounds.

The committee almost despaired but decided to keep its options open. When it seemed likely that the land could be sold for further development, Thomas Bristowe personally guaranteed the purchase money, but this did not become known until after his death.

Difficulties were resolved when the Raleigh Park Act was replaced by one allowing Brockwell Park to be created. Joshua Blades Blackburn died, thus enabling his heir, Joshua John Blackburn, to confirm the sale of the 78 acres which made up the first part of Brockwell Park.

A number of expenses incurred during the campaign were paid for by private means. These included the running of special trains from London bringing visitors to the area in order to demonstrate the suitability of the estate for a park.

Funds for the purchase came from many sources. The LCC contributed a substantial amount, as did the Vestries of Lambeth, Camberwell and Newington. The Charity and Ecclesiastical Commissioners also made contributions and there were many private donations.

Before the opening of the park, a few alterations and additions were made. A large lake was formed, suitable for swimming and deep enough for diving, with two smaller pools joined by waterfalls. Changing rooms for bathers and seats for spectators were placed around the lake. The kitchen garden was converted to a flower garden, with roses and Old English flowers mentioned in Shakespeare's plays, but the fruit trees remained for many years. Refreshment rooms were provided in the Mansion House, a bandstand was built nearby, and the stable yard behind the mansion was converted to a playground, with swings and roundabouts for younger children. Football and cricket pitches were laid out, as well as tennis courts.

Lt-Col Sexby, Chief Officer of the LCC's Parks and Open Spaces, was responsible for the alterations and additions. He commented: 'When it was bought for the people of London, it was already a park, not a park site.' People were thus able to use the park before its official opening.

There was great excitement in Brockwell Park on Whit Monday, 6 June 1892. The weather was lovely and crowds thronged the grounds to watch the opening ceremony, carried out by Lord Roseberry. Everyone could see because a raised platform had been built for the guests and dignitaries to stand upon. Lord Roseberry was fulsome in his praise of Thomas Bristowe and the role he played in securing the park for the people of South London, but sadly, the proceedings were marred by the sudden collapse of Thomas Bristowe and, shortly afterwards, his death.

It was decided to place a memorial to Mr Bristowe near the Herne Hill gates. It was unveiled in September 1893 and took the form of a large white-mountain limestone pedestal, supporting a bust of the late MP. Below it was a drinking fountain and, at its foot, a water trough for dogs. The memorial survived for many years, but was removed when the Herne Hill entrance was refashioned in 1958. It is thought that Thomas Bristowe's descendants took the bust, but it is not known what happened to the pedestal.

The park had many natural attractions, including splendid views towards London, the Victoria tower and the Houses of Parliament, and thence to Harrow and Highgate, and to the south, Crystal Palace and the Norwood and Sydenham hills.

In 1898, W.H. Hudson, author of *Green Mansions* and *Far Away and Long Ago*, noted in his book *Birds of London* that before the park was opened to the public:

... it had the most populous rookery in and around London. No large tree was without its nest, but after the Park opened to the public, many rooks went away. All that remains of this huge rookery are the rooks in the trees near the Herne Hill entrance.

He feared that the rooks would soon fly away, for in the previous two years the number of nests had dropped from 35 to 10. Sadly, his predictions proved correct. The rookery had disappeared by the turn of the century, the rooks driven away by the trains, traffic and the people.

It was impossible to enter the park from the Brixton area until 1895, when the tenant of Clarence Lodge agreed to an exchange of land to enable access through a new entrance from Arlingford Road.

In 1901, the rest of the Blades-Blackburn estate (43 acres) came on the market. Again a committee was formed, this time led by Norwood's second MP, Mr C.E. Tritton, and again an Act of Parliament was necessary to sanction the conversion of the estate into parkland.

The extension was opened in February 1903. Funds were contributed by the LCC, the Camberwell, Lambeth and Southwark Borough Councils, the Brockwell Park Extension Committee and private contributors.

Nearly one half of the new area was subject to leases previously granted by the Blades-Blackburn estate. In 1907 the lease of Clarence Lodge expired. The house, its outbuildings and gardens were demolished, and the area was converted to parkland.

In 1898, the tenancy of Brockwell House had become vacant, but there were still 21 years to run before the lease was due to expire. The Wellcome Physiological Research Laboratories were urgently in need of bigger premises to enable them to expand their research and the production of antitoxins. A new lease for 21 years between the vendors and Henry S. Wellcome was signed on 29 September 1898, due to expire at Michaelmas 1919.

Brockwell House was remodelled and converted from domestic to laboratory use. The old stables were modernised and new ones built with glazed brick walls and flooring paved 'with best stable brick'. Other animal houses were built, using the latest technology and materials conducive to the care and comfort of the animals. All premises were lit by electricity and there was telephone communication between the departments. The large paddock in the grounds was converted to a vegetable garden and the produce grown was used to supplement the fodder for the animals.

Despite the great outlay of finances to provide every modern facility in the new premises, there were many obstacles to overcome before the laboratories were registered by the Home Office and work could begin in earnest. The full extent of the value of their work was recognised during the First World War, when huge amounts of antitoxins were made to satisfy demands from the Armed Forces; antitoxins for diphtheria and tetanus, anti-gas gangrene sera and typhoid vaccines were produced.

The move to Herne Hill allowed research work to expand and, thus, staff numbers increased. One new member, A.T. Glenny, was recruited from Alleyn School and remained with the laboratories for the rest of his working life, making many important contributions in the field of immunisation.

At the time, diphtheria antitoxin was injected after the disease had developed. The work in the laboratories in Brockwell Park attempted to overcome the killer disease in potential victims through immunisation *before* the infection had a chance to develop. This was to culminate in the massive campaign in 1939/40 which practically eliminated the disease in Britain. For his work, Dr Glenny was elected a Fellow of the Royal Society and was awarded the Jenner and Addingham Medals for 'the individual who had done most in relieving pain and suffering in humanity.' Dr Henry Dale was another staff member at the laboratories, he became director in 1906 and went on to become a Nobel Prize winner for Physiology and Medicine in 1936.

The lease on Brockwell House and its grounds was due to expire in 1919, but because of the peculiar

The Bristowe memorial, 1930s. Thomas Bristowe secured Brockwell Park for the people of South East London, but died on the day of its opening.

Right: The rookery, Brockwell Park, 1890s. Before the estate became a park, it held one of South London's largest rookeries. The main part of the rookery was near the Dulwich/Norwood Roads entrance. When W.H. Hudson wrote his book on the parks and birds of London, he feared that the rookery was decreasing in size. Within a few years the rooks left, driven away by the constant noise of trains, traffic and people.

Below: Brockwell Park, Dulwich Road entrance. The last remnants of the rookery and the two lodges that guarded the estate entrance are visible.

Above: *A view of the Wellcome Physiological Research Laboratories. When the Blades-Blackburn estate became a park, Brockwell Hall and its surrounding land was already leased to Burroughs and Wellcome. The lease lapsed in 1918 and 4 years later the laboratories moved to Beckenham, Kent. All the premises were demolished. Whilst in residence in Brockwell Park, ground-breaking research had been carried out into life-saving vaccines*

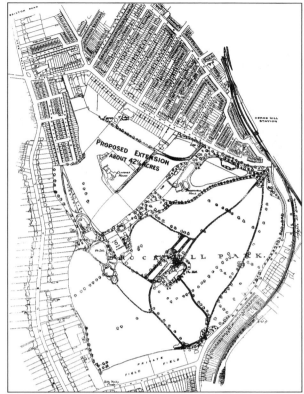

Right: *A map of Brockwell Park and its surrounding area showing the proposed extension of 42¹/₂ acres, 1899. The committee for the changes was led by Norwood's second MP, Sir C.E. Tritton. Funds were contributed by the LCC, the Camberwell, Lambeth and Southwark Borough Councils, the Brockwell Park Extension Committee and by private contributors. The new extension was opened in 1902 and over the years several other small purchases and adjustments were made.*

The entrance to Brockwell Park showing the two original park lodges, 1900. Horse trams and buses picked up passengers from the island at the junction of Norwood, Dulwich and Railton Roads, before continuing to Brixton, Camberwell or Norwood.

Above: *The bathing pool, Brockwell Park. Every Sunday morning the pool became a boating lake, many of the yachts were handmade, sometimes with paper sails*

Right: *The swimming and bathing lake, Brockwell Park, c.1920.*

Left: *The lido, Brockwell Park, 1948. Built by the LCC in the 1930s, the lido replaced swimming facilities in the lake, which was deemed to be a health hazard.*

A sizeable flock of sheep grazed in Brockwell Park from the First World War until the 1930s. They were moved around the park and kept the grass short.

circumstances created by the war, the premises were not vacated until 1922 when the laboratories moved to Beckenham, Kent.

The LCC immediately scheduled the demolition of the house and its outbuildings in order to turn the grounds into parkland. This move was strongly opposed by Mr Charles Woolley, who lived in Dulwich Road opposite St Jude's Church. He was one of Lambeth's first councillors and aldermen and in 1915 had given Lambeth a large collection of pottery, prints, maps and photographs, with the intention of them forming the basis for a Museum of Lambeth. Understandably, no moves towards creating a museum were made during and directly after the war, but he felt the vacant house would make an ideal place for such a project. Hopes were high when a letter from him was read to full Council, but a week later he died suddenly of a heart attack. Without him to lead the opposition, the house and outbuildings were demolished and the grounds converted to parkland.

The disappearance of the laboratories and the grounds deprived many young boys of a great sport. For a dare some would climb over the surrounding fence to pick up conkers from under the chestnut tree, or to get to a certain spot and return. If they could do either without being caught, they would win the challenge.

The demolition of Brockwell House was the beginning of the final stage in the creation of the park. Only the building of the lido and its halls was needed to complete its facilities. For years there had been complaints about the safety and condition of the water in the swimming lake. From time to time a vile smell was reported by swimmers and divers, and eye infections were said to occur in children and wildfowl. In 1937, the open-air swimming-pool, built by the LCC but charged to Lambeth Borough Council, was opened and the park's facilities were complete.

During the 1920s and '30s Brockwell Park was used regularly by local people. There were 41 tennis courts, several bowling-greens, numerous football

pitches and 13 cricket pitches, one of which was used for league cricket. At times, over 1,500 people gathered to watch these matches.

With such a large area of grassland, mowing could have been a full-time occupation, but a flock of 4–500 sheep cropped the grass, their hurdles being moved from place to place as necessary. At the end of the 1920s the park superintendent, Mr West, still found the sheep 'most useful'. They saved him 'a lot of mowing', particularly after rain, when 'the clay soil became very soft, and difficult to work upon.' The sheep had been introduced during the First World War. They and the people had become very used to each other and mixed together contentedly. At the time there were 38 staff members working in the park; among them must have been a shepherd.

Mr West also felt 'the speech ground' was 'as much an institution as the one in Hyde Park.' This feature has entirely disappeared from Brockwell Park.

Near the lake, which was popular with swimmers and, on Sunday mornings, with the owners of model boats, was a paddling pool for little children. The small ponds leading off the lake, known as duck ponds, were home to several species of breeding ducks and many visiting wildfowl. The aviary near the lake was a sanctuary for injured birds and the home of exotic pheasants, who found conditions suitable for breeding.

The park also boasted many unusual trees. Among them were Judas trees, swamp cypresses, strawberry and tulip trees, acasias, japonicas and prunus trees. There were also many trees and bushes now thought of as British, such as the lilac, laburnums, holm-oak and magnolias. There were also magnificent oaks, beeches, limes and elms. The walled garden remained one of the great attractions and each season the beds were set with flowers. The walls were covered with the last of the original fruit trees, climbing roses and creepers, and many old yews also remained. The garden was a haven for wild birds.

Near the Mansion House and 'Little Ben' (the clock tower presented by the second MP for Norwood, Sir Charles Tritton, to commemorate the 60th year of Queen Victoria's accession) was the

Brockwell Park boating and bathing lake, c.1920.

Left: *The old garden, Brockwell Park, 1904. This painted photograph was printed as a postcard and only cost 1p to send.*

Below: *The lake in Brockwell Park.*

Below: *The bandstand in Brockwell Park, early 1900s. This photograph was taken on a windy day and the young girl on the left is holding on to her hat.*

The aviary in Brockwell Park was home to exotic and, occasionally, injured birds. During the Second World War it was used to house rabbits and chickens. In the postwar reconstruction the aviary disappeared, after the foxes had had their share of the birds.

The old garden, Brockwell park, 1930s. The garden has been a restful retreat for families and individuals over the years. It was once the kitchen garden of the Mansion House and is sometimes called the rose garden after the roses that climb the trellis and walls. The small fish-pond with its fountain provided a focal point. This image is one of the many prints produced by the photographer/printer Harold Norman, who had premises at the junction of Railton and Dulwich Roads.

The old bandstand, Brockwell Park, early 1900s. A policeman stands to the left of the picture.

Right: *The drinking fountain, the clock tower and the bandstand, Brockwell Park, early 1900s.*

Below: *The souvenir programme for Lights o' Lambeth held in Brockwell Park, 17–26 June, in celebration of the Coronation of King George VI and Queen Elizabeth, 1937.*

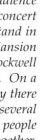

Right: *An audience gathers for a concert on the bandstand in front of the Mansion House, Brockwell Park, 1910. On a warm day there would be several hundred people gathered together.*

rustic bandstand and the dancing ground. On summer weekends, a band played to the crowds and, on one occasion, there were over 1,000 dancers, each of whom paid 4d. to enter the ground. However, it cost nothing to listen and sometimes there were thousands strolling in the park.

No event of national or regional importance passed without celebration on the site. The Silver Jubilee in May 1935 was an excuse for celebrations there. George V and Queen Mary were very popular and had visited the area on a number of occasions, both as Prince and Princess of Wales and as King and Queen.

Seven months later, the nation was plunged into mourning for the death of the King. The Coronation of his successor, Edward VIII, was planned for May 1937, and in Lambeth thoughts were turned to how best to celebrate the occasion. His abdication in December 1936 caused concern, but the original date for the Coronation, 12 May, was confirmed for the new monarch, George VI, and his consort Elizabeth. Thus, plans could go ahead.

The 35,000 pupils attending all schools in Lambeth were given commemorative cups and saucers and the Town Hall was illuminated. Public buildings and main street intersections were decorated, but the biggest celebrations took place in Brockwell Park. They lasted for three weeks.

The 'Tea for 5,000 Old Folks' event was shared with Vauxhall Park. People residing in Brixton and Norwood had tea in a marquee in Brockwell Park on four afternoons in June. Without doubt, the most spectacular event was the entertainment that took place each evening from 9.30p.m. to 11.45p.m. between 17 and 25 June – it was called Lights o' Lambeth, a musical fantasy. The great stage was based upon the Morton Gateway of Lambeth Palace, the twin towers rose to 60 feet and the frontage of the stage was 90 feet. A Hammond organ was installed and was a tremendous novelty for the audience, the instrument having only been introduced in Chicago in 1933. The St John Ambulance Brigade was in attendance and the Boy Scouts and the League of Frontiersmen provided the stewards.

The event began with an organ recital, followed by Queen Elizabeth's visit to Lambeth Palace in 1573. Then came a fanfare and a searchlight tattoo, with trumpeters from the Royal Artillery and Searchlight Units from the Royal Engineers. The National Anthem and a march was played by the Morley College Orchestra and the College Dramatic Society

'Little Ben' in Brockwell Park was a replica of the clock tower near Victoria Station, and was made by the same clockmakers in Croydon.

gave a 'peep' at Vauxhall Gardens in 1773. The performers were Samuel Johnson, David Garrick, Mrs Thrale, James Boswell, Oliver Goldsmith and Joshua Reynolds. The Battersea Polytechnic Operatic Society gave extracts from Sullivan's 'Mikado' and 'Yeomen of the Guard' and 'The Lost Chord' was sung by the Massed Choirs.

William Blake's 'Jerusalem' was sung by the boys of Archbishop Temple's school choir. There were Crystal Palace memories, fireworks and a display by the League of Health and Beauty. At 11.45p.m., the evening ended with a spectacular searchlight display. The audience could hear every word, for the pageant was amplified by tannoy; the South London Electricity Company supplied all electricity free of charge.

The Lights o'Lambeth was the last national 'spectacular' to take place before the war, but the council, encouraged by its success, organised the Symphony of Youth the following year. The most popular event was undoubtedly the cowboys and indians battle, fought by the local schoolboys.

Many changes took place in the park at the outbreak of the Second World War. The greatest was the almost complete disappearance of the children who had been evacuated to safe areas. They gradually returned but found that the military had taken over their previous domain and there were restrictions on their activities – partly due to military activity, but also because of a shortage of park staff.

Access to the ponds was restricted by fencing, but boys with home-made nets managed to break through to catch tiddlers for their own private ponds. The flagpole, presented by MP Charles Tritton to commemorate Edward VII's Coronation, was in a restricted area, and no longer used as a weather station. The aviary sported rabbits and chickens instead of exotic birds, and large areas of parkland were converted to allotments. Searchlight, anti-aircraft and barrage balloon sites were established. The Home Guard used the park for training and air-raid shelters were built around its perimeter with tanks of water being supplied for emergency use.

In spite of the wartime activity in the park, entertainments did not entirely cease. The LCC had a huge success when an open-air theatre was built near the Mansion House. The shows, comprising musical comedies, operetta, opera and ballet, were performed to great applause. Unfortunately, the theatre was destroyed by a flying bomb in the last year of the war and, later, the wreckage was dismantled and

Above: *The Mansion House, Brockwell Park, early 1900s. At this time the house was no longer a home and had become the park's refreshment rooms.*

Right: *The Mansion House was built in the early 1800s on one of the park's hills. It was the home of the Blades-Blackburn family until the estate became the premier park of South East London in 1892.*

The Norwood Road entrance to Brockwell Park. Until the early 1980s the lodge housed park staff. After the Second World War a modern house was built next door for staff families. Although the layout of the paths in the park are much the same, nearly all the trees have gone.

the orchestral pit was converted into a flower-bed.

For a few years, Battle of Britain Day (15 September) was celebrated in the park. Members of the Armed Forces, the Auxiliary Services, borough representatives, the churches and people from the surrounding area attended in large numbers to pay their tributes to 'the Few'.

Understandably, the reinstatement of Brockwell Park did not have priority in postwar Lambeth. Local people who had left the area due to evacuation, National Service or the bombing of their homes often did not return. Considerable rebuilding occurred and in some cases blocks of flats replaced individual houses and gardens.

The park never really returned to the great popular use it had seen in the pre-war years. Fewer staff were employed, but those who remained were a devoted and very hard-working band. The park reverted to a more natural state, but the formal flower-beds were laid out in a traditional manner. Dancing eventually returned to the newly-built bandstand and the bowling-greens and tennis courts had their regular players. The refreshment rooms also reopened in the Mansion House.

Eventually, the parkland taken by the allotments reverted to its original use, and the walled garden again became a sanctuary for those who loved peace and quiet, as well as for the wild birds. The model village outside the garden gates had deteriorated badly due to the combined influences of time, weather and vandalism, and was eventually removed. For a few years a small railway ran between the Herne Hill gates and the lido, which was popular during the weekends and holidays.

Postcards illustrate the great changes that took place at the original park gates, particularly those published by Harold Norman, whose business premises overlooked the Herne Hill entrance. Until 1996 the firm was remembered by its name-plate high up on the wall above its premises. The Norwood Road entrance to the park bears the most resemblance to the original entrance and even that has a modern house built next to it.

In the 1950s, the entire Herne Hill gate area was restructured. The house, built to replace the original gate lodges, was demolished and its place taken by the relocated, modernised toilets, fronted by a brick shelter. A brick wall was built facing onto Norwood Road. Raised flower-beds replaced the many bushes and trees and the Thomas Bristowe memorial fountain. Most of the low railings that originally surrounded the grassland and flower-beds had disappeared. Only those around the tennis courts, bowling club, the lakes, the walled garden, the Norwood gate area, the Mansion House area and the bandstand remain.

Since 1973 the Herne Hill Harriers have regularly used the park as a base for winter cross-country events. They host a 10k open road race there each year. Founded in Herne Hill in 1888, the Harriers have had many associations with the area. They were participants in the 1980s half-marathon, which started and ended in Brockwell Park. The race attracted many hundreds of runners, all of whom ran for their particular good causes.

In 1974, Brockwell Park was the venue for a flower show organised by the Lambeth Horticultural Society. It proved so successful that it was repeated the following year, expanded and very quickly became the nucleus of the Lambeth Country Show. Since then, one weekend in July, the park welcomes many thousands of Londoners to visit stalls exhibiting all manner of interests and activities, and selling a huge variety of goods, food and drink. Every council department has a tent to explain its work. The 'country comes to town' in the form of farm animals, horse shows and crafts. Vintage cars and engines, tractors and steamrollers are all on view. The end of the weekend is marked with a fair, which is very noisy and boisterous.

Over the years the park has gradually changed, both physically and in terms of its use. Sometimes this has been as a result of legislation, sometimes of policy. For example, legislation surrounding the protection of birds meant that the larger, more aggressive birds could not be controlled, and the crows, jackdaws, pigeons and gulls have largely ousted the smaller songbirds. This has been aggravated by the removal of bushes, which has lessened the areas for nesting and cover. Nestboxes were installed to counteract this, but nothing could replace the cover provided by foliage. The walled garden and the garden around the Mansion House provide the best sanctuaries for birds in the park.

Brockwell Park's well-being has been threatened several times in the last 20 years. Fortunately, most of the projects have been defeated. Riding stables, a horse ride and a cycle track were proposed but these were dropped, although some paths were marked to allow cycling. An athletics track was proposed which would supposedly only have used 60 acres; in reality, however, it meant cutting off and losing almost one-third of the flat part of the park. A proposal was made to change the names of all Lambeth parks and open spaces, including Brockwell. These harmful ideas were roundly defeated following massive campaigns. Out of these disruptions grew the foundation, and subsequent strengthening, of the Friends of Brockwell Park Society, which oversees and protects the interests of the park.

However, the society was not able to protect the physical well-being of the Mansion House one February night in 1990, when it was gutted by a fire, deliberately started by a young vandal. The house had been empty for years, despite the community making suggestions for its use. It was a Grade-II listed building, and thus deserved better protection. After some time, an agreement was reached and the

Above: *The Tulse Hill entrance to Brockwell Park. Compared to the other entrances this was a rather dull construction, probably because of the period during which it was built. However, the iron railings were beautifully made and well maintained.*

Left: *The Friends of Brockwell Park motif.*

The Herne Hill entrance to Brockwell Park, 1930s. The two original lodges have been replaced by a new lodge to house the park keeper and his family. This lodge disappeared during the park's renovation following the Second World War.

Left: *Ruskin Park during the winter, 1920s. The pergola is visible through the trees. This period was a time of transition, when older women still wore long dresses, and men never went walking without a hat.*

Above: *Ruskin Park just after its opening and before it was cleared of many bushes and trees.*

Above and right: *The old conservatory and house designed by William Blackburn, before the gardens were converted into Ruskin Park.*

Left: *Eight houses were demolished to make way for Ruskin Park, but many features of their gardens were kept. The beautiful old conservatory of one house was saved for a while, but was finally demolished, perhaps due to neglect. The nesting island on the lake remained a haven for wildfowl for many years, but during the hurricane of 1987 a huge willow tree fell over and formed a bridge over which foxes could cross.*

Mansion House was rebuilt and partially refurbished. At the time of writing no proper use has been found for it, but it does have better protection, including smoke alarms. At least one good thing came out of the fire – Henry Strachey's pictures of country scenes through the seasons have been cleaned, and hopefully will have better protection in future.

The hurricane of October 1987 caused many trees to be uprooted and still more damaged. The Friends of Brockwell Park and the Herne Hill Society donated money to replace some of the lost trees. Most of the replacements died, or were destroyed by vandals, and again replacements were provided. With added protection and care, it is hoped that these will survive.

Some of the new trees were planted at the time of the centennial celebrations in June 1992. Led by the Friends of Brockwell Park, the event was also attended by council and parliamentary representatives.

At the time of writing the lido has reopened under new management. Hopefully it will continue to prosper and its facilities expand.

A pathway in Ruskin Park which was known as the Avenue.

RUSKIN PARK, DENMARK HILL

Herne Hill's second park is situated on the Lambeth side of Denmark Hill, just above King's College Hospital and the railway. In the 1770s land, of which Ruskin Park is part, was purchased by a rich timber merchant, Samuel Sanders. Eight houses were built in the area which comprises Ruskin Park, one of which was the home of Samuel Saunders. The gardens of this group of houses were long and backed onto the Sanders estate.

At the beginning of the 1900s, speculative building and the consequent spread of London's population had encroached upon the outer suburbs, swallowing up much of the countryside. Camberwell, once an attractive village, had become so congested that parts were virtually slums, and the people were badly in need of open space. When the land of the eight houses and gardens on Denmark Hill came on to the market for development, alarm bells rang in the minds of the local people. Led by Frank Trier of Champion Hill, a local committee was formed with the intention of securing the land for conversion into a park. The committee was chaired by the Lord Bishop of Rochester; Herne Hill and Camberwell were then in the See of Rochester. Mr Frank Trier was the honorary secretary.

It was decided that if the objective was obtained, the park would be named after John Ruskin, who had

lived in the area for 50 years, 30 of them in a house on Denmark Hill. The hope was that support and funds would come from those who had known and worked with John Ruskin. And, indeed, this proved to be the case. The names of several such people appear on the supporters' list, Octavia Hill and Joan and Arthur Severn among them. The LCC, Lambeth, Camberwell and Southwark Borough Councils, the Commons and Footpaths Preservation Society, the Metropolitan Public Gardens Association and the City Parochial Foundation were the biggest contributors, and there were also many private subscribers.

Some £48,000 was paid for the 24 acres comprising the original park. The LCC's chief officer of parks, Lt-Col Sexby, designed the layout of the new park. He retained as many features of the original gardens as possible. Of the buildings, only the portico supporting the magnificent and beautiful wisteria of No. 170, and the stables and yard of its neighbour, later used by the park staff, remained. The Victorian conservatory, retained for several years after the park was laid out, has disappeared. The entrance to No. 170, however, can still be detected in 2003.

The design of the park included: a small ornamental lake, with resident wildfowl, and an island for nesting; a bandstand; a bowling-green surrounded by herbaceous flower-beds and paths; and a pergola, set with roses, wisteria and clematis, which was rebuilt after bomb damage during the Second World War. The park was landscaped with flower-beds, paths and lawns, its perimeter and paths being set with trees including chestnut, ash, lime, beech and oak.

The original contract stipulated that a children's playground was to be provided, set back some way from the houses to avoid any noise nuisance.

The park was officially opened in February 1907 by Cllr Evan Spicer, chairman of the LCC. It was a splendid occasion. Crowds gathered around the marquee and the raised platform was filled with top-hatted gentlemen, some with ladies. Union jacks and other flags flew, and the band played stirring music. The park grounds were bounded by Dane Avenue, later Ferndene Road, which bent around to join Dumberton Road, later part of Finsen Road.

In 1909, a further 12 acres of the Sanders estate came on the market. Frank Trier and a committee of local people determined that the newly-available land should be added to Ruskin Park. Through their efforts, the LCC was able to make the second purchase for £24,000.

Ruskin Park in the snow, showing the bandstand, the small lake and the island which was home to wildfowl.

Three years after the original purchase, in February 1910, the extension was opened by the chairman of the LCC's parks committee. Included in this was the area that the Sanders estate had allowed the small St Saviour's School, Herne Hill Road, to use for their sports and recreational purposes. A clause was included in the final agreement that this concession should continue, which it does at the time of writing. The 12 acres of the Sanders estate stretched to the new Herne Hill Road. When the second purchase was made, the section of Dane Avenue that reached to Dumberton Road was incorporated within the park, eventually becoming the pathway which now leads to Finsen Road from Ferndene. The perimeters of the 12 acres were planted with ash trees and the land was laid out for recreational purposes.

Not long after the opening of the extension to the park, the First World War was declared and the larger part of King's College Hospital was commandeered by the War Department and renamed the 4th London General. In the early stages, no-one expected the war to continue 'past Christmas', or that there would be so many casualties. As time went on, it proved impossible to accommodate the many injured servicemen in the King's complex, so huts for the convalescent men were erected in Ruskin Park.

The men in the park were visited by local people, and entertained in the newly-opened parish hall of St Saviour's Church. The son of a young boy who used to visit the soldiers found, in the attic of his house, mementos which had been given to his father by the servicemen. During the First World War the young boy had exhibited these mementos for 1d. a time, and bought cigarettes for the men in the park with the proceeds.

Not long after the end of the war, all traces of the huts and the bridge over the railway were removed, the land was restored, and the park returned to its intended use.

The park had a cricket club, with a pavilion near the path of one of the Ferndene Road gates. It held

regular events, and was well supported before the Second World War, and for a short time afterwards. Football matches were played in the fields, and the refreshment rooms near the bandstand were always a popular meeting place. The cricket club has long since disappeared and people have been known to question the purpose of the old practice bowling strips. Serious football has been replaced by groups of young people kicking a ball about and the tearooms, periodically vandalised, were finally demolished.

During the Second World War, Ruskin Park suffered its share of bomb damage. Incendiaries, exploded and unexploded bombs fell in the children's playground, on the bowling-green and tennis courts, and even in the 'trenches', but no one was injured. The park was eventually repaired, leaving no sign of damage, and most people would be hard-pressed to remember any untoward happening.

On the night of the 16/17 October 1987, the hurricane which hit the south-east of England caused the loss of trees in Ruskin Park and damage to others. The destruction was not as severe as it could have been, due to the park being situated under hills, but the loss left gaps and disfigurement. The old willow by the lake was blown down onto the island, leaving the wildfowl vulnerable. The Herne Hill Society donated a number of trees. Some survived, but most suffered the ravages of a too dry summer and vandalism.

Over the years the railings were removed from around the flower-beds, but another form of fencing was necessary to protect the beds from undisciplined dogs. At the time of writing the bandstand is rarely used, but tennis is played on the courts and bowls on the green. Many people walk through the park daily on their way to and from work. The pergola is much admired and children are taken to see ducks on the pond. Above all, hundreds of people visit the park each spring to see the magnolias, the Judas trees, the magnificent wisteria covering the portico, and the flowers of the thousands of bulbs blooming among the trees and shrubs that were so lovingly planted and tended by the park staff.

Lately, new hope for the park's preservation has come in the form of the Friends of Ruskin Park. Much depends on the strength of the Friends' endeavour, and the interest they can raise in the surrounding area.

The Friends of Ruskin Park work hard to preserve this beautiful open space in Herne Hill.

113

SUNRAY GARDENS

Herne Hill's third and smallest park, situated close to the meeting place of Red Post Hill and Sunray Avenue, was once part of the substantial Casina estate. Its residence, Casina House, designed by John Nash, stood at the top of Herne Hill, at its junction with Denmark and Red Post Hills. The house was demolished in 1906. Shortly before, it had been described as looking 'woe-begone', its grounds 'charming parkland', but 'doomed to be carved up, unless rescued'.

It was not carved up, however, until it was acquired, with neighbouring land, by the borough of Camberwell, under the 1919 Housing Act – known widely as 'the Homes Fit for Heroes' Act. The original plan for the new estate included a clause providing an open space for recreational purposes. When the time came for its development, the obvious choice was the area surrounding the lake at the lower part of the estate. At first it was called the Casino Open Space and was thought of more as a recreation ground than a park. It seems to have had no planned development, but to have grown piecemeal on a shoestring. The space had no formal opening and was never called a park but, in 1923, its name was changed to Sunray Gardens and it has been known as this since.

In the beginning it was suggested that the lake be filled in, but fortunately the idea was rejected – a park without a water feature was unthinkable. Instead, the banks of the lake were sloped to a depth of 9 feet. An unclimbable fence was then suggested, but that idea, too, was rejected, and low railings were placed along the lake edge. Paths were tarmacked and the grounds were planted with new trees and shrubs, especially in the areas adjacent to houses. Protective railings and gates were built along the perimeter of the gardens.

In 1925, two young swans were donated to the lake by the Royal parks. Later, one was exchanged for a swan from Ruskin Park – perhaps the original two were of the same gender.

Two years later, the Metropolitan Water Board stocked the lake with surplus fish from its reservoirs. With few predators, the roach, carp, perch, chubb and tench multiplied and the lake became overstocked. Despite the difficulties produced by this situation, no steps were taken to re-balance the stock, but a bomb exploding in the lake's depths during the war drastically reduced the fish

Sunray Gardens is Herne Hill's third park and was once part of the Casina estate.

population. It is reported that residents nearby were not concerned about rationing for days and young boys sold fish they had found for 2d. each. It is even recalled that fish were found in the fireplaces of some local homes having fallen out of the sky and down the chimney!

The fish population recovered, but the Sunray Anglers was formed in order to keep the fish under control. The club had 50 members, all local people, among them 20 pensioners, and for many years it prospered.

Over the years, the small park has undergone a number of renovations and alterations, some the result of staff changes.

During the 1987 hurricane, Sunray Gardens lost a number of trees. Some were replaced by the Herne Hill Society's funds and several did not survive – again as a result of the following season's dry weather and some vandalism. The swans have also gone – the last one was found to be dying of lead poising, not as a result of swallowing old fishing tackle floats, but from lead shot pellets.

Sunray Gardens has never attracted large crowds. Rather it is visited by local people, taking young children to the swings, pushing baby prams and toddlers' pushchairs, or walking the dog on a lead. In 2003 the park is often visited by individuals just wishing to quietly contemplate the passing of the seasons, to feed or watch the birds on the lake, or to walk through the park on their way home, to the village or to the railway station.

Despite not being particularly planned for, Sunray Gardens is a well-needed oasis on the edge of a densely populated area.

Sunray Gardens in spring. This pretty area of open land is the smallest park in Herne Hill. The gardens are the only remaining part of the original Casina estate.

Chapter 15

Chapter 15

∂◌∂

SPORTS AND LEISURE

INNS AND TAVERNS IN HERNE HILL

Most of the taverns extant in Herne Hill at the time of writing are over 100 years old and were built at the same time as the suburb. The oldest, the Half Moon, is the third inn by that name. The first Half Moon Inn was built in the 1650s, near the junction of the roads leading to Dulwich, Camberwell, Brixton and the Great North Wood, and the bridge crossing the River Effra. In such a spot the inn answered the needs of travellers from all directions.

The second Half Moon was leased from the Dulwich estate by the Webb family for many years. It was sold in 1868 with an unexpired lease of 26 years. The inn was described as having four rooms on the top floor, six on the first floor, with an assembly room and a bar and six rooms on the ground floor. There was also a large tea garden and a range of stabling. The tea garden was popular with visitors from London and the assembly room was the venue for banquets, social club gatherings, and parochial board meetings. When the lease expired in 1894, the third Half Moon was built, opening two years later, yards away from the site of the previous two inns.

After the River Effra had been bricked over and the railway constructed across the fields and crossroads, Half Moon Lane was straightened. When the lease on Springfield House expired, Stradella Road was laid out, and large premises with shop fronts facing onto the lane replaced the old inn and its gardens. Horse buses passed along Half Moon Lane to and from Dulwich, and the Half Moon became an official bus-stop.

The Half Moon and its surrounding area has altered beyond all recognition. At the time of writing the inn no longer has accommodation or a garden, but has kept its identity with a sign swinging in the courtyard.

Other established inns and taverns can be found on the borders of Herne Hill, including the Green Man at what is now Loughborough Junction and the George Canning at the meeting of Effra Road and Brixton Water Lane. The Fox Under the Hill stood at the junction of what is now Champion Park and Denmark Hill until it was destroyed during the Second World War. It was rebuilt a little further up, between Champion and Denmark Hills.

The location of the pubs meant that they were staging posts for the transport system of the day. Later, the courtyards of such inns were often the termini for horse-drawn transport services and, even in the twenty-first century, bus-stops are frequently named after the local pub.

The development of the railways saw new public houses appear in the Herne Hill area. Most were established before the turn of the century, often at the meeting place of two roads with the main entrance facing the transport thoroughfare. They were also built at the termini of bus routes, or near railway stations, to attract the custom of travellers.

Two taverns were built in the newly-developed Milkwood/Lowden Roads area – one, at the junction of Milkwood and Heron Roads, was called the Milkwood Road Tavern. It was ideally situated at the crossroads, near the shops and the bakery. The tavern was the first meeting place for the Herne Hill Harriers' road-running events, just after the association was formed in the back room of a nearby shop in 1889. The inn prospered over the years, but was destroyed by a bomb during the war. It was eventually replaced by a special school, which closed after only a few years.

The Herne Arms, at the bottom of Herne Hill Road, is said to have adopted the arms of the Herne family – prominent city merchants who were thought to have property in the vicinity. Others believe that the arms reinforce the legend of herons nesting on the hill and feeding in the River Effra. As was often the case, the Herne Arms predated the Parish Church, St Saviour's, which was later visible a little way up the hill from the tavern door. The church has since disappeared, but its school and parish hall remain.

The Prince Regent was built on the other side of the railway facing onto Dulwich Road and, opposite Herne Hill Station, was the Railway Arms. Both survived wartime bombing and the subsequent rebuilding programme. A tavern on the corner of

Railton and Mumford Roads survived the same hazards only to fall victim to the Brixton Riots.

The Brockwell Park Tavern, No. 133 Dulwich Road, was built when the road was being developed and it was probably more often frequented by the occupants of the smaller houses in the roads of the Poets' Corner, than those of the large houses of Dulwich Road.

The tavern was also used as a base for road-running events by the Herne Hill Harriers, before they moved to the Herne Hill Athletic Track.

INNS AND TAVERNS TO MUSIC HALL

Inns and taverns have always been found in London and its surrounding area, particularly along approach roads where travellers might stop to rest. Refreshments were served, including beer, wine and spirits, but drinking was not always the sole purpose of the establishments.

Among the taverns were those such as the Horns in Kennington, and the Father Red Cap in Camberwell, where the Manor Court and legal transactions were conducted. Hustings were held during elections and societies and clubs would meet in the establishments. It was not until the Victorian era that the purpose of the inns and taverns gradually changed.

Eating houses, clubs and restaurants opened to provide for the wealthier inhabitants of the area, and local inns and taverns became public houses, for those of more limited means. There were also shops selling alcoholic drinks but a number of these closed when licensing laws tightened and such bodies as the Salvation Army and the Total Abstainers showed interest in the reform of society and the well-being of family life.

In time, public houses began to provide entertainment and refreshments for those who were less affluent. This led to rooms in the pubs being converted, or larger extensions being added to premises, for the main purpose of entertainment. Refreshments began to take second place and so the music hall was born.

During the 1890s and 1900s, numerous music halls were built all over the country, far outstripping the conventional theatre and spawning a type of entertainment of such vivacity and vitality that its purveyors became better appreciated than most actors and actresses from the legitimate theatre.

Herne Hill did not have a music hall, but there were several within the local area, in Camberwell, the Elephant and Castle and Brixton. The nearest was the Metropole Theatre, which was built in 1894 on the corner of Denmark Hill and Coldharbour Lane. By 1900 it had become the Empire Theatre and, in the 1930s, the Odeon occupied the site. A century after the completion of the Metropole, a housing complex was constructed in its place.

A little nearer to Camberwell Green was Dan Leno's Oriental Palace. Dan Leno had his headquarters in Coldharbour Lane, near the junction of Herne Hill Road. Charlie Chaplin, a Lambeth boy, was a member of his company who later became an exceptional film comedian. Dan Leno, himself an outstanding and unique personality, died in 1904 at the young age of 43. He was most likely unaware of the impending phenomenon of moving pictures or that many music halls would in time be converted into cinemas.

Dan Leno's Oriental Palace was demolished in 1899 and was replaced by Camberwell's Palace of Varieties. This in turn became the Ritz Cinema, known in the 1940s as the Fleapit. In Edwardian times it lay between the Golden Lion pub and a row of shops. Later the shops were demolished to make way for Orpheus Street and subsequently the Post Office. The cinema and the Golden Lion were demolished and replaced by a shopping mall and bank.

Probably the most famous music hall within easy reach of Herne Hill was the Canterbury Music Hall in Westminster Bridge Road, which could hold huge audiences. The Canterbury, built as a conventional theatre, had an orchestra pit and a conductor, to provide accompaniment for the performers.

The music hall, vaudeville and conventional theatre fought hard to compete with moving pictures in the early 1900s, but they experienced a great resurgence of popularity during the years of the First World War. However, in 1927 *The Jazz Singer* saw sound synchronised with the moving picture and the knell of the music hall was sounded. By the 1930s, films had virtually killed off the music hall and people were flocking to cinemas by the thousand, many of them attending regularly once a week. During the same period, conventional theatre prospered. It was helped to some degree by an alliance with the railways, which provided joint cheap fares and matinée tickets, aimed for the most part at suburban housewives. Musical shows such as *Me and My Gal*, with its popular 'Lambeth Walk' broadcast so often on the wireless, and *The Crazy Gang*, helped to keep musicals and vaudeville alive.

THE MAGIC LANTERN TO THE CINEMA

The advent of photography in the 1800s ensured the arrival of the magic lantern, which enabled images to be shown on a screen. This became an immensely popular form of entertainment, both privately and publicly, and, as well as still images, rotundas with revolving panoramas were able to give the appearance of movement. Two of these, Crimean battle photographs and a journey from Niagara to London, were seen by over a million people.

By 1896 the first moving pictures were being shown, among them the Derby won by the Prince of Wales' horse and views of Brighton's beach and promenade. The Empire Music Hall showed an 'original, unsurpassed, unequalled Lumiere Cinematographe' in an 'absolutely true to life' series of 12 pictures, at great expense.

The magic lantern never entirely lost its popularity and the modern version of slide projection is used in both public and private domains.

The first decades of the twentieth century saw the production of numerous types of moving pictures and the creation of the first film stars. Initially, existing buildings were converted into darkened rooms with rows of fixed seats, but soon specially-designed cinemas were built, some with exotic names and extravagant interiors.

Brixton, Norwood, Camberwell, East Dulwich and Streatham all had cinemas. There were some spectacular ones within walking distance of Herne Hall or on the tram routes. In the 1930s the new Odeons were built to very specific designs – there was no mistaking them for cinemas belonging to any other company.

The Grand cinema in Railton Road, with its entrance almost opposite Herne Hill Station, was opened in December 1913. It is generally thought that the Grand was Herne Hill's first cinema, but this is not so. The first was a makeshift affair in one of the railway arches behind the Half Moon Inn. This faced Norwood Lane, long before the shops were built in what is now Norwood Road. The audience, paying only a couple of pence, sat on long wooden benches to watch the silent films being projected onto the screen. The performances were short and left enough time for an evening walk to Crystal Palace.

The archway cinema closed when the Grand opened. Hard wooden benches could not compete with the sophistication of fixed rows of seats and a permanent screen. The Grand, later the Pullman, survived the arrival of the 'talkies', the depression, two wars, evacuation and bombing, but it could not survive the coming of television. The small cinema closed in 1959. Much of the equipment remained in place when a bingo hall opened shortly afterwards. It prospered for a while, but closed in 1989. The empty building, already somewhat neglected, quickly deteriorated and eventually the pigeons took over.

Gallant efforts were made to rescue the Grand-cum-Pullman and there were hopes of turning it into a theatre. However, this was to no avail as, at the time of writing, the building is due for demolition.

Most of the cinemas within the immediate vicinity of Herne Hill have disappeared, only Streatham, Brixton and the Elephant and Castle have them. Films have remained a popular form of entertainment, but it is necessary to go further afield to see them. Many films are shown each week on television and there are reviews and advertisements concerning the latest releases in newspapers, on the radio and on television.

THE HERNE HILL HARRIERS

In the winter of 1888/89, a few friends met in the parlour of a confectioner's shop in Milkwood Road to discuss the formation of a running club. From that small beginning grew the world-famous Herne Hill Harriers, whose members went on to set records and win gold, silver and bronze medals for Britain in the Olympic Games in 1908 and 1912.

At first, road and cross-country events were the main interest, but soon the members began to compete in summer handicap racing, first as a junior club and then, in 1900, graduating to senior club status, entering and winning many international track events.

Over the years the Harriers have used several locations in Herne Hill as the start and finish points for events. The first was the Milkwood Road Tavern, which stood at the junction of Milkwood and Heron Roads.

They also met at the Half Moon and Brockwell Park Tavern until, shortly after its opening in May 1891, they began to use the Herne Hill Athletic Track.

In the 1920s, the Harriers joined with the Catford Cycling Club and held successful running and cycling events at the two stadia.

The Harriers continued to use the Herne Hill track until 1937 when the Tooting Bec Athletic Track opened. The move to Tooting Bec was chiefly because the new track had six lanes, whereas Herne Hill had only four.

The Harriers took some time to recover from the traumas of war, but despite that they added trophies to the list and reached National League status. They

The Herne Hill Stadium, 1902. A walking race featuring members of three different clubs: Jack Butler was (Polytechnic) world record breaker for 14 to 50 miles in 1897, and in 1902 and 1905. He competed at the 1905 Olympic Games, White City; Harry Otway was a founder member and secretary of the Herne Hill Harriers. In 1903 he won the Central Markets London to Brighton walk. Teddy Knott from Blackheath set the London to Brighton record in 1897.

Left: *An aerial view of Herne Hill Stadium, c.1948. The stadium could accommodate 15,000 spectators. The cinder track for running events was inside the cycling track and the rugby pitch in the centre. The long-jump pit can be seen on the left and the North Dulwich railway line is in the foreground.*

Left: *The London Olympics, 1948. One of the official cards produced to advertise the first Olympics held after the Second World War. The Herne Hill Stadium was the venue for cycling events. It had been a major task to return the stadium to the standard necessary for an international event as it had been occupied for five years by the Army and the ack-ack gun.*

Right: *The Harriers' runner, Joe Deakin, won the three-mile team event at the Olympics by 25 yards, 1908.*

The Donkey Derby, 1901. The line-up for the start of the very popular race at the Herne Hill Stadium

spent a period stationed at the Southwark Park Athletic Track, but returned to Tooting Bec Track after refurbishment.

In 1973 the Harriers returned to Brockwell Park, which became their base for winter cross-country events. At the time of writing they host an annual open-road race of 10k along its internal paths.

The young athletics team has gone from strength to strength and women have joined the ranks. At the time of writing the club plans to continue into the millennium and to excel over the next 100 years as they have done since their foundation.

THE HERNE HILL ATHLETIC TRACK

In May 1891 the Herne Hill Athletic Track opened in an area adjacent to Village Way, on the borders of Herne Hill. It was one of several large stadia developed during the late-Victorian period, in response to the great surge of interest in cycling. Putney, West Ham, Wood Green and Catford all had stadia, but all, except for Herne Hill, have since disappeared.

The Herne Hill Society logo.

The athletic track in Herne Hill became the venue for a variety of activities. The outer cycling track was initially banked and wooden, but later it was concreted. Inside the cycling track was a cinder-based running track and, in the centre, a football/rugby pitch and a large long-jump pit. Shortly after the opening, the Herne Hill Harriers began to use the new track.

Activities at the athletic track took some time to stabilise after the cessation of hostilities in 1918, but soon athletic and cycling events were being organised. At special events, such as those held on Good Friday and bank holidays, young local boys rushed to the track early in the morning, hoping to be among the few chosen to sell programmes and thus gain free entry. Sometimes there were as many as 15,000 spectators at these events.

At the outbreak of war in 1939, the Herne Hill track was taken over by the military and was the site of a contingent of the Army and barrage balloons. Then, in 1948, it was the venue for the cycling events of the London Olympic Games.

Shortly after the Harriers left Herne Hill for Tooting Bec, the cinder track was grassed over, making the area of the football pitch more acceptable in size. But this could not improve its status as an international venue and, at the time of writing, events at the stadium are usually local affairs, sometimes competitions between local schools and associations. The cycling track is also used less often as modern circuits are smaller than that at Herne Hill.

In 1988, an event commemorating the centennial of the invention of the pneumatic tyre was held at the stadium.

THE HERNE HILL SOCIETY

The Herne Hill Society developed from an exhibition and entertainments which formed part of a week-long celebration commemorating the centennial of St John's, Lowden Road, in June 1981. Before the end of the performance, given by the Balladmongers, a request was made for a repeat of the event the following month at St Paul's, Herne Hill, in aid of new surplices for the choir.

During the time of the exhibition, many people asked why the surrounding districts had societies, but Herne Hill was without. The question was put forward to see whether a society in Herne Hill would have the support of the local community.

As a result, a meeting was held the following March at the Lido Hall of Brockwell Park, after an article had appeared in the council's free press. The snow lay thick, but 20 people attended and ten became active members.

On 30 March 1982, an inaugural meeting was held at the church hall of St Philip and St James, Poplar Walk. The hall was full, discussion was lively and the chairman and a committee was appointed, with publicity, amenities and historical sub-committees. The constitution, prepared by the steering committee, was accepted.

Agreement was reached on the aims of the society, the format of meetings and the decision that matters affecting Herne Hill should be reported and discussed at meetings. Also, a newsletter would be produced.

Since then the society has met monthly, first at St Philip and St James' and then at Herne Hill's United Reform Church, Red Post Hill. Four newsletters are produced each year and a stall has been taken each July at the country fair held in Brockwell Park. The society itself has held an annual autumn fair. Members have also published booklets on the history of Herne Hill and its past residents, and also notelets and cards about Herne Hill, past and present.

The Herne Hill Society has maintained close associations with neighbouring organisations and there has been an exchange of speakers between societies on many occasions. At the time of writing it is apparent how closely linked the separate communities are and how the histories of each neighbourhood have long been intertwined.

Left: *The Station Approach, between Dulwich and Railton Roads, was one of the main shopping areas in Herne Hill, c.1910. This postcard was printed by Harold Norman, the biggest postcard producer in the area. His name-plate remained high above his premises for nearly a century, but was removed in the 1990s, apparently without protest.*

Right and below: *Welch, fruiterer and greengrocer, No. 122 Railton Road. In the early 1900s fruit and vegetables were seasonal and shops were often family concerns. Deliveries were made to local homes.*

Chapter 16

SHOPPING AND AMENITIES

THE HEYDAY OF LOCAL SHOPS

During the late-Victorian and Edwardian periods small, local shopping areas across the country boomed. Individual family-run businesses, where housewives carried out their day-to-day shopping, were the most common outlets. Saturday was the busiest day for traditional markets and department stores were confined to the more prominent high streets. The brand names that are taken for granted in the twenty-first century were in their infancy, or yet to be born, and chain stores were non-existent. Grocers supplied broken biscuits, loose flour and sugar, and butter, margarine and lard in slabs. Dripping could be purchased from the butcher's and was spread on bread and toast. Fruit and vegetables were available seasonally.

The main shopping area in Herne Hill was centred around the junction of Dulwich, Norwood and Railton Roads with Milkwood Road, Herne Hill and Half Moon Lane. In that small area almost everything necessary for ordinary living could be purchased. It is possible that Half Moon Lane was a little more exclusive than Railton Road.

The shopping area around the station and its hansom cab rank spread into Dulwich Road. The two roads here offered a great variety of businesses, including a tavern, coal merchants, a house-letting agency and insurance company, dining-rooms, printers, stationers, photographers, oilmen, livery stables and merchants catering for the needs of horses. There were also tailors, haberdashers, dressmakers, shoemakers and menders, ironmongers, butchers, bakers, fishmongers, grocers and greengrocers, hairdressers and barbers, and teashops for 'coffee, chocolate and ices'.

There was a fenced area with tall trees by the railway arches in Norwood Road, where garden sheds, greenhouses and garden implements were sold.

Opposite the Post Office and Fire Station at the bottom of Herne Hill was a terrace of shops with two-storey living accommodation above. This area, known as The Broadway, stretched around the corner

Flashman's, Dulwich Road, near Water Lane. Leather workers, locksmiths and basket workers were essential craftsmen before the mechanisation of transport.

into Half Moon Lane. There were 20 shops here serving a variety of needs; the largest being the undertaker, Crowhurst. In 1897 the Half Moon Inn, renamed the Half Moon Hotel, was rebuilt nearer the railway bridge than its original site. A terrace of shops, similar to those on The Broadway, was also constructed, and Stradella Road was laid out.

Further along Half Moon Lane there were more rows of shops. In Ruskin Terrace there was a dairy which advertised 'milk straight from the cow'. The cattle were stalled in a shed in Howlett's Road, behind the premises – now an art designers' centre. Until the 1920s, when trains began to bring milk into towns in large quantities and pasteurisation became compulsory, local dairymen had regular daily rounds. Before milk bottles became widespread, housewives or servants would take their jugs to the milk float and have them filled from the churns. On Saturdays, or at holiday times, the children of the family enjoyed this task. Before refrigeration, it was common to have two milk deliveries daily, especially in the summer when milk could so easily go off. Butchers, bakers and greengrocers delivered goods to customers by horse and cart, bicycle or handcart, at the same time taking orders for future deliveries. These practices continued until the outbreak of the Second World War.

Wills & Son, No. 67 Railton Road, a family firm specialising in bakery and confectionery. Chocolate was as popular in the 1900s as it is today. Note the orderly window display, which would have been important for attracting customers. On special occasions, shopkeepers made great efforts to celebrate.

There were also the itinerant pedlars who walked the streets with their goods, and who had their own particular calls. The best remembered was 'the muffin man'.

For many years a horse bus, and later a motor bus, trundled its way along Half Moon Lane to East Dulwich. The terminus was the courtyard of the Half Moon Hotel, where the tired horse would wait for its next journey. Shoppers climbed aboard with their heavy bags and were dropped outside their houses.

Shopping during the late 1880s and early 1900s must have been a more interesting and lengthy process than it is today. Goods such as Hydes Aesthetic Seeds for songbirds which are no longer available, could easily be purchased. Langtons, the family oilman, sold 'embrocation for all aches and pains', and Wedloch, the family butcher, sold his own 'calves' feet and heads, sweetbreads and prime pickled tongue'. Mr Collett, the fruiterer, greengrocer and potato salesman, waited on his clients daily and delivered his goods by box van. The newsagents, Williamson's, acted as a registry for the hire of servants. Mr Evans was the agent for the sale of tennis racquets and cricket bats. Osborne and Young catered for horse-drawn traffic and sold corn, hay and straw. They also 'foraged horses for gentlemen' under contract. A dyeing and cleaning works advertised as being '20 per cent cheaper than others in the trade' and a large bakery near Loughborough Junction catered for families and businesses; V.S. Pritchett played in the yard here as a child when he lived in Coldharbour Lane.

In 1899 Railton Road and Half Moon Lane shopping centres celebrated Christmas and the new century with festoons of decorations. Bunting and banners stretched from the upper storeys of shop premises and from lampposts and street signs. Shop proprietors tried to outdo one another with their decorative ingenuity; the fruiterers found it easier than the undertaker on the corner of Half Moon Lane, but even he, Mr Crowhurst, made an effort to brighten his entrance.

Railton Road shopping area, 1900. The street is decorated in celebration of the new year and the new century.

PUBLIC LIBRARIES AND ART GALLERIES

The Public Libraries Act was passed by Parliament in 1886 and was adopted by Lambeth's Parish Vestry the following year. Strangely, the adoption was initially opposed but, like the 1870 Education Act, it proved to be a most important measure. It opened up new opportunities for learning to the people of Lambeth.

The parish was divided into five districts with each district to be allocated a public library. The first to be opened was the Nettlefold Library in West Norwood, very near St Luke's Church. It was named after Frederick Nettlefold, a rich manufacturer of needles and an active Unitarian, who gave the land on which it was built. Within the first nine months of its opening, the statistics for borrowing were remarkable. There were almost 80,000 borrowers, with 13,000 children among them, and it was estimated that at least 500 people used the reading rooms daily. There were 13 daily newspapers available and 56 weekly and 33 monthly papers and magazines were regularly stocked.

The Tate Library at the Brixton Oval was the second to open. It was named after its founder, Henry Tate, the wealthy sugar refiner of Tate & Lyle fame. Founded in 1893, the library proved to be just as successful as the Nettlefold, and later held the borough's reference collection; this is quite separate from its archive at the Minet Library, Knatchbull Road.

The Carnegie Library, Herne Hill Road

The Carnegie Library opened in 1906 and was built on land given by the Minet Trust, formerly part of the Sanders estate. A grant for the construction came from the Carnegie Corporation of New York, from Andrew Carnegie's own funds. The corporation donated the money on the condition that the local authority would stock the shelves with books and guarantee the maintenance of the library.

Herne Hill's library was unique in its time. It was the first public library to allow borrowers to browse among the shelves before choosing a book. Previously, borrowers had had to ask the librarian at the desk for their required book. The experiment was so successful that soon other public libraries were adopting the method.

A sketch of the Carnegie Library by Alison Roache. Interestingly the library has no front door, only a barred gateway to the entrance hall.

From the outset, the library played an important part in the lives of local people. Its reading room and children's section were well used, particularly in the late afternoon, on Saturdays and at holiday times. During the First World War, the library lent books to convalescent soldiers recovering in the huts in Ruskin Park. During the Second World War, it shared its premises with an air-raid wardens' post.

The library only suffered a minor degree of bomb damage during the war but, fortunately, all the serious incidents occurred some distance away.

The advent of television saw reading take a lower priority and libraries were used less than before. The facilities were also deemed less important when it came to the borough's funding plans, thus there were fewer librarians and more assistants. Opening hours were curtailed and book stocks became subject to a policy of political correctness.

At the Carnegie Library, the children's books were moved into the main hall and the reference library became a dull area, despite a very good indexing system being housed in the hall.

At the time of writing there has been a move to close the Carnegie Library and four other branch libraries. This has evoked widespread opposition and a campaign to reverse the council's plan. Hopefully it will be successful and Herne Hill will keep its library. The building itself is a product of a bygone age.

The Carnegie Library is not the only library in Herne Hill. Another stands in Crossthwaite Road on the Blanchedowne estate. It was built in the grounds of the demolished Bessemer and Ruskin estates, which faced onto Denmark Hill and Sunray Avenue. Membership gives access to all Camberwell libraries, including the music library in Peckham Road.

In the past, companies such as Boots the chemist ran lending libraries. The books were mostly fiction and could be borrowed and returned to any library in the system. Herne Hill also had lending libraries. At No. 10 Milkwood Road there was a stationer, bookbinder and picture framer who ran the Milkwood Road Circulating Library, and nearby were the reading rooms run by St John's Church. The reading material consisted of newspapers, magazines and journals. Dulwich Village had its own

The Carnegie Library was built during the Edwardian period on land given by the Minet Trust. The site remained very countrified until Herne Hill Road was extended to Denmark Hill and the trees and bushes were replaced by houses.

Right: *The grounds of Dulwich Art Gallery.*

Below: *The entrance to Dulwich Art Gallery, early 1900s. Bomb damage during the Second World War and subsequent modernisation have made the building less visually charming, but facilities for the general public have improved greatly. The gallery is the oldest in the country and is administered by Alleyn's College of God's Gift.*

lending library supported by the well-to-do inhabitants of the area. A walk through Dulwich Park or to Camberwell gave access to municipal libraries and the reading room of the South London Art Gallery.

Dulwich Portrait Gallery

England's oldest picture gallery has always been within walking distance of Herne Hill. Access became easier when a bus from Herne Hill began passing the front gates. The gallery is owned and administered by Alleyn's College of God's Gift. Its original collection, donated by its founder, was enlarged by the Old Masters bequeathed by Sir Francis Bourgeois in 1811. He also left money for maintenance and the proper housing of the collection.

The gallery, built to the design of Sir John Soane, contains the mausoleum of Noel Desanfans who had originally purchased pictures for the King of Poland. Desanfans found himself left with the collection after the monarch had been deposed by the Russians. The tombs of his wife and his friend, Sir Francis Bourgeois, are also in the mausoleum. In 1825 a number of portraits of the Linley family were added to the collection, some of which were painted by Gainsborough.

The gallery had close associations with the Royal Academy and its schools. Pictures were regularly lent to the academy and, in 1815, academy students were allowed to visit for tuition and to copy pictures.

Public admission was granted in 1817, but only by advance ticket obtained from certain London print dealers. This limiting system was abolished in 1857 when the College of God's Gift was reorganised by Act of Parliament.

Over the years, the gallery was visited by many artists, including Turner, Constable, David Cox, David Roberts, Clarkson Stanfield, Cattermole and Van Gogh. John Ruskin was a very critical visitor and Robert Browning a more appreciative one. Stephen Poynter Denning was the gallery's keeper from 1821 until 1864.

The gallery suffered bomb damage in 1944, but by 1953 it had been restored and reopened with additional educational facilities.

At the time of writing the gallery opens six days a week, including Sunday afternoons, and volunteers staff the entrance desks and shop. Special exhibitions with a local theme, such as that held at the Gainsborough bicentennial, are always well supported by the public. A budget is not usually available for exhibitions but, fortunately, the gallery has a very supportive Friends' Society. In 1999 the building was closed to allow a thorough refurbishment to be undertaken. It reopened in 2000.

The South London Gallery

The South London Gallery had its origins in William Rossiter's attendance at the Working Men's College,

and his later position as manager of the South London Working Men's College.

In 1878 a free library was added to the college, the first in South London, and a few months later pictures covered the walls. Most of these were lent for several weeks by friends, but the loans sometimes extended into years. The free library's evening openings were said by the *Pall Mall Gazette* to be 'the only successful rival to the Public House'. The library became the South London Fine Art Gallery. Sunday lectures began and, by 1887, the gallery had moved to Camberwell. At first it occupied an old warehouse until, after fund-raising, it moved to Portland House in Peckham Road. A new gallery was built next door, part of which opened in 1891. This was completed with help from Passmore Edwards and the City Parochial Trust. The finished gallery was opened by the Prince of Wales and Duke and Duchess of York in 1893, at the same time as the central library, which was built opposite in Peckham Road.

The management of the South London Fine Art Gallery passed to the local authority who recommended an extension to include a reading room, office space and links with the school of art next door. The Passmore Edward's Gallery opened in 1900, one of its main features being its Sunday opening.

Bomb damage during the Second World War caused half of the South London Fine Art Gallery's exhibition space to be lost. However, at the time of writing it continues to hold its own collection, some from original donors and local artists, and maintains its connections with the Camberwell School of Art. From time to time it holds exhibitions, such as that in 1981 commemorating connections with John Ruskin and Victorian art.

The gallery was originally known as the South London Fine Art Gallery. It later dropped the 'fine' from its title and in 1992 was renamed the South London Gallery.

POSTAL SERVICE

The introduction of the penny post in May 1840 led to an unprecedented increase in letter writing. During the 1850s, in order to accommodate this growth, the Post Office divided London's postal area into ten districts. London's expansion continued and the postal services were used more and more, especially during the First World War. In 1917, postal districts were again divided, although the central areas remained unaltered.

With the exception of the first district in each area, the one nearest the City (i.e. Nl, El, Wl), the districts were numbered alphabetically, for example N2 is East Finchley and N22 is Wood Green, and E2 is Bethnal Green and E18 is Woodford.

The south-west and south-east postal districts differ from other London areas in that their continued expansion made it necessary to start again alphabetically – SW10 is West Brompton and SW11 is Battersea.

In South East London, the first sequence begins with SE2 (Brixton) and ends with SE18 (Woolwich). The second (with the exception of SE19 being Norwood) begins SE20 (Anerley) and ends SE27 (West Norwood). Thus, Herne Hill is SE24 and the small area north of Ruskin Park, and that around the Blanchedowne estate, within the Camberwell area is SE5.

In recent years, for the ease of a national automated postal system, postal codes have been introduced. Each code covers a very restricted area so that it is possible to tell within a few yards where a person lives.

In *Ye Olde Parish of Camberwell,* Blanche reported that before the penny post was introduced, letters were taken to points along the route of the Dover night mail, from where post was collected by local letter carriers. This system operated within a ten-mile radius of the metropolis. There were two deliveries a day in Camberwell and one in Dulwich. Some 30 postmen were employed in the Camberwell area and ten in Dulwich.

THE POLICING OF HERNE HILL

Herne Hill was so sparsely populated at the end of the eighteenth century that there was little known crime, but it is reported that 'footpads' and highwaymen sometimes robbed travellers on Denmark and Herne Hills. Armed and mounted watchmen were engaged to patrol the hills and were stationed at the triangle of land between Denmark and Champion Hills – the border between Lambeth and Camberwell Boroughs.

Herne Hill has never had a police station of its own but, as with most other services, since the early days of the Metropolitan Force, the area has been policed from Brixton, Camberwell and East Dulwich.

In the 1830s, a sergeant and eight constables marched from Westminster to set up Brixton's first police station. In 1857, after several moves, it was relocated to a new site and has remained there ever since, albeit with various alterations. In 1865 it became the headquarters for Lambeth and is now also the site of the stables for the mounted branch.

The first Camberwell branch of the Metropolitan Police Force was based at the corner of Camberwell New Road and Camberwell Green. The building was demolished in 1898 and a new station opened in Camberwell Church Road.

The East Dulwich branch was opened in 1884, and there was also a West Dulwich branch in Thurlow Park Road. Although parts of Herne Hill were initially policed by both these stations, in 1938 they were transferred to the Catford division. West Dulwich was closed in 1974 and Lordship Lane Police Station was opened in 1977 – at the time of writing it only polices the area of Herne Hill within the Southwark Borough boundary.

Charles Booth's inspectors walked the streets of London at the turn of the century and studied social conditions. They were accompanied by a member of the local police force who was familiar with the area. When Herne Hill was developing, streets on both sides of the hills were being laid out and not all of the houses were occupied. The inspectors concluded that because the residents were law-abiding and did not provoke police attention, the escorts knew less about the inhabitants of their area than was normal.

Many residents were absent during the day, some travelling each morning to the City by train. Inspectors particularly noted how quiet the Milkwood Road area was – the only people around were women, because the children were at school and the men either worked in Neville's Bakery or in the Brixton area. The inspectors also thought that the streets nearest the railway embankments in the north of the area appeared the poorest, with some of the houses being occupied by three families.

At the time of writing Herne Hill is policed by all three branches. Brixton Station covers the largest area, the East Dulwich Branch covers to the borough border and Camberwell police cover the lower area nearest to Camberwell Green. The liaison between all three branches works well.

In the period between the two world wars, policemen were very much in evidence on the streets. Much of the bad behaviour of young people was dealt with on the spot, sometimes, so it was said, with a 'clip around the ear'. A policeman was nearly always present in the vicinity of Brockwell Park and there is a well-known photograph of a policeman on duty in the park, taken standing next to 'Little Ben' *(see page 107).*

During the war, crime decreased considerably and the police force, including special constables, attended incidents with the other emergency services.

At the end of hostilities, and with the greater use of patrol cars, beat policemen largely disappeared from the streets and crime increased. The problems were redressed somewhat with the introduction of 'community policing' and beat policemen with special responsibility for particular areas. The area controlled by Brixton Police Station was divided into four – A, B, C and D. Each section appointed a committee of local people, who worked with the force to try to improve communication and conditions. The system has been helpful, but the social problems of the twenty-first century have made some aspects of policing difficult and care needs to be taken by the ordinary citizen.

Chapter 17

⋙⋘

THE CRYSTAL PALACE

The Great Exhibition of 1851, held in Hyde Park, was a phenomenal success. When the exhibition closed, Joseph Paxton, the designer of the building which had quickly become known as the Crystal Palace, formed a company to re-erect the building in Sydenham, on what he thought was 'the most beautiful spot in the world for the Crystal Palace.' The company was overenthusiastic and the new Palace was considerably bigger than the original. The budget was grossly over-spent and the company became saddled with a debt that it was never able to control.

On 10 June 1854, trains left London Bridge Station every few minutes and carried visitors to the newly-built station serving the Crystal Palace. Those travelling by road were advised to take one of two routes from London to Sydenham. The Queen, Prince Albert, the Royal children, the King of Portugal and his brother, the Duke of Oporto, drove through Herne Hill, along Half Moon Lane, to Dulwich, and thence to Sydenham Hill. Only those with special invitations or season tickets were able to attend the opening. The Government and representatives of the Church were in attendance, as well as foreign ambassadors. The Coldstream Guards and an Honourable Company of the Artillery were on parade. Clara Novello sang the National Anthem, hitting a high note that rang from end to end of the Palace and, after several speeches, the Queen and her party toured the building. The visit ended after the singing of Handel's 'Hallelujah Chorus' and an official announcement of the opening – all reminiscent of the Great Exhibition in Hyde Park three years previously.

Paxton's original water towers had proved unstable and Brunel's towers and the fountains were not ready for the opening on 10 June. Some two years later, the fountains were turned on in the presence of the Queen, the Royal party and thousands of spectators. Confusion reigned when strong winds blew spray over royalty and spectators alike, much to the amusement of the young Prince of Wales. The Palace, with its spectacular water display, was said to be 'the Eighth Wonder of the World'. For those living in South London, it was the most important centre of cultural entertainment they were ever to know, and for the people of Herne Hill, there was the advantage of being within walking distance. The Palace was visible from many locations and soon became part of the residents' lives.

John Ruskin deplored the new style of architecture in a pamphlet called 'On the Opening of Crystal Palace' and described the second building as 'a giant cucumber frame between two chimneys'. He had watched its construction, with alarm, from the family home on Denmark Hill. His only real contact with the Palace appeared to have been when he took his young cousin to a series of 'dreadful concerts' to help her recover from a broken engagement. It is hard to believe that he did not enjoy the regular firework displays, which were watched from high points in Herne Hill.

Henry Bessemer, who lived on his Denmark Hill estate adjoining the Ruskin's property for 35 years, could not have objected to seeing the Crystal Palace each time he looked south, for he bought the estate after the erection of the Palace. He had attended the opening of the Hyde Park exhibition, where he had shown a number of his inventions, including the results of his work on glass. He built many glasshouses for his produce and, with Charles Barry junr, built a domed conservatory, a pavilion and an observatory. He and his family would have enjoyed

A concert at Crystal Palace. The Handel organ was one of the finest in England and was destroyed in 1936.

The opening ceremony of the Crystal Palace performed by Queen Victoria on 10 June 1854.

the firework displays – he was well acquainted with pyrotechnics. It was he who made the round cannonball into the elongated shell, using his previous garden in Highgate as an experimental firing range.

The Bicknells of Herne Hill were certainly interested in Crystal Palace. One son, Henry Sandford, was a shareholder and director of the company. In 1864 he lent many paintings from his own collection to the 9th Annual Art Exhibition. They included works by Turner, David Roberts and Louis Haghe. The entrance fee to the exhibition was 6d.

Crystal Palace and its environs were painted by the impressionist artist Camille Pissarro, who was in England at the time of the Franco-Prussian War in 1870–71. Later, the author Émile Zola, in Norwood at the time of the Dreyfus persecution, photographed Crystal Palace and many other parts of Norwood. The negatives of these photographs were discovered almost 80 years later, in the attic of his granddaughter's home. Those that could be saved were regenerated, photographed and exhibited in England and France. An exhibition was held in Norwood and was viewed by many people, including some residents of Herne Hill.

Under the guidance of George Groves, Angus Manns and Charles Halle, music was introduced. Saturday afternoon concerts became a regular feature and, when the centennial of Handel's death approached, the great Handel festivals began. They became one of the most spectacular musical events of the year, with massed choirs of as many as 4,000 singers, many from South East London.

The Palace became a centre for ballooning and aeronautics. The first airship rose from the grounds and brought the traffic in Dulwich and Herne Hill to a standstill as it made its way to London. Crystal Palace was also the home of the Automobile Club.

The Brock's firework evenings became a regular feature after the first display attracted a crowd of 20,000 paying guests. They were watched from vantage points all around.

Every conceivable form of entertainment, from wild-west spectaculars to dog-and-cat shows, from flower shows to art exhibitions, and Boy Scout rallies, took place. Blondin walked on a tightrope to a backdrop of fireworks. The Palace hosted the Football Association's finals until Wembley Stadium was completed. But still the Palace could not pay its way and eventually the company went bankrupt. The Palace was purchased for the nation by the Lord Mayor of London's fund, just in time for it to be commandeered by the War Office during the First World War and turned into an onshore vessel of the Royal Navy. At the end of the war, it became a Services' discharge centre.

The Imperial War Museum was at Crystal Palace until 1924, when it moved to the Imperial Institute in South Kensington and eventually to Lambeth Road, where a site had been vacated by the Bethlem Royal Hospital. By the time the Palace was returned to the company, it was more than a little dilapidated, but with good management and hard work the grounds and buildings improved. Many of the previous activities recommenced, including brass band concerts, dancing and fireworks. Logie Baird broadcast from the Palace, sending out his first television transmission from the south tower, and motor racing began on a specially constructed track.

However, on the night of 30 November 1936, fire destroyed Crystal Palace and everything within it. The blaze was believed to have been caused either by a faulty electrical fitting or a carelessly dropped cigarette end, falling between the floorboards and igniting the dust below. Despite the efforts of staff and firemen from all over London, the glass melted and the iron buckled, leaving only smouldering ashes and the collapsed shell. The two water towers remained, standing sentinel.

And so ended the love affair of the people of South London with the Crystal Palace, which had endured since the day of its opening in 1854. Nothing was ever to take its place. The memory of the Palace was etched upon the community's mind. For generations the people of Herne Hill had walked there on summer evenings and after church on Sunday mornings. They had watched firework displays from every high spot in the district and sung in the choirs at the Handel festivals. They had attended Scout rallies and been inspected by Lord Baden Powell. They had visited flower shows and watched cricket and football matches, and, as children, had been taken to see the 'prehistoric' animals and the fountains.

For some years, the Brunel water towers stood as a reminder. They were demolished in the first phases of the Second World War as it was thought that they would act as pointers for enemy planes. The terraces and fountains disappeared under mounds of earth. After the war, the LCC, later the GLC, took over the management of the area for the educational and recreational purposes of the people of London. A national recreation centre was built, but it had little to do with the surrounding community. Crystal Palace remained in limbo, but in the 1960s the Norwood Society was formed for 'the protection and preservation of the amenities of Upper Norwood and District.' Soon the society had 400 members and was holding exhibitions about the Palace. The first, a ten-day exhibition, was hugely successful. It attracted visitors from as far afield as Canada and the United States and, as a result, Norwood, Massachusetts, was able to forge links with Norwood, London. The second exhibition was set up in 1966 and was called 'Living with the Palace'. The Duke of Edinburgh acted as patron for both events. The society fought for the preservation of the area's amenities, maintaining as high a profile as possible for the future use of the Palace site.

Paxton's remarkable underpass, which originally led from the high-level station to the Palace, remained intact throughout the years. The public are always astonished that such a place exists under the ugly bus terminus that now occupies the Crystal Palace Parade.

Interest is still high, not only in Norwood, but also in the surrounding areas, including Herne Hill. Another society, the Crystal Palace Foundation, was formed. It has a wide membership and has carried out much work to uncover some of the past glories of the Palace. The society has created a small but extremely interesting museum not far from the site of the lost Crystal Palace.

An aerial view of the Crystal Palace buildings and grounds, c.1930.

West Norwood Cemetery. Many of Herne Hill's inhabitants took up their final residence in this cemetery. Unfortunately, many of their headstones disappeared in Lambeth's 1970s clearance. A group has been established called the Friends of West Norwood Cemetery (inset) who aim to preserve the site.

Warmington Road. The home of the author, Richard Church (see page 136), where he spent some of his happiest years attending Dulwich Hamlet School and cycling out into the Kent and Surrey countryside. The dwelling now bears a plaque commemorating his family's time of residence.

Chapter 18

೦**⊚**⊚

RESIDENTS AND VISITORS

There are two past residents of Herne Hill who, by their purchases, did future inhabitants great good and, by caring for their own interests, unwittingly preserved for future generations one of the more pleasant London suburbs south of the Thames.

Residents are fortunate that the land they helped save from speculative builders was adjacent to that belonging to the Dulwich College estate, which has always been strict about excessive development. It was also fortunate that land adjacent to, and in the northern part of, Herne Hill was held by the benevolent Huguenot Minet family estate.

The two men were Samuel Sanders and John Blades. It is possible that the men might have known each other as their periods of residence could have overlapped and they were both successful business-men who bought estates in the area. Very little is known about Samuel Sanders and nothing about how he came to buy land and move to Denmark Hill. We do know that he was a timber merchant and probably had premises on the Lambeth side of the Thames.

Whatever the reason for his move to Denmark Hill, it can be surmised that he was a very astute businessman, for he purchased land that stretched back to the later Fawnbrake Avenue, up Denmark Hill and down Herne Hill. Within a few years Samuel Sanders was leasing land for 75 and 100 years to wealthy merchants and soon substantial houses were built on Denmark and Herne Hills, each with its own considerable grounds and its own carriage entrance. It was not until the 1870s that the leases on Herne Hill started to lapse and the second generation of houses started to appear.

It is not known when Samuel Sanders died or where he was buried, but it is certain that he should have some form of commemoration, for without him who knows what Herne Hill would now be like?

John Blades (1751–1828), the second unwitting benefactor, was a Londoner by birth and had established his glass-manufacturing business on Ludgate Hill by the age of 30. He married Hannah Hobson who was born in 1766. The couple had a son and three daughters before Hannah died in 1796 at the age of 30.

John Blades' glass-manufacturing business was very successful. He supplied spectacular glassware to the Royal Family, in particular to the Prince of Wales, later George IV, and to the Shah of Persia and the East India Company.

Being a City man, John Blades' church was St Bride's in Fleet Street, and his wife was buried in the crypt there. During his years of attendance a fire destroyed houses in Fleet Street and allowed access from the street for the first time. Blades was the first and largest contributor to the Lord Mayor's appeal for funds to buy the vacant land and enable access from Fleet Street for all time.

In 1809 John Blades purchased 60 acres of land 'in Brixton'. In 1827 his son, John Hobson Blades, died unmarried at the age of 31. It is possible that he was ill for some time before his death, because in 1826 when his father made provision for his mentally impaired youngest daughter, Laura, he did not name his son as guardian. Instead he arranged for a grant of custody with his daughter Caroline and his brother-in-law Joshua Hobson. The family was very close and cared for Laura until she died in Brockwell Hall at the age of 76. She was buried in West Norwood Cemetery.

John Blades died the year after his son and both were buried in the family grave at St Bride's. A memorial was erected. John had previously erected a memorial nearby to his three brothers, James, Perkin and Robert, all buried at St Bride's.

In early-Victorian times the crypt entrance was bricked up, probably during the time when church burials were no longer allowed. It was not until St Bride's was nearly destroyed during the Blitz that the crypt was rediscovered, together with the founda-tions of previous churches and Roman remains. The burial sites were recorded and remains reburied in new coffins. The crypt with the Blades' memorials can be seen by visitors to the church.

John Blades left a considerable estate, including the Ludgate Hill premises and the Brixton estate. It is also reported that Severndroog Castle, Shooters Hill, was part of the estate, but this is only mentioned in the London survey of St Mary's parish.

John Blades' eldest daughter, Elizabeth, married Joshua Blackburn of Bishopsgate, a manufacturer of 'Russian mats'. They lived at Brockwell Hall with John Blades and there their children were born; the first was Joshua Blades Blackburn in 1822.

Joshua Blades Blackburn became a Lincoln's Inn Barrister at Law and married Mary Ann, the daughter of a surgeon from Newcastle-upon-Tyne. It was Joshua who sold the land on which St Jude's Church was built and consecrated in 1868. He had returned the purchase money, donating it towards the building of the church. Later he gave the land on which the vicarage was built. He was probably influenced by the fact that his Aunt Caroline had married the first vicar of St Matthew's Church in Brixton and that the vicar appointed to St Jude's had been curate of St Matthew's. Later he was unable to agree to the sale of the first part of Brockwell Park, for he was said to be resident in 'an asylum'. However, he was reported as dying in Brockwell Hall in 1888 so his stay could not have been permanent. His wife, Mary Ann, had died six years earlier. Both were buried in West Norwood Cemetery, as were his mother, Elizabeth, and his younger brother.

The estate was inherited by Joshua John Blades Blackburn, the eldest son of Joshua and Mary Ann Blackburn, born in 1854. On inheriting it he was quick to agree the sale of the first part of the park and also allowed public access to the parkland before it was officially opened. He attended the opening of the park but sadly died only ten years later in 1898. He was also buried in the family grave in West Norwood Cemetery.

His successors agreed the sale of the rest of the estate to the LCC, subject to the leases on Clarence and Brockwell Houses. Brockwell Terrace, Clarence House and Brockwell House were demolished when their leases lapsed.

Nearly all of the participants in the formation of Brockwell Park, from the building of St Jude's to the final purchase, knew each other and shared a common concern – the care of the community and the local area.

Mention must also be made of two other estate bodies that protected and benefited Herne Hill and its environs.

At the time of the Reformation, Henry VIII confiscated all property and land belonging to the Church. This included the manor of Dulwich, which adjoined the parish of St Mary's, and the hunting grounds of the Archbishop of Canterbury. The manor was sold to Thomas Calton whose family in turn sold it to Edward Alleyn. It is alleged that in the early 1600s, on reaching the summit of Red Post Hill, Edward Alleyn fell to his knees to thank God for having allowed him to reach his destiny and find his home. He later founded a college for poor scholars and almshouses for needy men and women.

The hunting grounds were eventually acquired by the Minet family estate. Because much of the woodland had been felled at the time of the Interregnum, the land was felt to be more suitable for horticulture than housing.

The determination of the original purchasers and the management skills of their successors enabled Herne Hill to remain in a semi-rural state whilst neighbouring areas were being swamped by terraces of houses, roads and railways. Gifts of land and long leases with 'peppercorn rents' allowed churches, halls, libraries and open spaces to be created for community use.

George Allen (1832–1907)

George Allen was one of John Ruskin's pupils at the Working Men's Institute and was among the students John took painting in Dulwich and then for a substantial meal at the Greyhound. George became one of John's most trusted and loyal friends and one of the two pupils who helped sort through the thousands of drawings that Turner had left to the nation.

He became John's full-time assistant in 1857, a year after falling in love with and marrying one of the servants in the Ruskin household called Anne Hobbs. They lived in the lodge at the entrance to the Ruskin estate. After the death of John's mother and the sale of No. 163 Denmark Hill, they moved to Orpington from where George Allen conducted his business, his store of books housed in a shed in the garden. In 1890 he moved his offices to London.

John's father, John James Ruskin, had always acted as agent for his son's books but on his death John began to deal with this aspect himself. He set George Allen up as his publisher and gradually transferred his titles to the new company. The books were then sold at a fixed price. George Allen was a fine engraver and a capable publisher. He was also a knowledgeable geologist, mineralogist and botanist, all skills invaluable to John Ruskin. For the rest of their lives the arrangement between the men continued and at one time it was the only source of income for John.

Later in life, when John Ruskin was having difficulties with the Severns, George offered Ruskin a home with him. Nothing came of the offer and when Ruskin returned to Brantwood for good, George was never allowed to see Ruskin alone. He called Joan Severn 'the dragon', and generally did not like either Joan or Arthur – he thought them mercenary and they thought him grasping but had to admit that he was a good publisher and businessman.

Sir Henry Bessemer (1813–98)

Henry Bessemer was one of the most amazing men of the nineteenth century. Through his inventions and processes he helped to change the course of industrial life throughout the world. His steel process was compared to the invention of the printing press, the

Sir Henry Bessemer in his 80th year. Clockwise from top left the other portraits show him aged 36, 45, 56 and 70.

development of the compass, the steam engine and the discovery of America. He was honoured by kings and emperors, cities and scientific societies. He had towns named after him and was given the freedom of cities, including that of the City of London. He was made a Fellow of the Royal Society and after the refusal of Britain to allow him to accept the Legion of Honour from the French Emperor he was knighted by Queen Victoria.

Born in Charlton House near Hitchin, he showed early interest in metal casting, choosing to work in his father's foundry on leaving school. When the family returned to London he began to cast model medallions and sculptures and had his first commercial success casting cartoons and scrolls in cardboard.

He found a way of embossing stamp paper that could prevent forgery of deeds. The device was adopted by the Government Stamp Office but Bessemer received no payment and from then on he patented all but one of his inventions, of which there were over 110 in all.

He worked on the production of lead for pencils, typesetting, dyes for embossing stationery, a cotton version of Genoa velvet and found a way of producing 'gold' paint very cheaply, thus breaking the previous monopoly. For its production, he assembled a plant in his St Pancras garden in four separate units, which needed only five trusted associates to run. The process was never patented and remained secret for 50 years. The money from this enabled him to remain a free agent and to finance his own inventions.

He also worked on the production of sugar, fans for the ventilation of mine shafts, glass manufacture, centrifugal pumps for raising water, and exhibited four of his devices at the Great Exhibition in 1851. He worked on the simultaneous application of brakes on the carriage wheels of trains and, during the Crimean War, became interested in armaments, applying for a patent to eject elongated shells from smooth-bored guns – a device rejected by the War Department but accepted by the French. This led to his involvement in steel manufacture and, despite a lack of interest in his process from some industrialists, the War Department and the Admiralty, he made an immense fortune when he opened his own steel works at Sheffield. He granted licences under patent to manufacturers in England and overseas, thereby revolutionising industry and transport throughout the world.

Henry Bessemer and his family moved to Denmark Hill in 1863. They lived in a house described as 'charming and unpretentious', the grounds of which sloped down to North Dulwich railway lines. Within a few years he had built hothouses, forcing pits, cold frames, storage houses, vineries, peach and cucumber houses and a large conservatory adjoining his house for evening perambulations and the care of exotic ferns and plants. There was a park for deer, a small herd of Alderney cattle and a model farm. There was also a model of a ship's saloon, stabilised to prevent seasickness, a lake and a grotto, and later Bessemer Grange, built as a wedding present for his daughter. Charles Barry junr was the architect for the Grange, the pavilion and the conservatory.

On retirement Henry Bessemer returned to an early interest in optics. He built a steam-powered workshop and experimented with solar rays. He built an observatory with an adjustable revolving floor and roof and a telescope, but he died before his work on the lens could be completed.

One of his last projects was to design and build a diamond-cutting works with automated machinery to establish his grandson in business – another huge success.

He died in 1898 aged 85. He and his wife were buried in West Norwood Cemetery.

Elhanan Bicknell (1788–1861)
(In the National Biography)

Elhanan Bicknell was named after the American preacher Revd Elhanan Winchester, the original source of the name being one of 'David's mighty men'. He was born in Southwark, the son of a Unitarian serge manufacturer-cum-schoolmaster. After short periods teaching and farming he entered into partnership with a cousin and made a fortune in the Pacific whaling industry. He spent the money on his collection of art which included some of Turner's work long before it was fashionable. He was a close friend of David Roberts with whom he shared his Unitarian beliefs and, after one of his sons married Roberts' daughter, nine grandchildren. He attended the Essex Street Chapel in The Strand and was a contributor to the founding of the Effra Road Unitarian Chapel and school. Both chapels and halls were destroyed by enemy action during the Second World War and were only partially replaced.

Elhanan married four times and by the age of 37 had been widowed twice. He had 13 children and in 1818 moved to Herne Hill where, to accommodate his growing family and art collection, he extended his house considerably. He had one of the biggest and most important collections of modern art in Victorian England as well as an extensive library. Elhanan preferred modern art to the classics and on returning from a Continental tour stated that he had not seen a picture he would 'give a damn for'.

The house in Herne Hill had a full-sized billiard room and an impressive wine cellar. Elhanan was master of the City's Vintner's Company (1853–54) and when leaving office was complimented for his punctuality, attention to detail and his kindness to all members of the court. Five members of the Bicknell family were masters of the Company of Vintners and others were admitted to patrimony.

Elhanan and his third wife, Lucinda, kept 'open house', welcoming the writers (Dickens was one) and artists of the day as well as helping up-and-coming artists along the road to success. Elhanan, described as 'a biggish man, with a florid complexion, and a slight speech impediment', often lent his pictures for exhibitions in art galleries. Photographs show him to have been a confident, good-looking man.

All of his children received good educations and the benefits of wide cultural opportunities. They were reputed to have been above average in appearance and intelligence and several proved outstanding in their chosen fields.

Elhanan died in November 1861 at Herne Hill and was buried in the family vault at West Norwood Cemetery.

Clarence Bicknell (1842–1918)

The youngest of Elhanan and Lucinda Bicknell's children, Clarence was a member of the Church of England and a Cambridge graduate in 1865. On ordination he became a curate at St Paul's, Walworth

Elhanan Bicknell, a strong supporter of the Unitarian movement in Britain. The books on the table are by Priestly and Channing who were leading Unitarians.

Road, devoting himself to the needs of the poor of the neighbourhood, before joining an enclosed order in Shropshire.

When the order closed down, he began to travel and visited Ceylon, New Zealand, Morocco, Majorca and Italy. He became enchanted with the region of Bordighera on the Italian Riviera and remained there for the rest of his life. In 1878 he forsook his orders and, believing a common language to be more advantageous to the good of mankind than religion, he devoted himself to the spread of Esperanto. He studied the flora, the archaeology and prehistoric rock carvings of the area and produced *Flowering Plants and Ferns of the Riviera*, with his own watercolour illustrations, and *A Guide to the Prehistoric Rock Carvings in the Italian Maritime Alps*. Some 100 years later, descendants of Elhanan Bicknell journeyed to the Bordighera to commemorate the publication of Clarence's book on rock carvings.

Clarence established an international library and the 'Musea Bicknell' and on his death left his house, library and museum to the people of Bordighera. A collection of over 3,000 lithographs of his own watercolours of plants was left to the University of Genoa.

Henry Sandford Bicknell (1818–80)

Henry was born just after his parents moved to Herne Hill and was the only son of Elhanan Bicknell and his second wife. He followed his father's footsteps into the whaling business and shared his interest in art. He married Christine, the only daughter of David Roberts, and initially shared the artist's home in Fitzroy Square before moving to Effra Road, to Tulse Hill and finally to Cavendish House on Clapham Common. No less than 154 of David Roberts' paintings were displayed in the home, as well as those of other living artists. Henry also had a large collection of first editions and of letters and signatures of prominent people in many walks of life.

He organised the record-breaking posthumous sale of his father's estate and works of art and, later, that of his father-in-law's paintings. Before that sale, he arranged an exhibition of David Roberts' works at Crystal Palace where he was a shareholder and a director.

Henry and Christine produced a large family. However, she died in 1872 and Henry married again. He was treasurer of the Unitarian Church in Effra Road and, during the 1860s, one of the organisers of the nationwide petition for the admission of students of all denominations to the Universities of Oxford and Cambridge, not only those of the Church of England. The petition unfortunately failed.

He died rather unexpectedly in 1880 and was buried in the family vault in West Norwood Cemetery.

Herman Bicknell (1830–75)
(In the National Biography)
Herman was the third son of Elhanan Bicknell's large family to survive. He was a Unitarian and was educated in Paris, Hanover, the University College and St Bartholomew's Hospital, London.

At the age of 25, he joined the 59th Regiment in Hong Kong as assistant surgeon and from there transferred to the 81st Regiment in Lahore, serving throughout the period of the mutiny.

He studied Oriental dialects and travelled to Java, Tibet and the Himalayas, and returned home through the Indus and Palestine. When the Army transferred him to Aldershot, he resigned and from then on continued his studies and his travels to the Arctic, the Andes and to the Far East. He continually studied ethnology, botany and science. At one time he lived in the native quarter of Cairo and became so familiar with Islamic culture that he was able to join the annual pilgrimage to Mecca. He was the first Englishman to do so undisguised and later he also entered Fatima's shrine at Kum. He studied the scenes and life of Persia which enabled him to translate the poems of Hafiz.

Before Herman could complete his final manuscript, he died of cancer; his death hastened by injuries sustained in an accident during his second attempt to ascend the Matterhorn. It was said that he was a linguist of unsurpassed ability and had a brilliant and versatile brain. His brother, Sidney, saw his manuscript through to publication.

Sidney Bicknell (1832–1911)
Sidney was born in Herne Hill and was Elhanan's second son by Lucinda. David Roberts considered him 'a lout', but he was a highly intelligent and adventurous traveller and mountaineer.

He made ten ascents of Vesuvius, some during eruptions and one by moonlight at midnight. He crossed the Andes four times, visited the Himalayas and made a winter ascent of Mount Etna. He was in Naples at the time of Garibaldi's entry and saw some of the fighting in the Voturno, later publishing his account of the eventful tour. He was also a witness to many of the Franco-Prussian battles and one of the first Englishmen to make an ascent in a balloon.

When he tired of travelling, Sidney married and settled quietly in southern England. He built himself an observatory and studied astronomy. He had an extensive library on the subject of fungi, published a book of his findings and exhibited at the Royal Horticultural Society.

Sidney also studied archaeology and was a member of several scientific societies, including the Royal Geographical Society. He was elected a fellow of the Linnean Society. He was an enthusiastic photographer from the 1850s onwards and took several photographs, dating from 1859, of the Herne Hill house and grounds.

Sidney also spent time researching and studying his family's history. He died in Brighton in 1911 following an operation.

Thomas Lynn Bristowe (1833–92)
Norwood's first Member of Parliament, Thomas Bristowe, lived at Dulwich Hill House, Denmark Hill, his property neighbouring that of Henry Bessemer. The house lay between what is now Sunray Avenue and Red Post Hill.

Thomas Bristowe was very much a local man. The son of a Camberwell doctor, he was educated at King's College, The Strand, and became a successful stockbroker with an interest in railway stock.

He was a sidesman and warden at St Paul's Church, Herne Hill, and gave the use of his field for Sunday School treats and church fêtes. When he left Herne Hill he arranged for these functions to be held at Belle Vue, a house lying just above St Paul's.

He is best remembered for his management of the committee which saw through the purchase of the first part of Brockwell Park. During this time, he arranged for special trains to run to Herne Hill to demonstrate how badly a park was needed at the junction of the six roads and, when it seemed that the whole project would fail for lack of finance, he secured the continuance of the scheme with £60,000 of his own money.

Sadly, at the park's opening ceremony in which the chairman of the Parks Department of the LCC had been fulsome in his praise of the Member of Parliament's hard work in securing the space for the people of South London, Thomas Bristowe had a heart attack and died. He was buried in West Norwood Cemetery.

A bust on a pedestal with a drinking fountain below was unveiled as a memorial the following year. This was removed in the postwar years when the park was 'revamped'.

Anita Brookner (born 1928)
Born into a Polish Jewish family living in Herne Hill, Anita Brookner showed an early interest in art, visiting the Dulwich Art Gallery on frequent occasions. She received her further education at King's College and obtained a PhD at the Courtauld Institute.

Anita lectured on the history of art at Reading and Cambridge Universities and at the Courtauld Institute. She was the first woman to hold the Slade Professorship at Cambridge and became a fellow of New Hall, Cambridge, and King's College, London. She wrote on French art before turning to fiction in

1981, since when she has written many novels. In 1984, she won the Booker Prize for Fiction for her novel *Hotel du Lac*.

Hablot Knight Browne (1815–82)

Born in Kennington, Hablot was the younger brother of Lucinda, the third wife of Elhanan Bicknell. He lived with the Bicknell family on Herne Hill through-out his teens and attended St Martin's Lane School. There he won a Society of Arts medal for the best sketch on an historic subject and another prize for his 'John Gilpin's Races'. He was apprenticed to the engraver Finden, but found this monotonous, so with a friend he rented an attic in Furnival Court and both began to produce watercolours and to live on the proceeds. During this period he was introduced to Charles Dickens who engaged him as an illustrator – first for *Sunday as it was by Timothy Sparkes* and then for *The Pickwick Papers*. This was followed by *Dombey and Son*, *David Copperfield* and *Nicholas Nickleby*, using the name of Phiz to Dickens' Boz.

Richard Church

Hablot eventually illustrated all but the last four of Dickens' books, his last being *A Tale of Two Cities*. When preparing for *Nicholas Nickleby* the two men travelled to Yorkshire to see schools such as those portrayed in the book. Among other books illustrated by him were those by Charles Lever and William Ainsworth, notably *Old St Paul's*. He was described at the time as 'handsome and well-built, charming company with a quiet sense of humour.'

Hablot was one of 14 children and himself the father of five sons and four daughters. Much of his married life was spent in Croydon, then a small village in beautiful countryside 'ten miles from town' where the children had great freedom and every educational and cultural advantage. They were able to attend their aunt and uncle's 'open house' on Herne Hill and there see 'a profusion of art treasures, and meet men occupying distinguished positions in the art world.'

Hablot enjoyed riding and hunting, but not socialising with his neighbours for they were inclined to 'lionise' him. His doctor friend's influence secured him a permanent post as drawing master at the East India Company's Military College in Addiscombe (see *The Book of Addiscombe*). He especially enjoyed working in the evening by fire and candlelight with his family around him.

He continued working, despite suffering from a stroke, and exhibited until 1875, although not so successfully. Throughout his working life he exhibited at the Society of British Art and the British

Institute and entered two cartoons at the Westminster Hall Exhibition after a fire had destroyed the Parliament buildings.

He moved to Brighton where he died in 1882. Strangely, when leaving Croydon Hablot destroyed all his old correspondence with Dickens, Lever and Ainsworth; he declared that they were 'only about illustrations'.

One of his children, Edgar Browne, wrote a book called *Phiz and Boz* telling of Hablot Browne's life and his association with Dickens. Included was a chapter about his aunt's family, the Bicknells, which also gave glimpses of John Ruskin's eccentricities.

David Chadwick, MP (1821–95)

MP for Macclesfield from 1864–80, David Chadwick lived at The Poplars, Herne Hill. He became an accountant in 1843, later heading a firm of accountants and money lenders with offices in London and Manchester.

He was an associate of the Institute of Civil Engineers and president of the Manchester Statistical Society. He published books on finance and the distribution of parliamentary seats.

He was the agent for the Ironworks' manager who planned to corner the market in manganese and thus break Henry Bessemer's patents for the production of steel. David Chadwick was surprised when Henry Bessemer, who lived on Denmark Hill, called on him early one morning after overhearing a discussion outlining the planned takeover. The MP had to agree that the future lay in steel production and that his client would be ruined if Henry Bessemer retaliated by advertising in the City and also took legal measures against the Ironworks' manager. Within a few hours the manager agreed to Bessemer's terms and in the long run paid many thousands of pounds in royalties to Bessemer.

David Chadwick died at The Poplars in 1895.

Richard Church (1893–1972)

Richard Church was born in Battersea. His father was a postman with a passion for cycling and his mother a London School Board teacher, whose secret dread was the cycling trips her husband arranged!

Richard was a delicate child with poor sight. At seven years he was given a pair of glasses and 'overnight became a bookworm'. One Christmas he received a half-share with his brother in a tandem.

When it became necessary to leave Battersea, the family hunted for a new home by cycle and found it at No. 2 Warmington Road at the bottom of what became Ruskin Walk. Richard described the house as 'pretty, detached and double fronted, full of mirrors and with a drawing room painted in gold' – it had belonged to a theatrical entrepreneur. Herne Hill seemed like heaven after Battersea and when he was enrolled at the Dulwich Hamlet School Richard began three years of 'almost indescribable happiness' and there learned the value of self-education. Despite winning a scholarship to the Camberwell Art School, his father insisted that he became a boy clerk at the Land Registry. In the long run this proved beneficial, for he was helped in many ways by the people who worked there. Later, he was to become a publisher's reviewer and among the books he reviewed was Laurie Lee's *Cider with Rosie*.

Following his mother's death and his father's remarriage, Richard and his brother moved to the Champion Hill area – they took their bicycles with them and Richard continued his exploration of the Kent countryside and the study of its history, later writing about it in *Kent's Contribution*. He was a poet, a novelist and an award-winning autobiographer. *Over the Bridge*, *The Golden Sovereign* and *The Voyage Home* told of his life in Herne Hill.

He lived at one time in the grounds of Scotney Castle and later at Sissinghurst, where he died. A plaque commemorates the time he lived at No. 2 Warmington Road. This was requested in the 1980s by his eldest child, Polly Hunter, and Herne Hill councillors of both Lambeth and Southwark, but the placing of it was delayed until the required 20 years had passed since his death.

John Gregory Crace (1809–89)
John Diblee Crace (1839–1919)

The Craces were descendants of a line of decorators who were commissioned by monarchs, public bodies and private persons to decorate the interiors of palaces, castles, houses and private homes and public buildings.

John Gregory's father was Frederick, interior decorator of Windsor Castle, Buckingham Palace and Brighton Pavilion. John Gregory began working with Frederick at the age of 17, living at and running the business from Wigmore Street while his father lived in Brighton and worked on the pavilion. He became a full partner in the firm at the age of 21 and branched out into private work, arranging a showroom at Wigmore Street to encourage private patronage. He worked at Arlington, Devonshire and Chatsworth Houses, Tayworth Castle and Knebworth, as well as at Windsor Castle, Brighton Pavilion and Buckingham Palace.

John Gregory met and worked with Pugin at Alton Towers and the new Houses of Parliament, as well as at halls, abbeys and other castles. He contributed furniture and furnishings to Pugin's Medieval Court at the Great Exhibition and created a temporary structure for Queen Victoria and Prince Albert for a state ball for visiting dignitaries. He also decorated the Guildhall for a ball held at the time of the wedding of the Prince and Princess of Wales. He provided the furnishings for Government House in Perth, Australia, and designed the interior of the 1862 Great Exhibition building. In 1862 he sold his house in St John's Wood and moved to Springfield, Herne Hill, where he lived until his death in 1889. The Springfield estate stretched from just behind the Half Moon Inn to what is now Burbage Road. The estate was sold in the early 1890s by his son.

John Diblee Crace, the eldest of a family of 12 children, became involved in the family business in 1854 at the age of 16 when he was called home from school to take charge when his father became ill. He was involved in work at Windsor Castle for a state visit of Napoleon III and Eugenie in 1862. He also worked on the Great Exhibition in Cromwell Street and the interiors of Brunel's Great Western and the Great Eastern.

John Diblee travelled extensively in Europe, always studying architecture, interior decoration and materials, and on one journey accompanied the younger Charles Barry and his wife who lived nearby in Dulwich. As a result, he worked with Edward Barry on the crypt of St Stephen's Chapel in the Houses of Parliament. He decorated the India Office for a visit of a Turkish Sultan and worked at 142 Piccadilly and 9 St James' Square. He also worked at Knighthayes for MP Heathcote-Amory, at Longleat for the Marquis of Bath, Grosvenor House for the Marquis of Westminster, the Victoria Hall at the Victoria and Albert Museum, 18 Carlton House and Cliveden for the Astor estate, as well as redecorating the Brighton Pavilion. He also designed the furniture and furnishings for many of the houses he worked on.

In 1899 he sold the Wigmore Street premises and retired to his Gloucester Place house where he had moved following his marriage in 1873. His father had died and his own son was not interested in entering the business.

He was a contributing member of the Royal Institute of British Architects and a freeman of the Painters, Stainers Company in the City, as were both his father and grandfather. He took a consultative role and wrote articles and published books on decorative art.

John Diblee died at his home in Gloucester Place and was buried in West Norwood Cemetery with his father, very near to the grave of his grandfather Frederick Crace. All three men had lived until the age of 80.

Frederick Crace had made a considerable collection of maps, drawings and paintings of London which was then altering at a great rate. Many of the paintings were by Thomas Shepherd, whom Frederick Crace engaged to record his London before it was lost forever; he left the entire collection to the British Museum.

Henry Havelock Ellis (1859–1939)

Henry was born in Croydon but spent several years studying and teaching in Australia before returning to England in 1879. He then entered medical school and qualified some four years later.

His literary interests took precedence over medicine and he reviewed, translated and edited, publishing the *Mermaid Series of Elizabethan Dramatists* which caused a stir in the 1880s. He became particularly associated with the subject of sexual behaviour, publishing several works on the psychology of sex, marriage and social hygiene. Towards the end of his life he wrote his autobiography, *My Life*, published in 1939. He hardly had time to know its reception, for he died the same year.

He lived for a period in Holmdene Road when he suffered ill health. A short time later he moved to the Brixton area.

Professor Hans Eysenck (1916–97)

Born in Berlin into a theatrical family, Hans was brought up by his grandmother and was educated in Germany, apart from a short spell on the Isle of Wight. At the age of 18 he was taken with his class to hear Hitler speak and came to the conclusion that he was 'evil personified'. He left Germany with his mother and stepfather when he found that enrolment at Berlin University depended upon his joining the SS. He studied history at a French university before coming to England where he attended London University and gained a First in Psychology in 1938. At the outbreak of the Second World War he applied to join the RAF, but being an 'enemy alien' was turned down. Eventually he joined the staff of the Mill Hill Emergency Hospital, treating emotionally disturbed patients. After the war he joined the staff of the Maudsley Hospital, becoming head of the psychology department. He was a reader at the Institute of Psychiatry and later professor of psychology. He published many articles and books on his research findings, some causing much controversy, especially his findings on intelligence and his opinions on Freudian concepts.

He was a prodigious reader and was interested in extra-sensory perception and astrology. He published his autobiography *Rebel with a Cause* in 1990.

He lived in Dorchester Drive in the house originally constructed for an ice-cream manufacturer.

William Brodie Gurney (1777–1855)

Gurney was born in Stamford Hill and was baptised as an adult in 1796 at the Southwark Maze Pond Chapel (the original site is now part of Guy's Hospital). He was later associated with the Denmark Place Baptist Chapel in Coldharbour Lane. He began using shorthand in the early 1800s, attending trials, appeals, court martials, libel cases, addresses and speeches. Over the years he attended the impeachment of Lord Melville and the proceedings against the Duke of York, the trials of Lord Cochrane and Lord Thislewood, and the proceedings against Queen Caroline. He was formally appointed as shorthand writer to the Houses of Parliament in 1802.

William Gurney was secretary, treasurer and later president of the Sunday School Union and was present at its inauguration. He was joint editor of its youth magazine and its treasurer for 30 years. The profits from this were devoted to education and missionary works. He was on the board of the London Female Penitentiary, took Sunday services and was on the committee of the Westminster Branch of the British and Foreign Bible Society. He was treasurer of Stepney College and was interested in the anti-slavery movement, contributing towards the building of chapels in Jamaica. He lived on Denmark Hill and died there in March 1855.

William Innes (1905–99)

William Innes lived in Herne Hill for the greater part of his life. After the war he had a home in Hollingbourne Road, and subsequently in Ruskin Walk. He was a member of the Herne Hill Society and an active friend of the Horniman's Museum Society. A self-taught artist, he was past president of the London Sketch Club, honorary life member of the Pastel Society Council and member of the United Society of Artists. His work has been hung at the Royal Academy, the Royal Society of British Artists, the Royal Institute of Oil Painters and the Royal Society of Marine Artists.

In 1926 William Innes began his career as a short-hand typist with Carter and Co., situated near the Albert Embankment and the Doulton Potteries, in a company concerned with tiling and architecture. His time with the firm, interrupted by his war service as an RAF radar operator, lasted for 44 years. When he retired in 1971 he was a director and responsible for the tiling needs of many firms including Lyons, Kodak and Sainsbury's. He often worked in association with the firm's near neighbour, Doultons.

On his retirement he began a second career as a painter in oils and watercolours, becoming involved in societies and institutes in the art world. In both his careers he was assiduous in helping other young artists on the road to success.

Reginald V. Jones (1911–97)

The son of a Grenadier Guard, Reginald Jones was born in 1911 at No. 188 Railton Road. Shortly afterwards the family moved to Shakespeare Road but in 1931 returned to No. 194 Railton Road. He attended St Jude's School until he was eight years old when he transferred to the Sussex Road School. Considered 'rough', with 50 to 55 pupils in a class, it was 'well disciplined' with a growing academic reputation. He won a scholarship to Alleyn's College and later an open exhibition to study physics at Wadham College, Oxford, gaining a First and a grant to work for a doctorate. Whilst there he was disgusted at the Oxford Union's notorious resolution not 'to fight for King and Country'. He was intensely patriotic and remained so all his life.

After working at the Clarendon Laboratory on radar and infrared aircraft detection, he was appointed as Scientific Officer at the Air Ministry, eventually transferring to Intelligence. His work on the interpretation of Enigma code messages, on beams, radar, the interpretation of photographs and sketches of mysterious sites and fragments of scientific information smuggled out of occupied territories, was of immense importance to the defence of Britain. It is detailed in his book *Most Secret War*, dedicated to intelligence workers in Nazi-occupied Europe, reconnaissance pilots and those who carried out the resultant raids on V1 and V2 launching sites.

His work was recognised and honoured by Buckingham Palace and the USA, and was much appreciated by Winston Churchill.

He was concerned about the teaching of science in the postwar years and became professor of natural philosophy at Aberdeen University. He returned to Intelligence for a short while in the early 1950s before taking up his old post in Aberdeen.

Reginald never lost his affection for Herne Hill and stayed in touch with many people he had known as a child. He recorded his early life in his book and later gave more helpful details in response to a letter from the author.

He died suddenly in December 1997. A memorial service was held the following April. It was attended by many past and present colleagues, including the headmaster of Alleyn's College.

Henry Dawson Lowry (1869–1906)

Henry Lowry was born in Truro, Cornwall, in February 1869 and was educated at Queen's College, Taunton, and at Oxford. He began writing for the *National Observer* in 1891 and moved to London two years later. He also wrote for the *Pall Mall Gazette* and joined its staff in 1895. He was on the staff of *The Black and White Paper* from 1895 until 1898. He joined the staff of the *Morning Post* in 1897 and wrote as 'The Impenitent' in the *Daily Express*.

He began to publish works of fiction and non-fiction in 1893, beginning with *Wreckers and Methodists* and *Women's Tragedies,* both based upon his Cornish background. *A Man and Moods* and *Make Believe* followed in 1896 and *The Happy Exile* in 1897. In 1904 he published his first and only book of poems, *100 Windows*. He lived at No. 49 Dulwich Road, Herne Hill. He died after a short illness in October 1906 at the age of 37 and was buried in West Norwood Cemetery.

Ida Lupino (1918–95)

Born into a theatrical family in Herne Hill, Ida made her first stage appearance with her cousin, Lupino Lane, in a children's theatre company run by her uncle, Stanley Lupino.

She began training at RADA in 1936 and a year later was offered her first acting role in *Her First Affair*. She moved to Hollywood and appeared in several films, among them *The Light that Failed*, *They Drove by Night*, *High Sierra* and *Ladies in Retirement*. She won the New York Film Critics Award for her performance in *The Hard Way*. In 1949 she set up a production company and directed films, among them *Not Wanted*, *The Bigamist* and *The Hitchhiker*. She appeared on television and also directed programmes, including episodes of *The Fugitive* and *The Untouchables*.

William Henry Margetson (1861–1940)

A successful landscape and figure painter, William was born on Denmark Hill and was educated at Dulwich College before attending the South Kensington and Royal Academy Schools.

He moved to Berkshire, where he married another artist called Helen Howard Hatton. He exhibited at the Royal Academy and the Royal Institute and also illustrated books. He worked for *The Graphic*, the *Pall Mall* and *Cassell's Family Magazine*.

Roddy McDowell (Roderick Andrew) (1928–98)

Roddy was born in Herne Hill in 1928 and lived in a house at the top of Herne Hill Road. He attended St Joseph's School in Upper Norwood and entered the film world at the age of ten. He was in a number of British films before going to Hollywood in 1940. His first American role was in *Confirm or Deny* which was followed by a memorable appearance as Huw, the youngest son of a Welsh mining family, in *How Green Was My Valley*. This was followed with roles in *The Pied Piper*, *Lassie Come Home*, *My Friend Flicka*, *Keys of the Kingdom*, *The White Cliffs of Dover*, *Kidnapped* and *Green Grass of Wyoming*.

He appeared on the stage in America, his debut being in *The Young Woodley*. After a period touring, he returned to Hollywood in 1962 for roles in *The Longest Day* and *Cleopatra*. Later he appeared in *Planet of the Apes* and its several sequels. He was in over 130 films and made many TV appearances. He received several awards for his acting, including, in 1985, the American Cinema Foundation Award.

Roddy was a keen photographer and published some of his works in *Double Exposure* (Vols I–IV) and made a large collection of film and Hollywood memorabilia. He visited England a number of times and on one occasion returned to Herne Hill. He was seen gazing sadly at his old home; he said he remembered how happy he had been there.

Euphemia 'Effie' Chalmer Millais (née Gray)

Born in Perth in 1828, Effie Gray married John Ruskin in 1847 when she was 19 years old. They first met when Effie stayed with the Ruskins in Herne Hill on

The terrace of houses to the left of the line of shops was built on the site of the former home of Elhanan Bicknell. At the time when Dr Edward Nicholson was resident it was called Carlton House after his childhood home.

Carlton Parade shops, Herne Hill, between Frankfurt and Elphindale Roads, c.2000. This early-Edwardian development remains structurally the same as when it was first built, but there is no longer a butcher, a dairy, a baker nor a carrier.

her way to boarding-school. Effie's father had purchased John James Ruskin's family home in Perth. It was for her that John wrote his only children's story, *King of the Golden River*.

The young couple initially lived with the Ruskins in their Denmark Hill home before travelling to Venice, where they spent their happiest time together. Eventually John and Effie moved to Herne Hill, next door to John's childhood home. By then the marriage was known to be unhappy and unsatisfactory.

The younger Ruskins and the Millais brothers spent a holiday in Scotland together. Millais, deeply in love with Effie, found it difficult to complete his commissioned portrait of John. Effie had been the model for his highly acclaimed painting, 'Order of Release'. During the holiday, the young people were visited by Dr Acland, Ruskin's friend from his Oxford days, who was appalled at John's neglect of his young wife. John and Effie's marriage was eventually annulled and Effie returned to her family in Perth. One year later she met Millais again and they married. They had eight children and lived in Kensington.

Edward Chambers Nicholson

The couple did not meet Ruskin again but distressed him considerably by attending one of his lectures and sitting in the front row. Effie never forgave John Ruskin, despite her remarriage. She took her revenge when the mothers of the two girls that Ruskin later wished to marry contacted her. Her answers prevented the marriages taking place.

Edward Chambers Nicholson (1827–1900)

Nicholson was the son of a successful grocer. On the death of his mother he was sent to live with an aunt in South Carlton, Lincolnshire. After schooling in Uxbridge, he entered the laboratory world and spent his working life advancing the range of chemicals used in the industries of photography and dyeing, particularly the production of magenta dye. When the process and results were exhibited at the International Exhibition of 1862 in South Kensington, it was reported that 'nothing could surpass the splendour of the magnificent crowns of crystals' that he 'had contributed to the Exhibition'.

He later entered into partnership with two friends and colleagues, setting up an aniline dye factory in the Southwark area. A few years later the business was sold and Edward Nicholson retired to a life of leisure and gardening in Herne Hill. In the early 1860s he had purchased Elhanan Bicknell's estate and named the house Carlton House after the home of his early childhood.

Sidney Pike (1864–1907)

Pike was a London-born artist who lived at No. 35 St Saviour's Villas, Herne Hill Road. He exhibited 40 paintings at art galleries in London, the first one at the Royal Academy in 1880 and his last there in 1901.

His paintings were particularly effective when portraying autumn, spring and winter. He preferred painting landscapes to portraits and when he moved to the South Coast he painted scenes of the New Forest and the Bournemouth and Christchurch areas, as well as scenes along the banks of the Rivers Avon and Stour.

He regularly exhibited at the Bournemouth Fine Arts Society Exhibitions and was able to sell his works privately.

Pike was a restless man and only returned to the London area in 1897. He lived at No. 69 Elizabeth Street in Belgravia but moved to Chelsea and died there in 1907.

Christopher Pond (1826–81)

With Felix Spiers, Pond introduced catering to the developing town of Melbourne in Australia and to the Melbourne-Ballarat Railway. He helped finance and organise the first highly successful cricketing tour of an English team to Australia in 1862.

On their return to England the partners opened a restaurant at Ludgate Hill and from there introduced catering facilities at the stations of the Metropolitan and District railway line. This expanded country-wide onto the railways, with dining cars and station buffets. Eventually there were over 200 buffets at mainline stations. He and his partner built a multi-purpose complex in Piccadilly called the Criterion Theatre, Restaurant and Banqueting Halls which was the fictional scene of Sherlock Holmes' first meeting with Dr Watson.

Christopher Pond lived at The Cedars on Herne Hill. He died in 1881 and was buried in the family mausoleum in the West Norwood Cemetery.

Sir Victor Sawden Pritchett (1900–96)

Journalist, novelist, short-story writer, acclaimed autobiographer, critic, lecturer and broadcaster, V.S. Pritchett was born in Suffolk but spent most of his life in London. His father was a salesman who moved from job to job before setting up 'in business' and his mother was somewhat fey and impractical. The family moved 18 times in 12 years but remained in Rosendale Road long enough to allow Victor to attend Rosendale Road School and then Alleyn's College for three years. At 15 years he entered the leather trade as an office boy, gradually climbing the firm's ladder until, at the age of 21, he migrated to Paris. There he worked as a salesman and photographer before entering the journalistic field via the *Christian Science Monitor*. He travelled to Ireland and Spain and then returned to London to make his home.

His first novel was published in 1929 but he is best known for his many short stories which appeared in *The New Statesman* and *The Cornhill*, and in several collections, the first in 1933. He was highly regarded in America, his collections were published by Random Press and his stories in the *New Yorker*. He was an honorary member of the American Academy of Arts and Letters and of the Academy of Arts and Sciences.

Pritchett wrote studies of other authors, including Balzac and Turgenev, and many critical reviews, which appeared mostly in the *New Statesman*, of which he was a director. He edited the 1981 *Oxford Book of Short Stories*. He wrote his highly acclaimed *Cab at the Door*, followed by *Midnight Oil*. He was vice-president of the Royal Society of Literature and continued to write almost to his death at home in London in 1996. He was knighted in 1975.

Pritchett lived in the vicinity of Herne Hill on two occasions. His family moved to the Coldharbour Lane area, near a pickle factory, a large bakery, the Camberwell Skating Rink and St Matthew's School. There he swung on ropes from lampposts around Loughborough Junction, walked into Brixton and East Street Markets, sung music hall songs, played marbles and had fights on Denmark Hill. He cheered King Edward and his Queen when they laid the foundation-stone of King's College Hospital and shortly afterwards saw black-edged posters announcing the King's death. His father was advised to send him to a 'better school' but there appeared another 'cab at the door'.

His second period in the Herne Hill area occurred in his early teens, when the family moved to the newly-developing Rosendale Road. Pritchett played football in Brockwell Park and attended Rosendale School. At 12 he was transferred to Alleyn's College and there acquired a reasonable knowledge of French and German. At the age of 15 he was sent to work in the leather trade. He travelled to work by way of London Bridge and Dulwich Stations. The family moved to Bromley following the Zeppelin bombing of London.

He considered it was his time in Rosendale School and then at Alleyn's that turned him into a journalist and writer. At the time of the proposed changes to the names of many of Lambeth's parks and open spaces he was horrified and asked that his name be added to the list of protesters.

Sax Rohmer (Arthur Sarsfield Ward) (1886–1959)

Sax Rohmer was born in Birmingham where he was a very reluctant but short-term civil servant. He was later a journalist who wrote mystery stories, his most successful being about the wicked Dr Fu Manchu and his adversary, the Englishman, Nayland Smith.

Sax Rohmer is reputed to have spent many hours in Limehouse talking to a mysterious tall Chinese man called Mr King. He is said to have based the character of Dr Fu Manchu upon this gentleman. He also wrote another series about a detective, Morris Klaw, who solved his cases by sleeping at the crime scene.

He made a fortune from his books and later sold the rights to television, radio and film networks. His books were translated into many languages and sold in countless thousands – the several Fu Manchu films had a very popular following.

He married the sister of one of the Crazy Gang (Teddy Knox) and lived for a number of years at No. 51 Herne Hill on the corner of Danecroft Road.

There is now a blue plaque commemorating his residence; it was the first to be erected in Herne Hill. One day, the present owner of the house was clearing the attic and found some old printers' proofs which were later found to be the work of Sax Rohmer. It was her persistent campaign that resulted in the placing of the blue plaque in October 1985.

The Ruskin Family

John James Ruskin (born in Scotland in 1785) and Margaret Cox (born in Croydon in 1781) were first cousins. When Margaret was 20 years old she moved to Scotland to live with her uncle and aunt and there adopted her aunt's strict Presbyterianism. John James was then 16 years old. The two became friends and before John James left the family home in Perth for London they became engaged to be married. After initial difficulties in commerce, John James entered into a partnership in the wine business.

The firm Ruskin, Telford & Domecq had the agency of a Spanish sherry business. John Ruskin said later that his father knew more about sherry than any man alive. Eventually, John James made a fortune which supported a very comfortable lifestyle with Continental travel and the purchase of works of art. The couple only had one son, whose overindulgent upbringing enabled him to live life in an eccentric way without the necessity of earning a living.

John James and Margaret lived in Hunter Street after their marriage and one year later John was born. From then on their lives revolved around him. John James encouraged all his interests and perhaps unconsciously wished his son to fulfil some of his own frustrated ambitions. On John's birth, his mother dedicated him to the 'service of God' and decided he was to be a clergyman. Margaret educated him in the way she considered suitable, but in fact deprived him of much of the social and educational experience essential for a normal childhood.

In 1823 the family moved to No. 28 Herne Hill where they lived until John James felt a larger house was necessary to cope with the entertaining which accompanied John's growing reputation. In 1843, after considerable searching, John James purchased a house on Denmark Hill.

Margaret and John often accompanied John James on his business travels around the country and later the family travelled for pleasure on the Continent. When John attended university at Oxford, Margaret took rooms nearby and every weekend John James travelled to Oxford to be with his family.

When John's marriage to Effie Gray failed, John James arranged the annulment. John destroyed all evidence of Effie's presence and the family went on another Continental tour. The parents had not desired the marriage, although John James had settled an allowance on Effie. Margaret Ruskin had interfered on many occasions having always found it difficult to accept John's friendships with girls or women.

John James died in 1864. John felt guilty at his father's death, but also felt that he had never been allowed to be 'young'.

John James was an honourable and kind man. Those working in the domestic field often remained for many years. He left a considerable fortune to John who gave much of it away, sometimes in ways that would not have pleased his father.

Margaret Ruskin died in 1871 and joined her husband in the Shirley parish churchyard. John James had chosen the resting place because he had found flowers blooming there that had grown near his childhood home.

The home on Denmark Hill was soon sold and John departed for Brantwood via the lecture halls and rooms of Oxford University.

John Ruskin (1819–1900) lived through the reigns of three monarchs – George IV, William IV and Victoria. He was born in Hunter Street but four years later the family moved to No. 28 Herne Hill. His mother was his first teacher (he had to read a chapter of the Bible each day) but later he had additional tuition and spent a period at a Grove Lane Boys' School. His life was strictly controlled with no toys and no culinary treats and he was largely isolated from other children. Thus, he never learned to compete, converse or share with those of his own age. He saw his only friend during school holidays.

His father indulged John's interests in poetry, geology and painting; he had painting lessons from local artists Copley Fielding and James Harding. On family travels John James arranged for his son to see clients' art collections and grew to think most other children paled beside his exceptional son. Before entering Oxford as a 'commoner', John was compelled to attend King's College, The Strand, to redress the deficiencies in his educational standard.

At Oxford John gained the Newdigate Prize for Poetry, his father researching the subject for him. He was able to decide not to be a clergyman and met Henry Acland, who was to become a lifelong and wholly beneficial friend. Because John's time at Oxford was interrupted by a period of poor health, he gained only an 'Honorary Double 4th degree'.

Following John's graduation from Oxford the family began a Continental tour, during which time John wrote *Modern Painters* – largely a defence of Turner whom John had met when 14 years old and whose work he greatly admired. On Turner's death in 1851, John was named one of his executors. The book was an immediate critical success and over the years was followed by other volumes on various aspects of art and architecture.

John's relations with girls and women were uneasy and he came to prefer his relationships to be with older, married women or young girls, presenting no sexual challenge. His marriage to Effie Gray was disastrous and ended in annulment, and his relationship with the very young Rose la Touche was destructive for both and led to breakdowns in health. John's inability to have satisfactory relationships with women contributed to the frequent bouts of ill health he suffered, which eventually returned him to the control of a domineering woman. Nevertheless, when visited towards the end of his life by Charles Norton, an American friend, Norton said 'although old and stooping,' he was 'still one of the most interesting men in the world.'

He was considered a leading authority in the art world; his lecturing and interest in teaching led to his involvement with the Working Men's College and to his appointment as the First Slade Professor of Fine Art at Oxford.

He was responsible for many projects, including the founding of the Guild of St George in Sheffield, the Ruskin School of Drawing, the Art Collection at Oxford and the endowment of a Mastership of Drawing. He donated many works of art to various bodies and wrote many papers on the subject of art, as well as papers for the working man, which were later published in book form.

When his parents died, John sold the house on Denmark Hill and moved to Brantwood in the Lake District. There he spent the last 30 years of his life, occasionally touring on the Continent and visiting the Severns' house on Herne Hill, where his old nursery was kept in readiness for his visits which became infrequent towards the end of the 1880s.

To cater for the Severn family's needs he enlarged Brantwood and his estate. He became interested in local affairs and wrote his autobiography called *Praeterita*.

When he died, the press clamoured for burial in Westminster Abbey but his wish to lie in Coniston was respected.

A memorial to him was unveiled in St Paul's Church, Herne Hill, by William Holman Hunt, the last of the Pre-Raphaelites, and was constructed of 'Stones of Venice'.

John's wish that Brantwood and his treasures should be open to the public was not honoured for many years, in part because the terms of the will made its opening financially difficult.

Kathleen Saintsbury

Kathleen was the daughter of H.A. Saintsbury, actor and producer. He was the first Sherlock Holmes on the stage, a role he played no fewer than 1,400 times; his young messenger boy was Charlie Chaplin. As a child, Kathleen had been a member of Bramsby Williams' Company touring Canada. He was a friend of her father and had promised that whilst in his care he would ensure no harm came to her. Kathleen said Bramsby had kept his word and was immensely kind to her. She felt a deep affection and gratitude to her friend and mentor.

When she heard that he was alone and ill, she immediately retired from her theatre life and moved to Herne Hill. Kathleen said, years later, that the ending of her career was but a small price to pay for the gladness she felt in being able to return a little of the great kindness he had shown to her during her young life.

On one of Charlie Chaplin's rare visits to this country, Kathleen attended a reception given for him. He told her how pleased he was to meet her again and how warmly he remembered her father and the encouragement he gave at the beginning of his own long career.

Arthur Severn (1848–1931)

Arthur was the son of Joseph Severn and was befriended by John Ruskin. He travelled with him and Albert Goodwin on painting trips in the 1870s. He had spent time in Rome where his father later became British consul and was fluent in both English and Italian. He married Joan Agnew, a distant cousin of Ruskin, having been compelled to wait three years before proposing. From then onwards he lived either at Ruskin's childhood home (No. 28 Herne Hill), the lease of which was given to Joan as a wedding present, or at Brantwood in the Lake District.

Although a member of the Royal Institute and exhibiting many works, he never realised his potential as an artist because of the demands made upon him by his relationship with Ruskin and the financial difficulties of living between Herne Hill and Brantwood.

The marriage, which lasted for 55 years, was happy and produced five children. His final years were spent at No. 9 Warwick Square, London, where the family moved when the extended lease on the Herne Hill house lapsed.

He was buried at Coniston, next to the grave of his wife and favourite daughter, itself next to the Ruskin grave.

He is best known in Herne Hill for his paintings of the Denmark Hill and Herne Hill homes of Ruskin, particularly the two front views. As with many Victorian and Edwardian artists, his work was considered out of date after the end of the First World War but now his views of London are often reproduced on Christmas and birthday cards.

Joan Severn (née Agnew) (1846–1924)

Joan Severn was born into a family in straitened circumstances and was a distant relative of the Ruskins. At the age of 17 she visited the family on Denmark Hill for a fortnight and stayed a lifetime. She became companion and housekeeper to Ruskin's mother and indispensable to John.

She married Arthur Severn and was given the lease of Ruskin's childhood home on Herne Hill as a wedding present, from where she could oversee the Denmark Hill home. This arrangement did not last long as Mrs Ruskin died and John sold the Denmark Hill property.

During her married life the family moved constantly between Herne Hill and Brantwood, which was considerably extended to accommodate the needs of the five children.

Throughout the last 15 years of Ruskin's life, Joan was his constant companion, in some cases overprotecting him and preventing open contact with old friends. The terms of Ruskin's will as far as Brantwood was concerned were unclear and made it financially difficult to carry out his intentions. Consequently, the Severns had financial problems.

Joan Severn died at Brantwood in 1924 and was buried at Coniston with her daughter, who had died earlier, in a grave next to John Ruskin's.

Henry Simmonds (1818–98)

Born the son of a corn merchant in Maidstone, Henry Simmonds was apprenticed in 1832 for seven years to Joshua Johnson of the City Livery Company of Skinners. This was one of the original 12 great livery companies of the City. The Skinners were originally fur traders but for many years had not traded in this way; at the time of writing their work is mainly charitable.

In June 1839 Henry was admitted to the freedom of the company and later in the same year to the livery. He married and had five children. Following his first wife's death, Henry Simmonds remarried and moved to Aylesford House, Denmark Hill at the junction with Herne Hill. The couple had three daughters and the youngest, Alice Mary, was born whilst Henry was master of the Company of Skinners in 1871. At the christening ceremony, held in the Company's Court, a 'service of plate' to the value of 100 guineas was presented to her. Years later, after her father's death, she was admitted to the freedom of the company by patrimony. A son by the first marriage had already been admitted and members of the family for several generations have since been admitted.

Henry Simmonds was a City man who travelled daily to his place of business by carriage and sent his daughters to a local academy run by respectable single ladies. He supported many charitable causes, among them the Royal Home for Incurables. When he died, Alice Mary inherited his 'votes' for the admission of patients to the home. He was a great friend of Benjamin Disraeli and when it was founded in 1880 became an active member of the Primrose League – there was a branch in Norwood to which Alice Mary was elected a daughter. Henry Simmonds was a kindly and generous man. His grandson told how he and his mother went to see one of his grandfather's 'sea captains' who had married their head housemaid, for whom Henry had purchased a small house.

Aylesford House was set in substantial grounds. There was a home farm with cows and dairy and a large kitchen garden. It is thought that the house was named after the Kentish village near which he had spent his childhood.

After Henry's death in 1895, his wife continued to live there until she died. When the lease lapsed in 1902 the house was demolished and the site remained vacant for some years.

Alice Mary eventually married a solicitor called Francis Spencer Lewin. Two of his sisters were among the first trained female doctors and both served during the First World War in a hospital in Dieppe. Another sister was the wife of the Lord Chancellor in Asquith's 1916 Cabinet. John Everett Millais had lodged with the family at No. 25 Wimpole Street, whilst attending the Royal Academy Schools and awaiting his parents' return to England.

William Strudwick (1835–1910)

Born in the Edgware Road, William Strudwick lived variously in Newington, Thurlow Park and from 1890 at No. 12 Kestrel Avenue (now No. 44). He later moved to Croydon where he died in 1910. He was an exceptional photographer and in the 1860s recorded the area of old Lambeth which was lost under the new Thames embankment.

A collection of his photographs is held at the Lambeth Archives Department and another at the Royal Doulton Pottery Archives at Stoke.

Sir Mortimer Wheeler (1890–1976)

Born in Glasgow, the son of a journalist, Mortimer's early years were spent in Saltaire, where he studied the classics and became interested in archaeology. When the family moved to London he educated himself at museums and galleries before enrolling at University College in 1907. He became a Master of the Arts and gained a doctorate in literature, winning the Franks Scholarship in 1913. At the outbreak of war he joined the Royal Field Artillery, serving at Passendale in Italy and later in Germany. He won a Military Cross and a mention in dispatches.

He was appointed to the Royal Commission of Historic Monuments and took a post at the National Museum of Wales, excavating Welsh sites and then publishing *Prehistoric and Roman Wales*. Between 1934 and '37 he carried out his most famous excavation at Maiden Castle, publishing the results.

At the outbreak of the Second World War, Mortimer rejoined the Royal Artillery and was in the Eighth Army as a colonel and brigadier. In 1943 he was appointed Director General of Archaeology in India and later trained staff to excavate in Pakistan.

On leaving the Army he was honorary secretary, president, trustee and professor on a number of boards, institutes and at universities, and was the recipient of many honours. He published numerous books on archaeology and excavations.

Mortimer died in July 1976. He was a leading light in archaeology, but for the man on the street was best known for his participation in the radio and TV programmes 'Animal, Vegetable and Mineral'.

His family lived in Dulwich for years, but later moved to No. 12 Rollscourt Avenue. The house and its neighbours were destroyed during bombing in the Second World War. A small complex of maisonettes was later built on the site.

Bramsby Williams (1870–1961)

Bramsby Williams was born in Hackney and intended to become a missionary. He was instead diverted to a stage career via employment with a firm of tea merchants.

In 1896 he made his appearance on the London music hall stage and was an immediate success. Soon he appeared at the Tivoli and the Paragon and at other London and provincial music halls.

The following year he began his famous studies of Charles Dickens' characters, Mr Micawber, Peggotty and Fagin, and then moved on to monologues: *How we Saved the Barge, For a Woman's Sake, The Green Eye of the Little Yellow God* and *The Stage Doorkeeper*.

In 1903 he was invited to Sandringham by Edward VII, where he entertained with his mimicry and his Dickens' characterisations. He was one of those who was able to adapt to the changes that took place over the years. He made many appearances on the variety stage as well as touring in such plays as *The Shop at Sly Corner*, appearing on TV and in films. He published his autobiography in 1954.

His last years were dogged by ill health. He lived in a flat in the Mansions at the foot of Herne Hill and was cared for by Kathleen Saintsbury. He died in December 1961 at the age of 91.

Captain James Wilson (1760–1814)

James Wilson was born in 1760, the youngest of 19 children. He followed in his father's footsteps and went to sea. He crossed the Atlantic and fought in the Battles of Bunkers Hill and Long Island, returned to England and became a mate on an East Indiaman.

Lambeth Palace, St Mary's at Lambeth and Lambeth Pier. Charles Woolley lived in Dulwich Road for years and was a churchwarden of St Mary's. He conducted a very successful campaign to save Lambeth Pier when it was threatened with demolition.

He sailed to India but disembarked to set up a supply business. When the British troops were hemmed in by Hyder Ali's army and the French fleet, he was able to reach them with supplies on a number of occasions but, when taking them ammunition, he was captured by the French. At first he was treated reasonably well but the French commander sold the British prisoners to Hyder Ali for 300,000 rupees. James Wilson attempted to escape but was recaptured and, like other prisoners, was subjected to appalling cruelty, starvation, disease and torture. Only 30 of the men survived the ordeal and they were extremely ill.

When James Wilson recovered reasonably good health, he set about rebuilding his fortune and finally returned to England. On the journey he met a Baptist missionary with whom he had many arguments. He purchased a residence in Hampshire and began to enjoy country life and his new friends. Among them was another Baptist and as a result of long discussions and argument he was converted.

His past experiences enabled him to advise on the purchase of the *Duff*, the ship that was to take missionaries to the Pacific. It set sail in August 1796 with James Wilson as its captain. The voyage took two years and when he returned to England the people were glad to hear the first real news of their missionaries and the reception they had received. He was made a director of the new Missionary Society. He led a quiet life, for he had never fully recovered

his health after the extreme privations he had suffered in captivity. He bought No. 170 Denmark Hill in 1799 and became a deacon at his Walworth Road Church. He married a Miss Holbert and had five children. He died in August 1814 having been described as 'an indulgent husband, a kind and faithful parent and a considerate and pious master.'

The house on Denmark Hill was later owned by the Beneckes, with whom Felix Mendelssohn stayed in the 1840s. It was one of eight houses described as 'recently erected' by the young Mr Edwards in 1789, and was later demolished to make way for Ruskin Park. All that is left of the attractive house is the portico-cum-shelter, covered by an ancient and very beautiful wisteria, a sight to see in springtime.

Charles Woolley (1846–1922)

Charles Woolley was born the son of a doctor in Clapham. He was educated privately and then at King's College, London. He was an accomplished cricketer, oarsman and boxer when young and throughout his life maintained an interest in sporting events.

He was a City man, a director, president and vice-president, fellow, trustee, chairman and member of institutes, companies, associations, societies and clubs. He was master of the Worshipful Company of Turners and a fellow of the Royal Geographical Society, an author, local journalist, and he patented several of his own inventions. He was a councillor

Left: *Charles Woolley*

for the ward of Tulse Hill and one of Lambeth's first aldermen. He parted company with Lambeth Council when he opposed the selling of the Pedlar's Acre to the LCC for the site of the proposed County Hall. The Pedlar's Acre had been bequeathed to Lambeth Vestry in the 1600s by a pedlar who had taken refuge in the porch of St Mary's, Lambeth, and later prospered.

Charles was a licensed lay reader and churchwarden of St Mary's and a member of the Southwark Diocesan Conference. He was on the board of Waterloo Hospital and trustee, governor and member of local trusts including the Brixton Dispensary. He was involved in many events, such as the dinner for the poor at the time of Edward VII's Coronation, and in the saving of the old Lambeth Pier.

He was an authority on the history and architecture of London churches and over the years had made large collections of prints, maps, photographs, stoneware and glassware which he gave to Lambeth Council, hoping that it would form the basis of a Museum of Lambeth. When the Burroughs & Wellcome Physiological Laboratory moved from Brockwell Park, he proposed that the vacant house should become a museum. Unfortunately, he died suddenly before this could become a fact. The house was demolished and the grounds were converted to parkland.

Charles Woolley spent all his life in Lambeth. For part of his married life he lived in Haycroft Road, Brixton, and then moved to No. 35 Dulwich Road, just opposite St Jude's Church.

He was buried in West Norwood Cemetery, but unfortunately his grave was destroyed during the time of Lambeth Council's clearance policy.

VISITORS

Sir Henry Wentworth Acland (1815–1900)

Henry Acland was educated at Harrow and became a fellow of All Souls and an honorary student at Christ Church, Oxford. He studied medicine at St George's Hospital and was a gold medallist for Medical Jurisprudence. He was awarded fellowship of the Royal College of Physicians in 1850. He became professor of clinical medicine in 1851 and Radcliffe Librarian and was Regius Professor of Medicine at Oxford from 1858 until 1894. He was mainly respon-

sible for the founding of the medical school at the university and founding the Oxford Museum and Science Library. He was president of the General Medical Council from 1874 until 1887 and published papers on sanitation and medical education.

In 1860 he travelled to America as honorary physician to the Prince of Wales and was made a Knight Companion of the British Empire in 1884. He met John Ruskin at Oxford in the early 1840s and was a close and loyal friend to him. The two spent time together at Denmark Hill and in Oxford on many occasions.

Acland Crescent was named after him some 30 years after his death in 1900.

General William Booth (1829–1912)

Booth was the founder of the revivalist movement known from 1878 as the Salvation Army. The son of a Nottingham builder, William Booth possessed a rare eloquence and awareness of the needs of the poor in social and religious life. He underwent a religious conversion in a Wesleyan chapel in Nottingham in 1844 and, after a short period as a minister on Tyneside, he moved south and in 1865 founded the Revivalist Christian Mission in Whitechapel.

Shortly after his arrival in London, he was invited to preach at the Water Lane home of the Fosberys where he met his future wife, Catherine Mumford.

Although some of his officers were at times arrested for preaching in the open air, they continued their war against poverty, sweated labour and child prostitution, gradually helping to bring about a change of opinion.

In 1905 he was made a Freeman of the City of London. He received an honorary doctorate at Oxford, was a guest at the Coronation of Edward VII and opened a session of the Senate in America with prayers.

When he died in 1912, it is said that his funeral disrupted the City's traffic for most of the day – as it passed the Mansion House, the Lord Mayor was on the steps to do him honour. He was buried in the Nonconformist cemetery, Abney Park. Outside thousands of people gathered to pay their last respects.

The children of the Booth family followed their parents' footsteps into the mission. In the 1980s, the minister of the Railton Road Methodist Church visited Catherine Bramwell Booth, who was then over 100 years old. She was pleased to hear news of the Railton Road Methodists and remembered her grandparents speaking of their first meeting in Water Lane.

Sir Edward Coley Burne-Jones (1833–98)

Born into an influential family in Birmingham that included Rudyard Kipling and Stanley Baldwin, Edward became associated with the Pre-Raphaelites after meeting Rossetti and helping to decorate the walls of the Oxford Union.

He met William Morris and helped found the firm of Morris, Marshall, Faulkner & Co. He lived for a while in Rottingdean near his cousin Rudyard Kipling, before moving to The Grays in Fulham.

He travelled to Italy with John Ruskin in 1864. A loyal friend and supporter, he gave evidence for him in the Ruskin/Whistler trial and, at a time when Ruskin was having difficulty with the Severns, offered to build him a house in the grounds of his home.

He was fascinated by classical mythology. Most of his paintings reflected this interest and are thus immediately recognisable. Later, he illustrated books for Morris and the Kelmscott Press.

He was awarded the Legion of Honour and was knighted in 1894. He died in Fulham in 1898, an international figure.

Sir Henry Hallett Dale OM (1875–1968)

Henry Dale was educated at Leys School and Trinity College, Cambridge, taking his medical training at St Bartholomew's Medical School, London.

In 1904 he was appointed by Sir Henry Wellcome to the Physiological Research Laboratories at Brockwell Park. Two years later he became director, researching into ergot alkaloids with a team of pharmacologists. This work was to lead, in 1936, to a shared award of a Nobel Prize in Physiology and Medicine.

In 1914, just prior to the outbreak of the First World War, he and two colleagues left the park laboratories to become the nucleus of a body that later became the Medical Research Council.

He became a fellow of the Royal Society in 1914 and its president from 1940 until 1945. He served on the National Institute for Medical Research from 1928 until 1942, was a member of the General Medical Council for a decade from 1927 and a member of the Medical Research Council from 1942 until 1946. He was also a trustee of the British Museum from 1940 until 1963 and president of the British Council from 1950 until 1963.

He was knighted in 1932, having been made a Companion of the British Empire in 1919, and received the Order of Merit in 1944. He was presented with many awards and honours all over the world.

Sir Henry was one of the five original trustees appointed by Henry Wellcome when he set up The Wellcome Trust and, two years after the death of the founder in 1936, he became chairman of the trust until 1960.

Joseph Deakin (1879–1969)

Born in Skelton, Olympic gold medallist Joseph Deakin won his first race at a meeting celebrating Queen Victoria's Jubilee in 1887. He continued

Joe Deakin, 1901, with the medals and cups he won when he was with the Rifle Brigade in Northern Ireland.

running all his life, despite being gassed and blinded during the First World War. He joined the Army at the age of 18 and when stationed in Ireland won the national steeplechase and the one- and four-mile races at the same meeting.

Whilst serving in the Boer War he seriously injured his foot but on return to England joined the Herne Hill Harriers and trained at the Herne Hill Stadium.

He competed in and won national and international events and in 1908 he took part in the Olympics, winning his team event by 50 yards.

He worked until the age of 79 years and kept himself fit by continuing to run until his 90th year, when he competed in winter handicap races at the Surrey Athletic club.

He lived in the Loughborough Junction area, frequently visiting his married daughter, Josie Cleverly, and her family in Heron Road, very close to the site of the Herne Hill Harriers' first base at the Milkwood Road Tavern. Later, he and his wife moved to Tulse Hill where they shared a house with a younger daughter.

Stephen Poynter Denning (1795–1864)

Stephen Denning was keeper of the Dulwich Picture Gallery from 1821 until his death in Dulwich in 1864. He was an established portrait miniaturist and his best known painting was 'Princess Victoria – aged Four'. Bought by the gallery, it became particularly popular at the time of the Queen's death. He exhibited at the Royal Academy and at the British Institute in Suffolk Street.

He was a close friend of both Elhanan Bicknell and David Roberts and a frequent visitor to the Bicknells' Herne Hill home.

In 1841 he was commissioned to paint all but the two youngest children of Lucinda and Elhanan in their drawing-room. In the painting the cedar planted by Elhanan in 1818 can be seen through the window. The original painting is now in the print room of the Victoria & Albert Museum.

Charles Dickens (1812–70)

Charles Dickens was born in Portsmouth. His early life was marred by his father's imprisonment for debt in Marshalsea Prison and time spent in a blacking factory.

He later studied shorthand whilst working as an office boy, becoming a parliamentary reporter for *The Morning Chronicle*. He contributed articles to other papers and periodicals, republishing these as *Sketches by Boz*. His monthly instalments of the *Posthumous Papers of the Pickwick Club* were later produced in volume form. He was then only 25 years old. Whilst editing *Bentley's Miscellany* he serialised *Oliver Twist* and from then on continued editing publications and serialising his novels, many of which portrayed aspects of crime and the difficult social conditions of the age.

He led an exhausting life. Although his marriage ended in separation, he had a large family and a wide circle of friends. He toured the United States and Britain giving dramatic readings of his works, but had time for amateur dramatics and for philanthropic works, often in support of impecunious friends. He died suddenly in 1870, leaving *The Mystery of Edwin Drood* unsolved and unfinished.

His works were illustrated by a number of distinguished artists, among them Hablot Knight Brown (Phiz). Through Phiz, he visited the Herne Hill home of Elhanan Bicknell, as did other illustrators, George Cruickshank, George Cattermole and John Leech.

Dickens was also a friend of David Roberts, his daughter Christine, and son-in-law Henry Bicknell. The children of both families frequently went on holiday together.

Anthony Vandyke Copley Fielding (1787–1855)

Fielding was born into a family of artists. He was a teacher of art and a watercolourist who was very successful in his lifetime. In 1831 he was appointed President of the Society of Painters in Watercolour.

For a while he lived in the Camberwell area and the young John Ruskin was one of his pupils. He attended the Sunday morning gatherings held at the Bicknells' house on Herne Hill. Later, he would occasionally dine with the Ruskins at their home on Denmark Hill. His paintings hung on the walls of both the Ruskin and Bicknell homes. Those in the Bicknell collection were sold at the time of the record-breaking auction at Christie and Mansons, which took place some three years after Elhanan's death.

Dr Alexander Thomas Glenny, FRS (1882–1965)

An eminent immunologist, Alexander Glenny was born locally and was educated at Alleyn's College, Dulwich, from where he was recruited to work in the Wellcome Physiological Research Laboratories in Brockwell Park, moving with them to Beckenham, Kent, in 1922.

In 1904, at the age of 22, he began his life's work on the production of antisera and for 40 years led a team working on the control of infectious diseases through vaccination and immunisation. Glenny and his two colleagues were the first to suggest that children could be immunised against diphtheria and this led in 1939 to the immunisation of schoolchildren, practically eliminating the disease in Britain.

During the First World War, his team was able to produce large amounts of tetanus and diphtheria antitoxins, anti-gas sera and typhoid vaccines for the Armed Forces. Before and during the Second World War, the laboratories produced antitoxins which enabled members of the Forces to be protected from disease, particularly tetanus and those diseases prevalent in the tropics.

In 1944 Glenny was elected a fellow of the Royal Society and eight years later received the Jenner Medal of the Royal Society of Medicine. In 1955 he was given the Addingham Medal 'to the individual who has made the most valuable discovery for relieving pain and suffering in humanity.' He died at Fetcham, near Leatherhead, in October 1965.

Louis Haghe (1806–85)

Louis Haghe was born in Tournai, Belgium, the son of an architect. After a period at a drawing academy, he was apprenticed to a lithographer. As a result of teaching an Englishman the process, he was persuaded to migrate to England. His brother, Charles, also an artist, joined him.

Louis Haghe entered into partnership with a publisher called William Day of Lincoln's Inn Field and over the years his work raised the art of lithography to the highest level. His best known was the translation of the drawings of David Roberts, made on journeys to Spain, Egypt and the Holy Land. These were published over the years but later came together in books as *Picturesque Sketches of Spain* and *Sketches of the Holy Land, Syria and Egypt*. His work was the more remarkable because his right hand had been paralysed since birth.

Louis Haghe was also a successful watercolourist, which gradually became more important in his life. Like David Roberts, he had royal patronage and some of his work is still in the Royal Collection. He often travelled on the Continent with David Roberts, Samuel Prout and Clarkson Stanfield, and visited the Bicknell house on several occasions. His brother was always a constant companion.

He married, had a family and subsequently died in 1885. He was buried in the family grave in West Norwood Cemetery, not far from the graves of David Roberts and Samuel Prout. Years before, not long after the cemetery was opened, he had produced a lithograph of its entrance, drawn from the burial ground of St Luke's Church, West Norwood, just opposite.

William Holman Hunt OM (1827–1910)

Born in Cheapside, Holman Hunt entered the Royal Academy Schools of Art in 1844, later being elected an academician.

He was one of the founder members of the Pre-Raphaelite movement which was much derided by critics, including some of the Academy members. The movement's fortune changed for the better when John Ruskin wrote a letter to *The Times* in their support. Holman Hunt remained true to the movement's principles all his life.

His most famous picture is probably 'The Light of the World', copies of which were hung in churches and chapels throughout the country – one was hung in St Paul's Church, Herne Hill, and another in St Paul's Cathedral. Many of his pictures are still well known, including 'The Finding of Christ in the Temple', 'London Bridge', 'The Lady of Shalott', 'The Hireling Shepherd' and 'The Scapegoat'.

He remained a lifelong friend of both Millais and John Ruskin. He was also a friend of David Roberts but was critical of his painting 'The Simoon' because the Sphinx was placed untruthfully against the sunset. However, Dickens, for whom it was painted, praised it for its 'poetic concept'.

In February 1901, Holman Hunt unveiled the memorial in St Paul's Church to John Ruskin. Some 100 years later the memorial is still in evidence.

Holman Hunt was a frequent visitor to the Ruskins' home. He died in 1910 and was cremated, his ashes being interred in St Paul's Cathedral.

Adelaide Ironside (1831–67)

Adelaide Ironside was born in Sydney, Australia. She was the first Australian to travel to Europe to study art, intending to remain for ten years. She arrived in England in 1855 with letters of introduction from a well-known Republican Scottish minister, Dr Lang, to, among others, Sir James Clark (physician to John Keats and Queen Victoria – later to be her own doctor) and Joseph Severn. She travelled to Rome in January 1856 and soon established a reputation as a spiritualist medium and began

The headstone marking Adelaide Eliza Ironside's grave. She died of consumption in Rome in 1867 and was eventually buried in West Norwood Cemetery, as was her mother who died shortly afterwards. Co-lateral descendants of Adelaide and her mother and Australian friends organised and attended the laying of the new stone in 1985.

painting pictures seen in a crystal ball. Her mother persuaded her to pursue a more conventional occupation and she began to paint to support herself and her mother. In 1858 she studied fresco painting in Perugia, planning to fresco the walls of the new Parliament building and the university on her return to Sydney.

She met Joseph Severn, then living in Rome, and he became her friend and supporter. She also met the Prince of Wales who visited her studio and bought a painting for £500. She was granted a Papal audience, was awarded a silver medal and given permission to study private Vatican pictures.

She returned to London in 1862, and exhibited at the International Exhibition in Kensington, where her pictures were viewed to acclaim. They had previously been shown to William Leaf of Park Hill, Streatham, who was very impressed. She was asked to visit but was unfortunately ill and was advised to return to the warmer climes of Rome. She was heartened to find she had been elected a member of the Academy of Quirities but was frustrated that her home town would not purchase the pictures she had painted for it.

In 1865 she painted 'The Adoration of the Magi', which was exhibited in London and then in Dublin. Whilst staying with the Leaf family at Park Hill she met John Ruskin and became a friend and pupil. He often visited her at Park Hill or sent his carriage for her. She would have lessons at his Denmark Hill home or go driving with Joan Agnew, with whom she became firm friends. Mrs Ruskin found it hard to accept Adelaide's friendship with her son, although eventually she 'began to like her more'.

Adelaide's health was worsening. Sir James Clark recommended returning to Rome, but there her health continued to deteriorate and she died in April 1867. Among the condolences received by her mother were those from Joseph Severn, John Ruskin, Sir James Clark and the Prince of Wales.

Her mother returned to England to await passage to Australia but she too died of consumption the following year and both were buried in West Norwood Cemetery, the expenses being borne by William Leaf.

Felix Mendelssohn (Bartholdy) (1809–47)

Mendelssohn was born in Hamburg. His family fled to Berlin at the time of the French occupation, taking the name of Bartholdy and adopting the Christian faith.

Mendelssohn had every advantage in life – a loving and rich family, an excellent education and cultural upbringing. He was handsome, charming and fluent in several languages. He was a talented artist, a masterly pianist and organist, a very good conductor and a composer of works.

By the age of 20 he had composed symphonies and an opera and one of the finest Shakespearean compositions (the overture to *A Midsummer Night's*

Dream). He had conducted a performance of Bach's 'St Matthew's Passion', the first since the composer's death, which had to be repeated because more than 1,000 people had had to be turned away. He toured extensively in Europe, introducing his own and other composers' music to many. For a while he was director of Dusseldorf's musical life and then director of Leipzig's Gewandhaus Orchestra, later founding its conservatoire. But with the ascension of a new Prussian king, he was compelled to become director of the music department of the new Academy of Berlin, to compose to order, and therefore had to arrange for the Leipzig concerts to be conducted by others.

He found the pressure intense and was relieved to visit England to conduct concerts with the Philharmonic Society. He was finally able to leave Berlin to live in Frankfurt but shortly afterwards had a stroke. He was ill for several months. One day, feeling stronger, he went for a walk but it tired him too much. He had another stroke and died. It was said that an awful stillness prevailed in Leipzig – people felt that their king had died. Writing later, Groves (of *Musical Dictionary* and Crystal Palace fame) said of him, 'Never, perhaps, could any man be found in whose life there were so few things to conceal or to regret.'

Mendelssohn visited England on at least 11 occasions. The people took him to their hearts and he returned the affection by composing for them the first book of *Songs without Words* and organ sonatas. Two of his oratorios were given their first performances in England ('St Paul' and 'Elijah') and from his Scottish tour came 'The Hebridean Overture' and his 'Scottish Symphony'.

On his first visit, following an injury to his foot, he was invited to recover at Roselawn, the Norwood home of Thomas Attwood, organist at St Paul's Cathedral and a former pupil of Mozart. During this time, Mendelssohn gave an organ recital at St Paul's. The audience would not let him go, despite repeated encores, so the verger withdrew the organ blower, letting the air out of the organ.

On each visit to England he became more popular. All the musical world wished to meet him, but at times he withdrew from the public. On one of the last visits, he and his wife stayed with the Beneckes, banker relatives of his wife, at their home on Denmark Hill, the site of which is now in Ruskin Park. To amuse the children he played the piano and while so doing composed 'Camberwell Green' which later became known as 'The Spring Song'. There is a pedestal in Ruskin Park to commemorate his visit.

Sir John Everett Millais (1829–96)

Millais was born in Southampton but spent his childhood in Jersey and Brittany. At the very young age of 11 he was admitted to the Royal Academy Schools. Until his family's return to England he boarded with the Lewin family in Wimpole Street. The younger son of the family was later to marry the daughter of Henry Simmonds. The son of that marriage inherited drawings, sketched by Millais, of the younger members of the Lewin family at play.

Millais was a founder member of the Pre-Raphaelite movement. His picture 'Lorenzo and Isabella' was one of the movement's first, based on a poem by Keats. His 'Christ in the House of his Parents' was strongly criticised, but following Ruskin's letter in support of the movement, his fortunes changed.

Millais met the Ruskins 'for breakfast' and they became friends. They visited each other often before going on holiday to Scotland together, accompanied by Millais' brother. He had been commissioned to paint John but found it difficult for he had fallen in love with Effie. His portrait of John hung in the drawing-room of the Ruskins' house on Denmark Hill – John's father had wished to throw it out but John said it was good and had cost money so it was kept.

Millais did not meet Effie again until a year after the young Ruskins' marriage had been annulled, although shortly after their return from Scotland he had painted her younger sister.

Millais and Effie married in 1855. They were both in their mid-twenties. The first years of their successful marriage were spent in Perth and they later had eight children.

During the 1860s Millais illustrated several of Anthony Trollope's books and the two became close friends. Despite Dickens' vehement criticism of Millais' 'Christ in the House of his Parents' they were close friends.

One of his most famous works, 'Bubbles', was painted to prove that it was possible to paint a bubble. It was the original purchaser of the work who sold it to Pears, the soap manufacturer, for a greatly increased price.

Millais became a very successful portrait painter and was knighted by Queen Victoria. He was the first artist to receive a baronetcy. He was elected president of the Royal Academy in 1896, but died shortly afterwards of cancer of the throat. He was buried at St Paul's Cathedral and there is a statue to him in the grounds of the Tate Gallery in London.

John Nash (1752–1835)

Nash, who was said to be the son of a Lambeth millwright, was the favoured architect of the Prince Regent and was of Welsh extraction. He trained as an architect but became disillusioned. He was persuaded by a fellow pupil to return and soon built up a large practice with patronage of gentry and royalty.

His best known work was the laying out of Regent's Park and the wide roadways leading from Carlton House to the park. He was also remembered for All Soul's, Langham Place, and his work on Buckingham Palace and the Brighton Pavilion.

He lost favour on the death of George IV in 1830 and was dismissed from his work on Buckingham Palace and the Board of Works. He was associated on a number of occasions with Humphry Repton and in the 1790s the two men were commissioned by Richard Shawe to develop the Casina estate. The grounds were laid out by Humphry Repton and the house was designed by Nash. It was demolished in the Edwardian period and the area was redeveloped in the early 1920s.

He retired to the Isle of Wight in 1830 where he died five years later at the age of 83.

The Pite Family of Architects

Alfred Robert Pite (1832–1911)

Alfred Pite was articled to the firm of William Gilbee Habershon and became a partner in 1860. He was the architect of the Don Pedro Railway in Brazil in 1856. When the secretary of the Suburban and General Dwellings Company misspent the monies subscribed for the promotion that would become the Milkwood/Lowden Roads estate, Habershon & Pite undertook the development. Alfred Pite was the chief architect of the project. His two sons were also architects associated with Herne Hill and its environs.

William Alfred Pite (1860–1949)

William Pite was educated at King's College and was articled to Habershon & Pite in 1876. He won the Pugin Studentship in 1883 and studied architecture abroad, before qualifying in 1890.

He was a member of the Architectural Association and on the council and board of examiners of the Royal Institute of British Architects. He is best known for ecclesiastical and hospital building, as far apart as Cardiff, Penzance, Walsall and Epsom. He won the countrywide open competition with his design for the new King's College Hospital, Denmark Hill, and was the hospital architect from 1905 until 1937. He retired to live in Eastbourne and died there in 1949. He was also architect of houses in outer London, some Barnado homes and war memorials.

Interestingly, Kathleen Pite, his daughter, became matron of King's College Hospital in 1937. She had trained at King's and been a nursing sister there before becoming matron at the Samaritan's Hospital in 1932.

Professor Arthur Beresford Pite (1861–1934)

Arthur was also educated at King's College and was articled to the firm of Habershon & Pite, later winning the Donaldson Medal and the Soane Medallion. For 23 years he was professor of architecture at the Royal College of Art in South Kensington and was appointed professor of architecture at the LCC Brixton Technical College.

During this time he designed the parish hall of St Saviour's Church, Herne Hill Road, built on land donated by Sir Robert Sanders MP. Completed just prior to the outbreak of the First World War, the hall was used for many unplanned purposes, including the entertainment of convalescent soldiers from King's College Hospital, Ruskin Park and St Gabriel's College. Since the demolition of St Saviour's Church the hall has had another use – every Sunday the congregation meets and it becomes a church.

There is a plaque near the entrance of the hall commemorating Beresford Pite's contribution to the area, as there is to commemorate William Alfred Pite in the chapel of King's College Hospital.

Samuel Prout (1783–1851)

Born and educated in Plymouth, Prout was 14 years old when he met John Britton (an antiquarian) in his father's bookshop. After initial failure he moved to London and for two years he stayed at John Britton's home, contributing illustrations to his series of books, *Beauties of Britain*.

He began to travel on the Continent, his reputation growing with the publication of lithographs in his books *Illustrations of the Rhine*, *Facsimiles of Sketches made in Flanders and Germany* and *Sketches in France, Switzerland and Italy*. It was the first of these that led to his meeting with the Ruskins and their first Continental tour.

Although successful as an architectural and marine artist and as painter in watercolour to William IV and Queen Victoria until his death, he remained comparatively poor. He suffered ill health and never sufficiently increased the price of his works to make much difference, but he was happily married with numerous children.

Much of his married life was spent in the Brixton area. He moved to De Crespigny Terrace, where the Salvation Army Training College now stands, to be close to his friend John Ruskin.

He had many friends in the art world, among them David Roberts and Clarkson Stanfield. His works were hung in the Bicknell and Ruskin homes which he visited quite frequently. He travelled with artist friends on the Continent. He had a wide range of patrons, many of whom bought again and again.

He died suddenly in February 1851 at his easel, after spending the evening celebrating John Ruskin's birthday.

Humphry Repton (1752–1818)

Repton was the outstanding landscape gardener of his time. He was involved in the layout of over 200 parks and gardens and was also famous for his *Red Books*, in which he illustrated his clients' gardens and his plans for their reconstruction. He was also the author of several books on the subject of gardens and their reconstruction and was responsible for the expression 'landscape gardening'.

Born in Bury St Edmunds, he was educated first at Norwich Grammar School and then in Holland. On his return to England, he married in 1773, had 16 children and studied botany and gardening. When his commercial enterprises proved unsuccessful, he moved to Romford, Essex. This was his home for 40 years where he set up as a landscape gardener adopting informal layouts. He received commissions from his many friends as well as from the gentry and noble families. His first big project was the grounds of Cobham in Kent and among his many successes were the gardens of Woburn Abbey, and those of Russell Square, Bloomsbury. His plans for Brighton Pavilion were accepted by the Prince of Wales but were dropped because of the Prince's financial difficulties.

In 1811 he was involved in a road accident. This restricted his activities and he died in 1818.

Portrait of David Roberts, drawn on stone, 1844.

He was associated with John Nash on a number of occasions, as were two of his sons. In the 1790s the solicitor Richard Shawe commissioned both men to create the Casina estate. Humphry Repton laid out the grounds of the estate, at its lowest part designing the lake from the natural springs of the area. Casina House was demolished during the Edwardian period and the grounds were redeveloped in the early 1920s to become what is the Casino estate at the time of writing.

David Roberts (1796–1864)

Roberts was not a resident of Herne Hill, but was so closely associated with the Bicknell family and friends that he almost became one. He lived most of his life in Fitzroy Square, London.

Born in Edinburgh of a poor family, he was apprenticed at the age of ten to a house painter. The skills learned stood him in good stead when working as a theatre scene painter. After a few years touring with theatre companies, he left Scotland for London with his new wife and found work at The Old Coburg, Drury Lane and Covent Garden.

He began to exhibit, to travel on the Continent with artist friends and, in 1830, spent a year in Spain. The drawings he executed there were lithographed by his friend, Louis Haghe, and published as *Picturesque Sketches of Spain*. He was then able to leave the theatre altogether and to work and travel as he pleased. He visited the Middle East and his work was again lithographed by Haghe and published as *Sketches of the Holy Land, Syria and Egypt*.

His painting output was high. He was a member of the Royal Academy, an honorary member of the Scottish Royal Academy, and of other bodies in Europe and the United States. He was honoured in many ways, had friends in many fields and was an executor of Turner's will.

Prior to the embankment of the Thames he painted a series of views of London before 'its beauty was lost forever' under the granite, bricks and mortar of the new banks. His last painting was of St Paul's on Ludgate Hill, the subject of his very first painting of a London scene.

His marriage was a failure. His wife, an alcoholic, returned to Scotland, leaving him to care for his daughter, Christine, who eventually married Elhanan Bicknell's son, Henry. Roberts and Bicknell were joint grandparents of nine children.

When he died in 1864, David Roberts was interred in the Bicknell vault in West Norwood Cemetery, but in 1875 was transferred to a grave next door, the move occasioned by the striking of a medallion in his honour by the Art Union of London – one of only 29 struck between 1843 and 1884.

Dante Gabriel Rossetti (1828–82)

Rossetti was the son of an Italian refugee who was a professor of Italian at King's College. He was educated at King's College and later attended the Royal Academy Schools. He left soon afterwards because he felt the teaching methods inappropriate. He studied with Ford Madox Brown, shared a studio with Holman Hunt and was a founding member of the Pre-Raphaelite movement. After criticism of the movement by the Academy, he refused to exhibit there again and instead sold his work privately.

He was a very difficult eccentric and was befriended by John Ruskin. He caused disruption when staying on Denmark Hill by working at night and sleeping all day. He married his model, Elizabeth Siddal, whose work John Ruskin considered superior to Rossetti's. When she died shortly afterwards of consumption and an overdose of laudanum, Rossetti was distraught, burying a book of his unpublished poems with her. Not long afterwards he exhumed the coffin, extracted the poems and sent them off for publication. At the time he lived at No. 16 Cheyne Walk.

Rossetti later shared a house with William Morris and also shared his wife. He became very reclusive towards the end of his life and moved to Birchington in Kent, where he died and is buried.

When Elizabeth Siddal was advised to go abroad to warmer climes for the sake of her health, Ruskin

Approach of the Simoon, Desert of Giza, 1838. One of David Roberts drawings made at the time of his first visit to Egypt. It was lithographed by Louis Haghe and was criticised by Holman Hunt because the Sphinx was falsely placed against the sun. However, Dickens, for whom it was painted, praised it for its 'poetic concept'.

paid for her journey and treatment and made her an allowance throughout her stay.

Joseph Severn (1793–1879)

Joseph Severn had travelled to Rome with John Keats in 1820. He is remembered for his care of the poet until his death a short time later of consumption, and for his sketches of Keats, particularly the last 'drawn to keep me awake' at 3 o'clock one morning. He was granted an award by the Royal Academy in recognition of his care of the poet, which enabled him to live and work in Rome for several years, becoming fluent in Italian. He became the centre of the British art circle in Rome and was so again on his return as British consul in 1861.

It was in Rome that John Ruskin called upon him with a letter of introduction. He introduced Ruskin to the art treasures of Rome and to many people in its art circle. During the years that Joseph Severn spent in England the two friends met and visited frequently.

While he was consul, he gave Adelaide Ironside a letter of introduction to John Ruskin, which led to their friendship and her many visits to Herne Hill.

Joseph Severn was happily married and had six children, the last two being twins. One was Arthur, who married Joan Agnew, a distant cousin of Ruskin.

On return to Rome as British consul, he found a difficult political situation with the division of Italy and the intrigues of the Papal Government, but in the years before his retirement he helped many of his compatriots, as well as many Italians. His work was recognised by King Victor Emmanuel who made him an Officer of the Order of the Crown of Italy and awarded him a pension.

In his retirement he was able to collaborate with information about Keats and Shelley for new editions of their works. He was intensely gladdened that Keats, 'The Bright Star', had 'not written on water' and to find that the new edition of Keats' work was dedicated to himself.

He died in 1879, and was eventually buried in the old cemetery in Rome, next to Keats, 'numbered among the immortal Poets of England'; his own services to freedom and humanity were also recognised.

John James Sexby (Lt-Col VD) (1847–1924)

John James Sexby was employed by the Metropolitan Board of Works at the age of 20 and by 1880 was Associate Surveyor of Parks and Open Spaces. When the board's work was taken over by the LCC, a separate parks department was established and in 1892 Sexby became its chief officer. During his time with the LCC there was a great increase in the number of London parks and open spaces and by the time he retired in 1910, Sexby was responsible for over 5,000 acres of London's parkland. One of his first projects was to lay out Brockwell Park in 1892 and one of his last to lay out Ruskin Park in 1907. A flower garden in Peckham Rye Park was named after him.

He wrote extensively on the history of London's parks, gardens and open spaces. There is a chapter on the history of Brockwell Park in his book, *The Municipal Parks, Gardens and Open Spaces of London*.

Another of his great interests was the Voluntary Army (the forerunner of the Territorial Army). He was a founding member of the Lambeth and Southwark Volunteers, starting as a private and rising in the ranks to take charge of 'A' Company in 1880. He won many prizes for shooting over the years and in 1884 was presented with 'a very handsome dress sword and an illuminated testimonial' for his services to the company. He was awarded his Victoria Decoration in 1892 and when he resigned from the volunteers he was honoured by being permitted to retain his rank and to wear his uniform on formal occasions.

He died in 1924 at Melbourne House, South London.

Elizabeth Eleanor Siddal (1829–62)

Siddal was born in the Old Kent Road area; the daughter of a cutler, she spent a period working as a milliner. She was introduced to the Pre-Raphaelite group and modelled for Millais and Rossetti. She was encouraged to paint by Ford Madox Brown and Rossetti. Ruskin settled an allowance on her of £150 a year in exchange for her output.

She suffered from consumption and Ruskin arranged a consultation for her with his friend Dr Acland. He also paid for her journey to France and for her stay there.

She married Rossetti shortly after her return from France but died of an overdose of laudanum in February 1862.

Sir Evan Spicer (1849–1937)

Evan Spicer lived at Belair, Gallery Road, in Dulwich Village. He was head of the family firm of paper manufacturers and the father of a sizeable family of sons and daughters. He was a kindly man and when the lake in his grounds froze over, he arranged with the headmaster for the boys of Dulwich College, of which he was a governor, to have a half-holiday so that they could skate on the ice.

As a governor of the Dulwich College estate, he was also able to arrange the 500-year lease (at a peppercorn rent) for the Congregational church, built at the top of Red Post Hill. He was an ardent Congregationalist.

He was chairman of the LCC and helped smooth the transition of ownership at the times of the purchases of Ruskin Park and the second part of Brockwell Park, as well as of Norwood Park.

He took pride in his garden and was always concerned to prevent further encroachment of building upon open spaces. He was knighted in 1917 and died at the age of 88 in 1937.

Lt-Col J.J. Sexby

William Clarkson Stanfield (1793–1867)

One of the finest marine artists of the Victorian era, Stanfield was born in Sutherland. He went to sea and spent much of his time painting seascapes before being 'press-ganged' into the Navy.

He was fortunate in meeting Captain Marryat (of 'Mr Midshipman Easy' and 'Children of the New Forest' fame) who advised him to make a career in painting. When he finally left the Navy he became a scene painter at Drury Lane Theatre where he met David Roberts and built a name for himself as one of the leaders in that field.

He frequently exhibited at the Royal Academy, painted many marine pictures and illustrated books.

Among his friends were Charles Dickens, Captain Marryat, David Roberts and Elhanan Bicknell, in whose house a number of his pictures were hung. One of his pictures, 'Pic du Midi D'Ossau in the Pyrenees, with Smugglers' was sold for 2,550 guineas in the posthumous record-breaking sale of the Bicknell collection.

Sir Charles Ernest Tritton (1892–1906)

Norwood's second Member of Parliament (from 1892 until 1906) lived at Broomfield in Norwood. He was elected following the death of Thomas Bristowe and resigned from the Commons because of his opposition to the bill for Tariff Reform.

He is best remembered in Herne Hill and Norwood for his work in securing the second purchase of Brockwell Park as well as his presentation of the clock tower, 'Little Ben', to celebrate the Golden Jubilee of Queen Victoria's accession and the flagpole to celebrate the Coronation of Edward VII. Both are landmarks in the park at the time of writing. He is also remembered for his support of the purchase of Ruskin and Norwood Parks.

He was chairman of the Princess Christian Hospital for the British wounded and was on the board of the British Home for Incurables at Crown Point. He was also president of the Norwood Cottage Hospital and vice-chairman of the Hospital Sunday Fund and the London City Mission (and was on its Finance Committee). He was vice-president of the Church Missionary Society and the British and Foreign Bible Society. In his business life, he was senior partner in the Brightman Company (Billbrokers and Banking Agents) and Director of the United Kingdom Temperance and General Provident Institute.

Joseph Mallard William Turner (1775–1851)

Born in Maiden Lane, near Covent Garden, Turner's early years were marred by his mother's instability. His father, a barber, did his best to give his son an education and then some art tuition. In later years, he moved into his son's household, acting as steward and general factotum, until his death in 1830.

Turner was one of the greatest artists this country has ever produced. When he died, he left to the nation more than 300 oils, 20,000 drawings and a fortune to found a charity for needy artists and an art gallery. People were surprised at his wealth, for he lived frugally, and even more surprised to find that he had two homes – the occupants of each being unaware of the other residence.

He was buried beside the tomb of Sir Joshua Reynolds and other painters in St Paul's Cathedral. On the day of the funeral, thousands lined the streets to watch the cortège pass by – it took three hours to reach the cathedral from his home in Queen Ann Street. Among the mourners were many living artists, including David Roberts.

At one period of his life, his work was reviled by critics, despite his being appointed an academician in 1802 and the professor of perspective six years later. This changed when Ruskin's *Modern Painters* was published, in which he gave Turner his unqualified support. Turner had many patrons and travelled extensively in Britain and on the Continent and over the years exhibited many pictures at the Royal Academy. His appearances on 'Varnishing Day' were legendary.

Years before Ruskin's support effected a change in public opinion, Elhanan Bicknell had purchased a series of Turner's paintings, featuring aspects of the whaling fleet. He later sold them but over the years purchased a number of the artist's works which he displayed in his Herne Hill home. These were either bought direct from Turner or from his agent, Thomas Griffiths, who lived on Crown Point.

Turner was a frequent visitor at the Bicknells' 'at homes' and evening dinners. There is a famous caricature by Count D'Orsay of Turner drinking tea at the Bicknells' home. Turner was also a friend of David Roberts and was often a guest at the dinners held at his house in Fitzroy Square.

Turner himself never returned the hospitality, except to allow visitors to his gallery at Queen Ann Street. Ruskin first met him at the home of Thomas Griffiths; although still a boy he had been an admirer of Turner's work for some time and considered meeting Turner one of the key events of his life. The Ruskin family owned many of Turner's paintings. John was given one for his 21st birthday and, of course, he inherited the family paintings. Turner was an occasional visitor to the Ruskin home. John, and occasionally his parents, visited Turner's gallery in Queen Ann Street. John's father was a little annoyed when the reading of Turner's will revealed that the only legacy for John was a 'mourning ring'.

Sir Henry Wellcome (1854–1936)

The son of an American farmer/preacher, Henry Wellcome was born in Garden City, Minnesota. His first steps into the pharmacy world were working in the family drugstore. He then spent a period with a pharmaceutical firm and graduated from the Philadelphia College of Pharmacy in 1874. He was engaged by a leading pharmaceutical company to promote the sale of drugs abroad and sometimes published papers on his observations made whilst travelling. He was then invited by another Philadelphia graduate, Silas Burroughs, to work with him in Britain.

The two men joined forces and created the firm of Burroughs, Wellcome and Company, initially to sell new 'compressed medicine' tablets. Over the years the company received many accolades and awards for excellence and eventually the business expanded throughout the world.

Silas Burroughs, who became a British subject in 1890, died in 1895. In 1894 his partner had formed the Wellcome Physiological Research Laboratories, which in 1898 moved to Brockwell Park. In 1898, the lease on a ten-acre site in Brockwell Park had become vacant. It had another 20 years to run before expiry. The site, with the Victorian-built Brockwell House, stables and outbuildings, was leased by Henry Wellcome, for the use of the Wellcome Physiological Research Laboratories.

At the time, the purpose of the laboratories was to carry out research into the cause and treatment of infectious illnesses, particularly diphtheria, one of the commonest causes of child death in the Western world. In the event, the laboratories remained in Brockwell Park until 1922 because of the peculiar circumstances of the years of the First World War. In 1896 Henry Wellcome had formed the Wellcome Chemical Research Laboratories in Snow Hill, and later built the Wellcome Research Institute in Euston Road, originally a museum for his historic medical collection. When the Snow Hill premises were destroyed by enemy action, the company also operated from Euston Road.

Henry Wellcome died in 1936, having created The Wellcome Trust. Over the years the trust distributed millions of pounds, funding many research projects and becoming one of this country's largest charitable organisations.

There is no known record of Henry Wellcome having visited Herne Hill, but it is unlikely that he would have contemplated buying the lease of the Brockwell Park site without seeing the location and all that the purchase would entail.

Andrew Carnegie (1835–1919)

Carnegie was neither a Herne Hill resident nor a visitor, but he deserves mention because his corporation donated the Carnegie Library, Herne Hill Road, to the people of Herne Hill. He was the son of a poor Scottish family that emigrated to the United States in the mid-nineteenth century.

When working as a messenger boy for the Pittsburgh Telegraph Office (for $2.50 a week) he was given access to a private library. Every Saturday he borrowed a volume and was soon of the opinion that a library was the most valuable facility a community could possess. He became involved in railways, steel manufacture and the oil industry and grew to be very wealthy. In 1901 he sold his corporation for $89 million and, after setting up a pension fund for his workers, he devoted his wealth to the founding of free libraries and the endowment of universities and educational facilities in the United States, Canada and the British Isles. Some 660 libraries were endowed in the British Isles.

His corporation was approached for help in setting up a library in Herne Hill Road. The Minet Trust had given the land and the Carnegie Corporation funded the building of the library, with the provision that it be stocked and maintained by the local authority. Andrew Carnegie died in Massachusetts in 1919.

Left: The people of Herne Hill strolling in Brockwell Park, c.1900. Note the fine clothing worn by the lady with the baby carriage and that all of those pictured are wearing hats.

Below: The swimming and bathing lake, Brockwell Park, c.1920.

Below: *During the Edwardian period, at the height of the production of postcards, dozens of photographs were taken of the lake in Brockwell Park and many of the park's other features.*

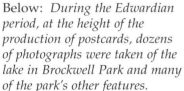

ACKNOWLEDGEMENTS

The author would like to thank her many friends in Herne Hill and its neighbouring areas for their assistance in the compilation of this book. She would also like to thank the institutions where research was carried out and the staff who, over the years, have helped with the gathering of information about Herne Hill, past and present. The author would particularly like to thank her niece, Katie Broadie, who typed the manuscript. Also thanks to those friends who lent many photographs, maps and illustrations, particularly Keith Holdaway, Kevin Kelly and Sheila Northover. Thanks are also due to Yvette Williams, then archivist at Lambeth, who set the author on the research road in the 1970s.

SUBSCRIBERS

The Abbott Family, Herne Hill, London
A.G. and M.A. Anderson, Barkston, Lincolnshire
F.M. Anderson, Herne Hill, London
Marcus C.F. Antill, Herne Hill, London
Ken, Dorothy and Victoria Baker, Poplar Walk
The Baldwin Family, Danecroft Road, Herne Hill, London
Betty B. Barnes, Crawley, West Sussex
Peter R. Beach, Potton, Bedfordshire
Oliver H. Beach, Denmark Hill, London
Trevor J. Beach, Lyndhurst, Hampshire
Mrs Margaret Bennett, Herne Hill, London
The Reverend Garry and Mrs Phyll Bennett, West Wales
Julian Bentham and Victoria Almey, Kestrel Avenue, Herne Hill
Edmund Bird, Herne Hill
Barry and Jackie Blunt, Herne Hill, London
Anthony and Valerie Bond, Brighton
Dr C.G. Bottom, Herne Hill, London
Briggs, Rollscourt
John W. Brown, Local History Publications
Venis V. Buckle
Sheila M. Burke, Dorking, Surrey
Brian Carr, Herne Hill, London
Tony Cartland, Herne Hill, London
Margaret Carvell, Herne Hill, London
Sonia Castro, Herne Hill, London
Paul and Kathy Chambers
Arthur, Valerie, Elizabeth, Genevieve and Richard Chandler, Herne Hill
Patricia V. Clark, Herne Hill, London
John Clark, Dulwich, London
Harold C. Clark, Chichester, West Sussex
David and Linda Cleverly, Herne Hill, London
Rosemary Comber, Upper Norwood, London
Tessa Cooney, Herne Hill
The Cooper Family, Herne Hill, London
Norman D. Cox, Herne Hill, London
Michael, Carole, Katherine, Matthew and Elizabeth Coyne, Herne Hill

Mark and Hanny Cruttenden, Herne Hill, London
D. and M. Damant, Herne Hill, London
Andrew Davidson, Herne Hill, London
James D. Davidson, Dulwich, London
De La Salle Brothers, Herne Hill, London
De La Salle Brothers, Oxford
Michael and Christine De Luca, Herne Hill
Gerard Dickinson, Herne Hill, London
Len and Irene Dobbs, Herne Hill since 1958
Margaret H. Doherty, Herne Hill, London
Ian Dunn, Herne Hill, London
George Vaughan Ellis RIBA, Cornwall
Graham A. Feakins, Herne Hill, London
Steve and Buffy Fender and Family, Herne Hill
Blaise, Verity and Alban Fenn, Herne Hill, London
Jane and David Fenwick, Tunbridge Wells
Eva M. Fluch, Herne Hill, London
Jean and Ron Ford, Rosendale Road, Herne Hill
Gordon Fowkes, Herne Hill, London
Wendy and Tim Franey, Herne Hill
Betty and Bruno Freddi, John, Paul and Angela
Peter M. Frost, East Dulwich, London
John T. Gardner, Upper Norwood, London
Clifford German, Herne Hill, London
Heather Gilmour, Herne Hill, London
Eve Guttentag, Herne Hill, London
Robin and Maria Haig, Sydney, Australia
Mr David Hamley and Mr Brian Hamley, Norman House, Dulwich Road, SE24
Angus Hanton, Dulwich Storage Co.
Doris E. Harris, Herne Hill
John Hawks, Poets Corner, Herne Hill
Terence M. Higgins, Herne Hill, London
Adrian Hill, Herne Hill, London
Keith Holdaway, Streatham, London
Robert Holden, Herne Hill
John Hopkins, Herne Hill, London
Mary Howard, Holcombe, Somerset/previously Fawnbrake Avenue
Derek J. Howell, Herne Hill, London
Daphne C. Hunter, Herne Hill, London

Nigel Hunter Jones MCIOB, Dorchester Court, Herne Hill, London
The James Family, Herne Hill, London
The Jeyarajah Family, Herne Hill, London
Hugh and Angela John, Herne Hill, London
The Kain Family, Herne Hill
Molly Kerridge, Herne Hill, London
Ann Kerrigan, Herne Hill, London
Sarah Kerrigan, New Mexico, USA/previously Fawnbrake Avenue
Robin Key and Liz Harwood,
Bernice Maria King, Poets Corner, Herne Hill, London
Elizabeth M. King, Herne Hill, London
Lawrence David King, Poets Corner, Herne Hill, London
Ronald David King, Poets Corner, Herne Hill, London
Ronald James King, Poets Corner, Herne Hill, London
Rosemarie E. King (née Kays), Poets Corner, Herne Hill, London
Brian Kippax, Chislehurst, Kent
Alice and Joseph Lane, Herne Hill, London
Robin Langley, North Dulwich, London
Miss G.M. Law, Dulwich, London
Sandra Leavy, Herne Hill
Anthony and Katya Lester, Herne Hill
Lord Lester, of Herne Hill
David Lipscomb, Herne Hill, London
Mr R.J. Loft, Herne Hill, London
Dr E.C. Loft, Herne Hill, London
Mr C.J. Loft, Herne Hill, London
Margaret and Len Logan, Herne Hill
Mr and Mrs D.C. Long, Herne Hill
Ana Lowin, Railton Road, Herne Hill
Robin Mason, Herne Hill, London
Mrs Gunilla Mattsson-Willis, Herne Hill, London
Daniel, Penny and Conor Maurer, Herne Hill, London
Pritti Mehta, Herne Hill, London
The Meredith Family, Herne Hill, London
M.J. Metherall, Surrey
Brian and Pamela Mico, Herne Hill, London
The Mistry Family, Herne Hill
Eve Mitchell, Herne Hill, London
Mark and Monique Montague-Drake, and Luke, Yoann, Naomi, Anastasia, and Jean-Luc
Christina L. Morgner, Herne Hill, London
Pat Mulcaster, Herne Hill, London
Jack Murray, Brockwell Park
Agnes and Tommi Muttonen
Dr P.C. Nicholas, Tregony, North Dulwich
Sheila Northover, Herne Hill
Bernard Nurse, Herne Hill, London
Karen Lorraine O'Regan (née King), Poets Corner, Herne Hill, London

Allan D. Orchison, Herne Hill
David J. Osborne, Halifax, West Yorkshire
Olwyn and Joan Owen-Price, Herne Hill, London
John Henry Palfreman, Brantwood Road, Herne Hill
Mr and Mrs J.M. Parkin
John Parrish, Herne Hill
Rodney and Margaret Pinder
Arthur and Trixie Popham, Herne Hill
Brian T. Press, Brixton, London
Mr Oliver Ray, Herne Hill, London
Peter J. Reeve, Carver Road, Herne Hill
Jeffrey J. Rumble, St Feock, Cornwall
Helle J. Sampson and Joanne E. Tuckey, Herne Hill, London
Bernard and Pamela Secrett,
Anne Sharpley, Herne Hill, London
Maureen B. Shbero, Herne Hill, London
Geoffrey Shepherd, Chevy Chase, Maryland
John Shepherd, Evesham, Worcestershire
Andrew Shepherd, Loughborough, Leicestershire
Stuart Sinclair, Herne Hill, London
Mary Slater, Herne Hill, London
John Smallwood, Waterloo, London
P.L. Spencer, London, SE21
Mrs Joan Ann Spooner, formerly of Deerdale Road, Herne Hill
David B. Stacey, Herne Hill, London
Philip Stavrinou, Herne Hill, London
Neil, Chris, Ruby and Millie Stone-Sharp, Herne Hill, London
Sidney and Brenda Swann, Brixton, London
David and Beth Taylor
Brigid Taylor, Tulse Hill, London
The Taylor-Knobel Family, Herne Hill, London
Marjorie Telford, Herne Hill, London
The Telford Family, Herne Hill, London
Isabelle Teresa, Regent Road and Norwood Road
Dr Cecelia M. Theodore and David R. Miller, Herne Hill, London
David Thompson, Herne Hill, London
Ruth Thompson
D.E. Thorogood, Eastbourne, East Sussex
H.J.O. Tudor
Joan Turner, Herne Hill, London
Bob Wallace, Herne Hill, London
Mr and Mrs P. Whall, Herne Hill, London
Jane E.K. White, Herne Hill, London
Danny White and Helena Myska, Herne Hill, London
Frank and Penny Whitford, Narborough, Leicestershire
P.E. and A.M. Whitworth, Herne Hill, London
Mrs Pamela Williams, Herne Hill

Community Histories

The Book of Addiscombe • Canning & Clyde Road Residents
Association & Friends
The Book of Addiscombe, Vol. II • Canning & Clyde Road
Residents Association & Friends
The Book of Axminster with Kilmington • Les Berry
and Gerald Gosling
The Book of Bampton • Caroline Seward
The Book of Barnstaple • Avril Stone
The Book of Barnstaple, Vol. II • Avril Stone
The Book of The Bedwyns • The Bedwyn History Society
The Book of Bickington • Stuart Hands
Blandford Forum: A Millennium Portrait • Blandford Town Council
The Book of Bramford • Bramford Local History Group
The Book of Breage & Germoe • Stephen Polglase
The Book of Bridestowe • R. Cann
The Book of Bridport • Rodney Legg
The Book of Brixham • Frank Pearce
The Book of Buckfastleigh • Sandra Coleman
The Book of Buckland Monachorum & Yelverton • Hemery
The Book of Carharrack • Carharrack Old Cornwall Society
The Book of Carshalton • Stella Wilks and Gordon Rookledge
The Parish Book of Cerne Abbas • Vale and Vale
The Book of Chagford • Ian Rice
The Book of Chapel-en-le-Frith • Mike Smith
The Book of Chittlehamholt with
Warkleigh & Satterleigh • Richard Lethbridge
The Book of Chittlehampton • Various
The Book of Colney Heath • Bryan Lilley
The Book of Constantine • Moore and Trethowan
The Book of Cornwood & Lutton • Compiled by the People of
the Parish
The Book of Creech St Michael • June Small
The Book of Cullompton • Compiled by the People of the Parish
The Book of Dawlish • Frank Pearce
The Book of Dulverton, Brushford,
Bury & Exebridge • Dulverton & District Civic Society
The Book of Dunster • Hilary Binding
The Book of Edale • Gordon Miller
The Ellacombe Book • Sydney R. Langmead
The Book of Exmouth • W.H. Pascoe
The Book of Grampound with Creed • Bane and Oliver
The Book of Hayling Island & Langstone • Rogers
The Book of Helston • Jenkin with Carter
The Book of Hemyock • Clist and Dracott
The Book of Herne Hill • Patricia Jenkyns
The Book of Hethersett • Hethersett Society Research Group
The Book of High Bickington • Avril Stone
The Book of Ilsington • Dick Wills
The Book of Kingskerswell • Carsewella Local History Group
The Book of Lamerton • Ann Cole & Friends
Lanner, A Cornish Mining Parish • Sharron
Schwartz and Roger Parker
The Book of Leigh & Bransford • Malcolm Scott
The Book of Litcham with Lexham & Mileham • Litcham Historical
& Amenity Society
The Book of Loddiswell • Reg and Betty Sampson
The New Book of Lostwithiel • Barbara Fraser
The Book of Lulworth • Rodney Legg
The Book of Lustleigh • Joe Crowdy
The Book of Lyme Regis • Rodney Legg
The Book of Manaton • Compiled by the People of the Parish
The Book of Markyate • Markyate Local History Society

The Book of Mawnan • Mawnan Local History Group
The Book of Meavy • Pauline Hemery
The Book of Minehead with Alcombe • Binding and Stevens
The Book of Morchard Bishop • Jeff Kingaby
The Book of Newdigate • John Callcut
The Book of Nidderdale • Nidderdale Musuem Society
The Book of Northlew with Ashbury • Northlew History Group
The Book of North Newton • Robins and Robins
The Book of North Tawton • Baker, Hoare and Shields
The Book of Nynehead • Nynehead & District History Society
The Book of Okehampton • Radford and Radford
The Book of Paignton • Frank Pearce
The Book of Penge, Anerley & Crystal Palace • Peter Abbott
The Book of Peter Tavy with Cudlipptown • Peter Tavy
Heritage Group
The Book of Pimperne • Jean Coull
The Book of Plymtree • Tony Eames
The Book of Porlock • Denis Corner
Postbridge – The Heart of Dartmoor • Reg Bellamy
The Book of Priddy • Albert Thompson
The Book of Princetown • Dr Gardner-Thorpe
The Book of Rattery • By the People of the Parish
The Book of St Day • Joseph Mills and Paul Annear
The Book of Sampford Courtenay
with Honeychurch • Stephanie Pouya
The Book of Sculthorpe • Gary Windeler
The Book of Seaton • Ted Gosling
The Book of Sidmouth • Ted Gosling and Sheila Luxton
The Book of Silverton • Silverton Local History Society
The Book of South Molton • Jonathan Edmunds
The Book of South Stoke with Midford • Edited by Robert Parfitt
South Tawton & South Zeal with Sticklepath • Radfords
The Book of Sparkwell with Hemerdon & Lee Mill • Pam James
The Book of Staverton • Pete Lavis
The Book of Stithians • Stithians Parish History Group
The Book of Stogumber, Monksilver, Nettlecombe
& Elworthy • Maurice and Joyce Chidgey
The Book of Studland • Rodney Legg
The Book of Swanage • Rodney Legg
The Book of Tavistock • Gerry Woodcock
The Book of Thorley • Sylvia McDonald and Bill Hardy
The Book of Torbay • Frank Pearce
Uncle Tom Cobley & All:
Widecombe-in-the-Moor • Stephen Woods
The Book of Watchet • Compiled by David Banks
The Book of West Huntspill • By the People of the Parish
Widecombe-in-the-Moor • Stephen Woods
The Book of Williton • Michael Williams
The Book of Witheridge • Peter and Freda Tout and John Usmar
The Book of Withycombe • Chris Boyles
Woodbury: The Twentieth Century Revisited • Roger Stokes
The Book of Woolmer Green • Compiled by the People of the Parish

For details of any of the above titles or if you are
interested in writing your own history, please contact:
Commissioning Editor Community Histories, Halsgrove
House, Lower Moor Way, Tiverton Business Park,
Tiverton, Devon EX16 6SS, England; tel: 01884 259636;
email: katyc@halsgrove.com